D0846169

Reprints of Economic Classics

THE RIGHT TO THE WHOLE
PRODUCE OF LABOUR

THE

RIGHT

TO THE

WHOLE PRODUCE

OF

LABOUR

BY

ANTON MENGER

WITH

AN INTRODUCTION AND BIBLIOGRAPHY

BY H. S. FOXWELL

[1899]

REPRINTS OF ECONOMIC CLASSICS

AUGUSTUS M. KELLEY · PUBLISHERS

NEW YORK 1970

First Edition 1899

(London: Macmillan & Company, 1899)

Reprinted 1962, 1970 by

AUGUSTUS M. KELLEY · PUBLISHERS

REPRINTS OF ECONOMIC CLASSICS

New York New York 10001

· · · · · · · · · · · ·

I S B N 0 678 007144

L C N 68 54737

· · · · · · · · ·

PRINTED IN THE UNITED STATES OF AMERICA
by SENTRY PRESS, NEW YORK, N. Y. 10019

THE RIGHT

TO

THE WHOLE PRODUCE

OF LABOUR

THE ORIGIN AND DEVELOPMENT OF THE
THEORY OF LABOUR'S CLAIM TO THE
WHOLE PRODUCT OF INDUSTRY

BY

DR. ANTON MENGER

PROFESSOR OF JURISPRUDENCE IN THE UNIVERSITY OF VIENNA

TRANSLATED BY M. E. TANNER

WITH AN INTRODUCTION AND BIBLIOGRAPHY
BY H. S. FOXWELL, M.A.

PROFESSOR OF ECONOMICS AT UNIVERSITY COLLEGE, LONDON;
LECTURER AND LATE FELLOW OF ST. JOHN'S COLLEGE, CAMBRIDGE

London

MACMILLAN AND CO., LIMITED

NEW YORK: THE MACMILLAN COMPANY

1899

INTRODUCTION

Dr. Anton Menger's remarkable study of the cardinal Dr. Menger's work.
doctrine of revolutionary socialism, now for the first
time published in English, has long enjoyed a wide
reputation on the Continent; and English students of
social philosophy, whether or not they are familiar with
the original, will welcome its appearance in this translation. The interest and importance of the subject
will not be disputed, either by the opponents or the
advocates of socialism; and those who know how
exceptionally Dr. Menger is qualified for work of this
kind, by his juristic eminence, and his profound knowledge of socialistic literature, will not need to be told
that it has been executed with singular vigour and
ability. Hitherto, perhaps because it was not generally
accessible to English readers, the book has not received
in this country the notice that it has met with elsewhere.
Yet there are reasons why it should be of peculiar
interest to English economists. The particular method
of criticism adopted by Dr. Menger, and indeed the
whole scope of his inquiry, will be almost entirely
novel here; while on its historical side the work is

mainly distinguished from previous essays in the same
field by the importance it assigns to an unquestionably
original but too-much-neglected school of English
writers. I venture to offer a few introductory remarks
by way of explaining the nature and results of Dr.
Menger's inquiry, and its special claims on the attention
of Englishmen. I do so as one who has always felt
that the work of this little English School was of first-
rate significance in the history of socialism, and that a
critical examination of their teaching must form part
of the training of every serious student of the social
question ; and as one, therefore, who has special reason
to appreciate the laborious researches Dr. Menger has
made into his subject, and the masterly way in which
he has handled it.

Its general
scope.

The work before us, then, is at the same time a
history and a criticism. It deals, not with socialism
in general, under all its aspects, but with a single claim
or first principle of socialists, the asserted right of the
labourer to the whole produce of industry; or, if we
prefer to express it in its negative form, the denial of a
right to "unearned" income. Dr. Menger does not
exaggerate when he says of this principle that "it is
the fundamental revolutionary conception of our time,
playing the same part as the idea of political equality
in the French Revolution and its offshoots." "Both
conceptions," he goes on to remark, "are of a purely
negative character, and contain no positive principle
for the reconstruction of an economic order; but seeing

that the masses are most easily united on negations, an immense revolutionary power must be ascribed to both" (p. 160). This claim of labour to the whole produce of industry, without deduction of any kind, has, in one or the other of the various interpretations that may be put upon it, served as the foundation of most of the protean forms of modern socialism ; and there can be no question that it well deserves to be singled out for careful and express treatment. In the terse and compact little volume before us, which is understood to be a portion of a larger forthcoming work, Dr. Menger has undertaken this important task, and has devoted himself almost exclusively to an examination of the history and validity of this formidable claim.

It will be understood, therefore, that Dr. Menger does not profess to cover the whole field, either of socialistic theory or socialistic experiments. His book is in the main abstract, and contrasts strongly with the detailed examination of particular situations, schemes, and problems, so dear to the English mind. He gives us nothing of the picturesque or emotional side of socialism, no highly-coloured pictures of the seamy side of the modern economic *régime*. In place of these more familiar, and to many more congenial, topics, we find two concurrent inquiries, each of a somewhat general character, and mutually illustrating one another. We have a cold, rigorous analysis of the fundamental principles, apparently so plausible and axiomatic, upon which socialistic proposals rest, exhibiting relentlessly,

A history and a criticism.

but without bias, their insurmountable inconsistencies; and this is accompanied by an historical account of the part played by the most notable of these principles in modern literature and politics, tracing it from its origin in the English school of Thompson and others, down to its latest developments in theory and legislation.

1. DR. MENGER'S CRITICAL METHOD

The criticism.

On the historical, as well as on the critical side, Dr. Menger's book deals with much that, if not entirely new to English economists, has certainly been too much neglected by them. But it is his critical method which will probably appear most unfamiliar, at least to those whose reading has been confined within the narrow pale of what used to be called the "orthodox" school. It may therefore be worth while to glance at the purpose of his criticism, the standpoint from which it sets out, and the general character of its results.

Juristic rather than economic.

Dr. Anton Menger is a jurist by profession, and it will be gathered from the title of his work that it is the juristic rather than the strictly economic aspect of socialism in which he is most directly interested. Yet it would be altogether misleading if we were to say that his criticism was concerned with law in the English sense of the term. The whole discussion deals not with positive law, but ideal right; with relations of *Jus, Droit, Recht*, not of *Lex, Loi, Gesetz*. The English language is significantly weak in words, and especially in adjectives, which will readily mark this distinction; and this makes it the more difficult to convey the corresponding ideas to an English reader. The term Right is full of ambiguity, and boxes the philosophical compass from the ethical imperative of Kant in the one direction to the material, actionable title at law in the other: and we have no adjectives which bear precisely the same relation to Right as the adjective legal does to Law. But the distinction is absolutely essential for our present purpose. Dr. Menger's inquiry is not concerned with the structure of positive law, but with the system of ideal right.

Not concerned with positive law but with ideal right.

Neither the actual legal structure of societies, nor the prevailing notions of equity, have hitherto received adequate recognition at the hands of English economists. But of late years, perhaps owing to the influence of the realistic school, there has been a distinct tendency to look more closely into conditions of law and custom; and this has been especially noticeable in the case of those investigations of particular economic questions which are more and more displacing the quasi-abstract text-books that formerly appeared in such profusion. In most of these recent monographs we find that the legal conditions occupy a prominent place, and together with other matters of fact, historical and descriptive, receive much of the attention once devoted mainly to abstract considerations. Economists recognise that in all economic inquiries, certain legal conditions are necessarily assumed, whether or not they are explicitly set forth. They are aware that the whole circle of economic life in civilised societies rests upon, and is powerfully modified by, the actual system of legal relations, or body of positive law, which forms the skeleton, so to speak, of the social organism.

In the case of certain specific bodies of law this connection must be obvious to the dullest observer. The effect of poor laws and factory laws on the position of labour, of market and contract law on commercial dealings, of monetary law on the movements of price, is too direct to be ignored. But it is equally real, if less evident, in the case of the whole system of positive law, and especially, of course, in regard to that part of it which relates to property. If the anarchists, in their vivid perception of the economic significance of law, have exaggerated its power to control the distribution of wealth, the economists as a body have unduly minimised it. The physicians of the last generation have sometimes been blamed for unduly pursuing anatomical to the neglect of physiological studies. The economists unquestionably fell into the opposite error. They were too apt to take their "political anatomy" for granted, if not altogether to ignore it; and this applies with special force to that part of social anatomy which should deal with the general system of law. Hence, though they certainly did not under-rate the importance of such specific laws as those determining tariffs and taxes, there is a marked failure to appreciate the economic effects of the more fundamental and general law of property and contract. This is one of the respects in which the English economists of this century compare unfavourably with their great master Adam Smith ; and it is here perhaps that we may find an explanation of their almost complete indifference to the pregnant issues which were being raised by contemporary socialists. In this respect, however, distinct progress has been made since the rise of the historical school. If much still remains to be done, economists are at least alive to their deficiencies, so far as concerns the study of positive law. It is generally recognised now that whether our purpose is to effect practical reforms, or merely to get at the scientific explanation of the existing situation, an examination of the legal conditions is indispensable.

But this is not enough. We must go beyond the study of positive law to the study of the conceptions of ideal right on which it is based. It has been said that the science of one age is the common sense of the next. It might with equal truth be said that the equity of one age becomes the law of the next. If positive law is the basis of order, ideal right is the active factor in progress. To use the Comtian phrases, there is a dynamical as well as a statical jurisprudence, and both are vitally important to the economist. The whole aims and objects of economic policy and legislation, the trend of all movements for social reform, revolutionary or progressive, must depend upon the prevailing sense of ideal right, upon the notions of justice and fairness,

Ideals of equity not less important.

more or less coherent, which recommend themselves to
the governing body of opinion at any time as axiomatic
and unquestionable. Vague and intangible, perverse or
impracticable as they may seem, these notions of right
are none the less real and resistless in their sway.
They are themselves, no doubt, not unaffected by
positive law, as Maine and others have shown. But
in progressive societies they are a living, and in the
long run, a dominant force. Their growth is slow and
secular; revolutions and counter-revolutions may run
their course, while they remain but slightly changed;
but as they gradually develop, they fuse and trans-
form the whole structure of positive law, and alter the
face of civil society. If the supreme purpose of the
economist is to obtain some insight, however limited,
into the future course of economic evolution, and so to
lessen the social friction and waste of energy incident
to its progress, he should surely examine, with not less
care than he bestows on the institutions of positive law,
these notions of ideal right of which positive law is
only a belated and imperfect, though wonderfully
elaborated embodiment.

Their
gradual
evolution.
That there are such underlying ideas of right, and
that the whole tenour of legislation is silently, unconsciously moulded by the accepted views as to what is
economically and constitutionally fair and just, will not
be disputed. Crystallized into catching phrases, we
meet with these current ideals of equity at every turn.
One man, one vote; a living wage; a fair day's wage

for a fair day's work ; equality of opportunity; *à chacun selon ses œuvres;* property is a trust; a man may do as he likes with his own; *caveat emptor; laissez faire,—* these and many others will be familiar to us as effective instruments of economic and political movement. If they are modified, the legislation of all free countries will reflect the change; until they are modified no forcible revolution will have more than a superficial and transient effect. That they do change would be readily allowed; but I doubt whether either the extent or the importance of the change is generally realized. The instances above mentioned may serve to remind us that ideas of fairness vary from age to age as well as from class to class in the same age ; and the history of opinion on Usury, on Slavery, on Property in Land, on the rights of Traders, on Competition, on Individual Responsibility, is full of examples in point. It would be hard to say whether the average man of to-day would be more astonished at the medieval ideas of corporate responsibility and vicarious punishment, than the medieval would be at our anarchical competition and flagrant usury. But it is certain that each would find the other's notion of fairness positively scandalous. We are always apt to overlook the variable, subjective character of this notion. In settled organic stages of society, the change is too slow to be perceptible. And even in periods like that of the Renaissance, when the change is most rapid, and the conflict between institutions and ideals most marked, men have been able to objectify their fancies, and to

persuade themselves that they were part of an unalter-
able order of nature.   This illusion is for ever dispelled
so far as scholars are concerned, for its history has been
written.   But the average man is still too prone to believe that his view of fairness is eminently " natural," and
admits of no question.   In England we are under great
obligations to Dr. Cunningham for the excellent work
he has done towards removing this prejudice.   With
the decay of the " classical " economy, and of the whole
system of thought founded on the philosophy of natural
law, we may expect the prevalence of a more genuine
historical feeling, and the general appreciation of the
fact that even our perceptions of fairness themselves
are, like other social elements, in a state of continuous
evolution.

How it
affects
social
stability.

It is hardly too much to say that in the gradual
development of these ideals of right, and in the relation
between their development and the development of
positive institutions, we have the key to social stability.

That form of society is most securely rooted in which
these movements are fairly concurrent; in whose legal
structure and economic relations the prevailing notions
of equity or axioms of justice are most faithfully
mirrored ; and where they are carried out in similar
degree on all the various sides of social life.   In these
respects our own time does not compare favourably
with the Middle Age.   Not only is our age one of
exceptionally rapid change, but our ideals are changing
even more rapidly than our institutions, so that we live

in an atmosphere of social ferment and revolutionary proposals. What makes the situation still more critical, and forms to my mind the peculiar danger of modern societies, is the startling contrast between their political and economic development. In politics, equality; in economics, subordination. One man, one vote; why not also one man, one wage? This contrast, which must be brought home to the dullest at election time, is full of social unsettlement, and is quite sufficient to account for the unrest characteristic of our day. How different was the inner harmony of the system of the Middle Age, where the economic order found its parallel in the political order, and was even reflected in the spiritual order, and projected in the conception of another world. The medieval conditions resulted in a long period of organic and stable society; the modern mark an age of transition, perhaps of revolution.

It seems clear that great change is inevitable either in our social philosophy or in our social institutions before we can arrive at that general consonance between them which social stability appears to require. The first impulse is to believe that our ideals must prevail, and the institutions go by the board. Principles of equity seem so axiomatic and imperative, until equally obvious but conflicting ones are proposed, that we are apt to invest them with something like religious obligation. It is this impulse that has given us modern socialism, with its vigorous criticism of the classical economics, and its revolutionary crusade against the

existing order: and the impulse is so natural that the
socialistic movement has grown with singular rapidity,
and is regarded with more than benevolent neutrality
by large masses who do not adopt the party label.   But
before making catastrophic changes in a social order
which at least has the merit of having survived, and of
having thus shown itself compatible with steady progress, it would seem only reasonable to direct a portion
of our critical activity to an examination of the principles
upon which the new order is to rest.   It is surely worth

Purpose
and signifi-
cance of
Dr.
Menger's
inquiry.

while to inquire how far these principles are consistent
with one another, and how far all or any of them are
capable of incarnation in a practical coherent system of
rights, adapted to human nature as we know it, or are
likely to find it in our time.   This is precisely the
object which Dr. Menger has proposed to himself in
this brilliant sketch.   To me at least it seems difficult
to exaggerate its importance.

Dr. Menger's criticism, then, presents itself as the
obverse of the socialistic attack.   It differs in two
respects from the ordinary criticism of the historical
school.   It deals not so much with actual legislation,
as with socialistic projects ; and it is not so much concerned with their ethical and economic as with their
juristic foundation.   From first to last, the inquiry
proceeds from the juristic standpoint.   It is confined to
the examination of those claims of right in which
socialist writers have embodied their ideals of equity,
and which form the backbone of their systems.   It

would be doing great injustice to the scholarly analysis
of Dr. Menger to compare it with the turgid and
irregular dissertations of Proudhon. But the purpose of
both writers is to detect the inner fundamental contradiction which underlies a great deal of the popular thought
on economic subjects. Proudhon made some pretence
of applying his criticism indifferently to both the communistic and the economic systems of social philosophy;
Dr. Menger deals only with the philosophy of socialism.

This term socialism is often used in this country Socialism
with a vagueness for which there is no excuse, as in and its two
the well-known phrase, "We are all socialists now." claims.
Dr. Menger, like Mr. John Rae, attaches a precise
meaning to the word. He understands by it not the
natural revolt against a morbid excess of commercialism,
which seeks to infuse existing social relations with a
more human and healthy spirit, but the campaign for
social reconstruction, the revolutionary socialism that
challenges the very principles upon which modern
society rests. For him Marx, not Ruskin, is the type
of the socialist. Socialism in this sense, the only one
really distinctive, has been well defined by Mr. Rae, in
terms which Dr. Menger might have drafted himself.
"It is not only a theory of the State's action, but a
theory of the State's action founded on a theory of the
labourer's right—at bottom a demand for social justice—
that every man shall possess the whole produce of his
labour." [1] It is this famous but ambiguous claim, lying

---

[1] John Rae, *Contemporary Socialism*, 1884, p. 13.

as it does at the root of all modern socialism, strictly
so-called, which forms the central subject of Dr.
Menger's inquiry; though he has a good deal to say of
another claim, perhaps more familiar in actual history,
the right to subsistence. To both these claims, but
especially to the first, he gives a most searching scrutiny
from the standpoint of jurisprudence. That is to say,
he studies them in their relations to other claims
asserted by the same school of writers, and generally
inquires how far they could form part of a consistent
system of legal right upon which it would be possible
to base the economic relations of an actual human
society.

The jurisprudence of the Have-Nots. Jurisprudence, he tells us, is in effect a mere reflection
of traditional legal conditions. Hence, its doctrine of
natural rights has been developed mainly from the
point of view of the propertied classes. As Adam
Smith puts it, in words whose significance was not lost
on Charles Hall, " Civil Government, so far as it is
instituted for the security of property, is in reality
instituted for the defence of the rich against the poor,
or of those who have some property against those who
have none at all." [1] Thus, just as socialists speak of a

---

[1] *Wealth of Nations*, bk. v. c. i. part ii. This view of Government
explains the position of the anarchist, so far as anarchism is intelligible
at all. But it is clearly inappropriate to modern conditions. It might
as truly be said of some democratic governments to-day that they are
a machinery by which those who have less property may compensate
themselves at the expense of those who have more. The tables have
been turned.

bourgeois political economy, so one may speak of the theory of rights in its orthodox form as a *bourgeois* jurisprudence. But in the course of the last century a rival jurisprudence has made its appearance in the shape of socialism—the jurisprudence of the Have-Nots, of the proletariate. This new philosophy of right still constitutes, in Dr. Menger's opinion, the real essence of socialism. He considers the economic form assumed by socialism in its later developments to be a mere outward husk, mainly due to the influence of the harsh and one-sided doctrine of Ricardo; a reaction against what its founders called "the New School of Political Economy," and the rest of mankind "the Dismal Science." With the revolution that economic teaching has undergone in the last fifty years, the force of this reaction is correspondingly diminished; and the jurisprudential element in socialism resumes its original importance.

For the details of Dr. Menger's analysis of this socialistic jurisprudence the reader will, of course, turn to the work itself. That the new philosophy of right should contain fundamental inconsistencies is only what we might expect if we consider its historical development. On the one hand, like the crude political economy which it attacked, it was founded upon the highly individualistic theory of natural right; while on the other, it was a reaction against unprecedented individual license, in favour of collectivist organisation for the general welfare. The earlier philosophies, like those of Owen

Its contradictions and their ultimate issue.

and Thompson, were more inclined to protest against self-interest and competition, and to inculcate a spirit of altruism and a system of communism.   The Marxian socialists have appealed very frankly to the most primitive of the individualistic instincts, and have laid more stress on the confiscation of existing forms of property than on the nature of the new system of distribution. Dr. Menger works out this conflict of discordant elements with great patience, acuteness, and research, in so far as it is exemplified in the claims of right which the various socialist philosophies contain, and the inadequate measures by which they propose to realise their principles.   Upon the whole, he leaves us with the conception of two great principles which dispute for primacy, the right to subsistence and the right to the whole produce of labour. These two claims he clearly shows to be inconsistent both in theory and in practice, in spirit and in effect; and after an interesting review of the degree of success with which they have respectively figured in socialistic projects of law, he comes to the final conclusion that it is the right to subsistence rather than the right to the whole produce of labour which social development tends to realise. In other words, we are tending more towards communism than anarchist individualism.

The inquiry essential.   An inquiry of this kind may seem somewhat too abstract to English readers, by nature averse to discussions of principle, and prone to take refuge from what Adam Smith called "disagreeable metaphysical arguments" in the more congenial examination of detailed practical schemes. If the sobering study of detail possessed the same fascination for the world in general as it seems to have for men of the Anglo-Saxon type, this English habit might perhaps be as sufficient as it is certainly safe. But there are large masses of mankind who are of more imaginative temper, more apt to be stirred by ideas, more under the dominion of phrases, who take these apparently axiomatic principles for the colours under which they make war on society. For this reason alone we could not afford to neglect the study of these socialist ideals, even if it were not of high intrinsic interest from a scientific point of view. When we consider the profound importance of the issues at stake, and the immense mass of human happiness and misery depending upon a right solution of them, the most matter-of-fact minds will perceive the practical value of a careful discussion of first principles. Take, for instance, the two claims of the right to subsistence, and the right to the whole produce of labour, and imagine the hopeless confusion and ruinous unsettlement that must result from the attempt to give complete legislative expression to these claims, if they are, as analysis clearly shows they are, radically inconsistent and contradictory. Just as we may avoid widespread physical desolation by rightly turning a stream near its source, so a timely dialectic in the fundamental ideas of social philosophy may spare us untold social wreckage and suffering.

2. DR. MENGER'S HISTORY

The
history.

Dr. Menger, however, does not by any means confine himself to this formal discussion of the socialist philosophy of right; nor do I know that this is the portion of his work which will be of most interest to English readers. I ventured to call attention to it first, because it reveals the main purpose of the author, and because from its very novelty and originality it seemed to require some preliminary introduction. But the larger part of the book is occupied by the brilliant piece of historical research upon which the more formal and systematic

Traces the develop- ment of a socialist claim.

discussion is founded. It is an attempt, Dr. Menger tells us, to trace the gradual development, in the various socialist schools and parties, of the conception of a new right—the right to the whole produce of labour—and to set forth the series of actual proposals by which men have tried to give a practical embodiment to this right during the last hundred years.

Difficulties of the inquiry.

Now it is a comparatively simple affair for the socialist to criticize existing society. He has to do with familiar institutions, realized on a grand scale, institutions which have lasted long enough for their defects to have become notorious, so long that the real advantages they secure are supposed to be part of the nature of things, and taken as matter of course. But the critic of socialism is heavily handicapped. Socialism, in the revolutionary sense, can hardly be said to have any established institutions. It eludes scrutiny. Such embodiments as it has achieved have been either too transient to leave a definite impression on the camera of history, or too exceptional in their conditions to possess much value as illustrations of general principle. We may know that they failed to realize the ends they were designed to serve ; we can only guess at the crop of evils they might have brought forth in due time, had they really taken fair root. Even their very failure to survive is not as conclusive as it would be in the case of more substantial experiments ; for it may always be said that they were never tried on a sufficiently large scale. It is the same to some extent with the theories of socialism. Socialists make merry at any differences of opinion or treatment which exist among economists ; but we shall hunt in vain through expositions of socialism to find one which even remotely approaches in detail and consistency, or in general acceptance, the ordinarily received *corpus* of economic science. Hence the critic of socialism has no definite objective. He has to reply to a desultory, guerilla attack : the socialists have the advantage of *franc-tireurs*, their position is constantly shifting and always obscure. So many socialists, so many social philosophies.

This endless diversity of theories and projects is a further burden to the critical historian. It obliges him, if he would be reasonably thorough and comprehensive, to glance at a very wide range of topics. The inquiry, too, must necessarily be international. International relations have influenced the growth of socialistic thought from its very origins, so that its history must at least take account of English, French, and German developments. Add to this that the literature of socialism is much of it inaccessible and obscure, clandestine, unfamiliar even to socialists themselves, and the difficulties of systematic criticism are sufficiently apparent.

Dr.
Menger's
success.

Dr. Menger's success, in the face of such difficulties, is certainly remarkable. He has contrived to give us a most effective and vigorous study of the historical evolution of the socialist doctrine of Right, from its early origins in Godwin and the English School, down to its latest manifestations in modern politics and legislation. It may be doubted whether so much valuable work has ever before been compressed within the same narrow limits. The picture is necessarily somewhat broadly sketched, but it is sketched with singular accuracy and learning; and though Dr. Menger, with rare self-restraint, is careful not to obtrude the mass of detail study upon which it is based, scholars will not fail to appreciate the elaborate and thorough character of his researches. It is a masterly piece of exposition throughout.

Dr. Menger seems equally at home whether he is dealing with the English, French, or German schools of socialism, and treats all three with equal fulness. The account of the French School is particularly well done, and is evidently based upon most minute and laborious studies. But so far as the work is polemical, we may consider that its main object is to assert the originality

of the English School at the expense of that of the better Promin-
known and more self-asserting North-German School. ence assigned to
Certainly this is the more novel side of Dr. Menger's the English School.
monograph ; and it is not perhaps too much to assume
that it was the occasion of its publication.   On account,
then, of the prominent part which the English School
plays in his work, as well as of its peculiar claims on
the interest of English readers, and because it has
always had a strong fascination for myself, I venture
to make some special reference here to this part of
Dr. Menger's inquiry.   In the whole story of human
thought upon social subjects there is no passage which
has been more critical, or more fruitful of wide-reaching
consequence.

3. The English School of Socialists

We may regard socialism as a protest against the Socialism
extravagances of the individualistic movement of the a reaction : English in
Renaissance and the Reformation, against the disintegra- its origin.
tion of the settled order and inner harmony of medieval
life.   This protest was constantly noticeable at periods
of change, as, for instance, after the Civil War ; and it
became general and acute during the ferment of thought
caused by the American and French Revolutions, and
during the terrible sufferings of the masses, nowhere
more severe than in England, which resulted from the
industrial revolution and the Great War.   As a reaction
against the anarchy of individualism, socialism naturally

developed in proportion to the exaggerations of the
fashionable philosophy; and when this found its *reductio
ad absurdum* in the extreme *laisser-faire* of the "New
School" of economists, about the early 'forties, the tide
of socialist influence reached its first high-water mark.
If this is a true view of the nature of the socialist
movement, it is not surprising that it should have
originated in England; and even those to whom
socialism is the gospel of the future have no ground
for national self-glorification on this account. It is
only natural that the reaction against the power of
modern capital, and the mischiefs incident to license
and absence of control, should begin in the country
where that power first made itself felt, where its license
was most unbounded, and where it attained the most
striking proportions. English genius perhaps does not
so commonly show itself in work of pure originality as
in the successful adaptation to useful purpose of ideas
derived from other races. But this is not so true in the
region of politics, and especially of social politics. It is
notorious that all the great *remedial* measures which have
proved the most effective checks to the abuses of capitalistic competition are of English origin. Trade Unions,
Co-operation, and Factory Legislation are all products of
English soil. That the *revolutionary* reaction against
capitalism is equally English in its inspiration is not so
generally known. But the present work establishes this
point beyond question. It conclusively proves that all
the fundamental ideas of modern revolutionary socialism,

and especially of the Marxian socialism, can be definitely traced to English sources. It was a handful of English writers, brought up in the classic country of capitalistic production, and reflecting upon the terrible wreckage of the early pre-regulation period, who laid down the broad lines of thought upon which socialistic criticism of capitalism has ever since proceeded. Original, independent, trenchant, and radical as they were, this little school of writers stand apart, clearly distinguishable from the various groups of contemporary social reformers, as well as from that English socialism whose form was determined by foreign influences. Not content, as the common English habit is, to attempt to palliate the miseries of the time by specific and detailed legislation, they challenged the very principles upon which the system of society rested : and while others were absorbed in the advocacy of social Utopias, they devoted themselves to asserting the inherent defects and injustice of the existing system, and demanded that these defects should be dealt with by radical and preventive, rather than by regulative and remedial methods.

Of this English School, the chief names are undoubtedly those of Godwin, Hall, Thompson, Gray, Hodgskin, and Bray. It will seem to many that Robert Owen should be added to this list. But though it is impossible to exaggerate the importance of the Owenite movement as a propagandist and remedial agency, and as a means of giving asylum and resonance to socialist ideas, Robert Owen himself was not remarkable as a

The English School : Godwin at its head.

militant and destructive thinker. Thomas Spence and Tom Paine, and even William Cobbett in some respects, might have a stronger title to be regarded as leaders of the revolutionary movement. Much more, I think, may be said, especially from the point of view of Dr. Menger's argument, for the claims of William Ogilvie. His remarkable book on the *Right of Property in Land,* which at once fascinated and shocked respectable Sir James Mackintosh, is often quoted by Godwin, who adopts Ogilvie's very phrases, and must have recognized in him a kindred spirit.[1] But in spite of the undoubted ability and influence of Ogilvie's work, we may here follow Dr. Menger in placing Godwin at the head of the English Socialist School. " Godwin," he says, " may be regarded as the first scientific socialist of modern times, in whom are to be found in germ all the ideas of modern socialism and anarchism." Traces of these ideas, no doubt, exist here and there in many of his predecessors, not merely in Ogilvie, Spence, and Paine, but in other minor writings, some of which are entered in the Bibliography appended to this book; and socialistic yeast even lurks, where perhaps it might least be suspected, in that wonderfully catholic work, the *Wealth of Nations.* Still Godwin fairly deserves the position assigned to him by Dr.

---

[1] Godwin adopted from Ogilvie his comparison of Rents to Pensions, and his description of hereditary wealth as a premium paid to idleness. "Whoever," says Ogilvie, "enjoys any revenue, not proportioned to industry or exertion of his own, or of his ancestors, is a freebooter, who has found means to cheat and rob the public" (p. 46). His argument really goes further than his conclusion, and would logically exclude the right of inheritance.

Menger. By its philosophic completeness, its rigorous and fearless, if somewhat puerile logic, and its admirably lucid exposition, the *Political Justice* may fairly entitle its author to be regarded as the Adam Smith of socialistic speculation.

Dr. Menger's account of Godwin in the text is so full, and the *Political Justice* is so well known, that I need say little of it here. It was an attempt, Godwin tells us, to systematize political views and principles after the new light thrown upon them by the discussions in France and America. From French speculation, he says, he derived a bent towards simplicity in political constructions; and possibly this, too, was the source of that confirmed optimism, that faith in the unlimited possibilities of social improvement, and the irresistible sway of intellectual conviction, which is the most striking character of the work. These premises were required to give even a superficial plausibility to his social philosophy. It was a combination of the purest communism with the most anarchic individualism. "The subject of Property," he says, "is the keystone that completes the fabric of political justice"; and in his last book (viii.), where he treats of property, we have an epitome of the whole. Individuals have no rights, neither has society : hence he cannot admit the claim of labour to the product of industry, except on its negative sides. In the established system of property he saw the root of all social evil, and attacked it with unsparing vigour. For it he would substitute a system

The Political Justice.

of equal property, where distribution is determined by
want, or "the capacity of the subject." In the Arcadia
he imagined, this system would require "no restrictions
or superintendence whatever." "It grows out of a
simple, clear, and unanswerable theory of the human
mind, that we first stand in need of a certain animal
subsistence and shelter, and after that, our only true
felicity consists in the expansion of our intellectual
powers, the knowledge of truth, and the practice of
virtue." Here we soar quite out of sight of the work-a-
day world. Godwin only appeals to that very rare class
of mind which is mainly swayed by intellectual considerations : his book, for ordinary men, was destitute
of motive force. He was too dispassionate in temper,
too extravagantly optimistic in his belief in the ultimate
empire of reason, too innocently blind to the impulses
that animate the average man—in short, too hopelessly
impracticable and unworldly ever to lead, or even to
stimulate, a revolutionary movement. A glance at the
admirable portrait of him by Maclise goes far to explain
why his book, with all its brilliance, was so ineffective.
The subject of that portrait could have had no serious
relations with the world of affairs. His political insight
may be measured by his adoption of that most chimerical
of all Utopias, an anarchical communism. Here is
Godwin, who regards want as the only equitable title to
property, objecting to any control over the individual
disposition of property, even in bequest. Contrast this
with the position of that statesman socialist, Saint-

Simon ; who, with views on the equities of property not very different from those of an average British juryman, was a strenuous advocate of heavy death duties.[1] However, Godwin was perhaps saved by his extravagances. The *Political Justice* appeared in 1793, at the height of the Reaction and the Terror, and no book even of that perturbed period was more profoundly subversive and revolutionary in its teaching. But the Government, who rigorously prosecuted many lesser men, felt that they could afford to ignore Godwin. A man who dwelt in regions of thought so far removed from the world of everyday life was quite harmless for all immediate practical purposes, and Governments do not trouble themselves about the future. Godwin's influence on the socialistic movement was, in fact, almost wholly indirect; and I am inclined to think that it might have been almost inappreciable, but for the elaborate development of his views by William Thompson, and the existence of a great propagandist agency for Thompson's ideas in the Owenite Co-operative societies.

In Charles Hall we come to a writer of a very different, and to my mind, far more stimulating quality. The *Political Justice* may be said to have had an academic origin. It was an attempt to systematize

Charles Hall : his chief work.

[1] Robert Owen, too, when candidate for Marylebone in 1847, advocated the replacement of existing taxation by "a graduated property tax equal to the national expenditure"; notwithstanding his well-known general preference for voluntary methods (Holyoake, *Sixty Years of an Agitator's Life*, 1893, i. p. 122).

political views and principles after a period of ferment
and criticism, which had disturbed the symmetry and
acceptance of the traditional systems. Hall's inspiration
was derived from direct contact with human misery in
the exercise of his calling as a physician. His book is
not the result of a philosophic desire to bring political
science up to date, or to draft a more perfect scheme of
society. It springs directly from a burning sense of
injustice and wrong, and a first-hand acquaintance with
widespread, undeserved suffering and destitution. The
more grave social abuses generally leave their mark on
the public health, so that medical men can hardly fail
to observe them; and Hall is one of the most notable
examples of a long series of physicians who made a
noble use of their opportunities, and play an honourable
part in the history of English industrial reform. Forced
by his daily duties, he tells us, to observe the deplorable
condition of the masses at that time, he was led to
reflect upon the causes which had brought it about. He
finds the cause in what he calls Civilisation; and hence
the title of his remarkable work, *The Effects of Civilisation
on the People in European States.* By Civilisation, Hall
practically means just what Godwin means by "the
established system of property," viz. a certain legalized
inequality, with the consequences incident to it. His
central idea is that Wealth is Power over the labour of
the poor; leading under the then-existing conditions to
inequality and oppression. This at least, as he very
forcibly and impressively argues, is the usual effect of

civilisation, though not a necessary one. It really results, he maintains, from the arbitrary and forcible assumption of land which has prevailed in most societies. Accordingly his remedy is a more equal distribution of land; towards which end he makes somewhat hesitatingly the several proposals which Dr. Menger has summarized in the text. Regarded in bare abstract, Hall's argument may not appear specially noteworthy, or to entitle him to distinction from the crowd of land-nationalisers whom we always have with us. Nothing but a study of the book itself will give an adequate idea of the restrained intensity of its purpose, the rigorous march of its argument, and the grandeur of its general conception. But the dominant effect perhaps which it leaves on the mind is a sense of the existence of a great impersonal power, arising out of faulty social institutions, necessarily operating to degrade the masses; a power of whose nature victims and instruments are alike unconscious. This impression is the more vivid on account of the scientific spirit and transparent sincerity of the work. Hall everywhere keeps his indignation in check, and never suffers it to provoke him to personal or class attacks. His criticism is inexorable and relentless, but not passionate or intemperate. Nor is the discussion disfigured by theoretical jargon, trumped up to give a pseudo-scientific basis to conclusions really derived from a hasty and partial induction. In these and many other respects, Hall's *Effects of Civilisation* is honourably distinguished from Marx's *Kapital*. It is not so well adapted to appeal to a popular audience as the more famous work, nor I think was it written with this intention ; but it has just the kind of originality and force which turn the current of cultivated opinion in new directions.   It was undoubtedly influential amongst the Owenite socialists, who constantly recommend it to the societies ; and it must be held to entitle its author to a permanent place in the history of one of the most important movements of modern thought.

Not in-
fluenced by
Godwin.
I am inclined to doubt whether Hall was acquainted with Godwin's writings.   Neither in his principal work, nor in the *Observations on Malthus* which he appended to it, is there any reference to Godwin.   Hall was one of the first writers to see through the imposture of American liberty, about which Godwin and his friends were so warmly congratulating themselves.   He points out that it is idle for the States to object to the mere titles of nobility, when they are laying the foundation for the substance of the evil in the steady growth of an aristocracy of wealth.   Again he observes (p. 272) that " many able and good men have seen the evils attending the great inequality of property ; but not being aware that they were destructive to the degree that we have demonstrated them to be, they have suffered other con- siderations to overbalance them in their minds."   So candid a writer as Hall, who refers freely to friends and opponents, would surely have made an exception in favour of Godwin here, had he read his work.   It is still more remarkable that there should be no reference to

Godwin in the *Observations on Malthus*, considering the
well-known relation between these two writers, and
the common interest Hall and Godwin had in rebutting
Malthus's main conclusion. It is true that Godwin,
like Hall, pleaded the remoteness of the pressure which
Malthus apprehended; but their general arguments are
essentially different. Godwin immediately leaves the
material question of more or less food, and passes to the
visions of intellectual progress, of "triumph of mind
over matter," on which he really relies. Hall, who is
too serious to indulge in mere speculation, meets
Malthus on his own ground, and keeps close to the real
issues. The question of remoteness seems to him vital
for practical purposes. It is an enormous gain if we
can "lay the reprieve at one hundred years." But this
physical limit may be extended by political action.
"Nature's remedy, colonisation," should be adopted;
and "marriage may be regulated by law." If all fails,
and over-population ensues, its evils will be less in a
state of equality than at present. In any case, the
denial of the right to existence is unjust and iniquitous.
It is not Nature's laws, as Malthus asserts, that doom
the labourer to starve; that cruel doom is brought on
him by the rich. He produces six or eight times what
he requires in order to live, but this is taken from him
by those who produce nothing. In fine, Hall says that
Malthus's system "will operate as an encouragement
to those who were too much before inclined to oppress,
to push their tyranny still further,—but I am very far

from thinking this was the design of the author" (p. 349).
This is a far more practical reply to the objection on
the ground of over-population than Godwin's. I have
referred to it at some length, because the tract seems to
be unknown; and it appears to me to confirm the view
that Hall was an essentially independent thinker, and
that he was unaware of previous work published by
Godwin on somewhat similar lines.

Closer affinity with Paine and Ogilvie.

If, indeed, we are to find a precursor for Hall, we
must look to Tom Paine, and especially to Paine's
Agrarian Justice. This notable essay, which resembles
Hall's work in its incisiveness and fearless logic, presents
civilisation under just the aspect in which it appeared
to Hall. "Poverty," says Paine, "is a thing created by
that which is called civilised life. It exists not in the
natural state." "Civilisation therefore . . . has operated
two ways, to make one part of society more affluent,
and the other part more wretched, than could have
been the lot of either in a natural state." "The condition of millions in every country of Europe is far
worse than if they had been born before civilisation
began, or had been born among the Indians of North
America of the present day." "The contrast of affluence
and wretchedness continually meeting and offending
the eye, is like dead and living bodies chained together."
He attributes these mischiefs to "the landed monopoly."
The diagnosis and the agrarian remedy remind us of
Hall. But Paine lacks Hall's intensity and economic
insight. He is pre-eminently a politician; "the founder

of political ideas among the people of England," as Holyoake styles him; but he cannot claim to have seriously raised the social question, as we now understand it. The merit, or demerit, the fame in any case, which attaches to this achievement, must I think belong to Hall. Godwin and Ogilvie stated the formal issues with some precision, Ogilvie with some practical conception of what was at stake. But both writers had a certain academic air. Dr. Bain says of the *Political Justice*, "It was a splendid ideal or political romance, and may fitly be compared with the *Republic* of Plato. It set people thinking, made them dissatisfied with the present state of things." [1] Without pretending to put the *Political Justice* on the same level as the *Republic* of Plato, we must admit that it was rather the dream of a philosophical optimist than the bitter cry of protest against injustice and suffering. It was much better calculated to set scholars thinking, than to turn the widespread dissatisfaction of serious men into revolutionary channels. But Hall was the man to preach a social crusade. His book does not seem to have been noticed by the authorities, owing to its very small and private circulation, or it would no doubt have been suppressed. It is difficult to say what might not have been its effect had it been more widely read. As it was, Hall's influence, though limited and indirect, was very considerable. His work was carefully studied by the leaders of the Owenite societies, and had much to

[1] *Life of James Mill*, p. 435.

do with the rise and shaping of that critical socialism which was the life-blood of the movement in the second quarter of this century.

William Thompson.

I pass now to the better-known William Thompson,[1] who, perhaps, deserves by the completeness of his exposition, the wide influence of his writings, and the devotion of his life and fortune to the movement, to be regarded as chief of the English Socialist School. Socialistic propagandism has been mainly carried on by men of Celtic or Semitic blood, and Thompson appears to have been an Irishman, a native of County Cork, where he died at Clonnkeen in 1833, aged about fifty, according to Minter Morgan. In 1827, he tells us that for about twelve years he had been "living on what is called rent, the produce of the labor of others"; as an Irish landlord, in fact. For twenty years, like Combe, he was a vegetarian and teetotaller. His life was spent in advocating and aiding the formation of Owenite Co-operative Societies; and he left the great bulk of his property by will in 1830 to be applied to the same purposes. The will, however, was successfully contested by relatives on the ground that "immoral" objects were included in its benefits; and very little of his property seems actually to have been used as he had directed.

[1] Thompson must be distinguished from William Thomson, editor of the *Chartist Circular*, who describes himself in *The Age of Harmony* as "Founder of Fifty Economical Societies, and Secretary to the Protecting Union of the Hand-loom Weavers of Scotland." Thomson appears to have been a Glasgow man.

The immediate occasion of his principal work was a Occasion
discussion with a gentleman of Cork, "celebrated for and spirit
his skill in the controversies of political economy," who *Inquiry.*
descanted on the blessings of the inequality of wealth,
a theme which was developed with great extravagance
by Mrs. Marcet and other worthy but maudlin writers
of the period. But the foundations of his views were
laid long before. He was a pupil and an enthusiastic
admirer of Bentham, "who has done more," he says,
"for moral science than Bacon did for physical science";
and he describes himself as merely working out the
applications of his master's principles. In Owen's
system of equality he hoped to realise Bentham's conception of a maximum of happiness. There is indeed a
tendency to formal enumerations and elaborate classification in Thompson's work which was probably derived
from Bentham; but not much else, I think, except the
perpetual insistence upon a rigorous, systematic and
impartial calculation of utility, upon which all its
argument proceeds. There was another obvious influence
which was at least equally potent in forming his views.
From first to last his work is saturated with the spirit
of Godwin, though the teachings of Bentham no doubt
gave him a practical turn and a regard for facts and
detail conspicuously wanting in the author of *Political
Justice.* Like Godwin, Thompson shows a strong
preference for purely voluntary methods, and hopes for
great results from the development of the intellectual
side of human nature. But he distinctly advocates

communistic organisation as against individual economy. He is filled with almost the Owenite detestation of competition as the root of all social evil ; though he goes so far with Godwin as to admit that a genuine system of *laisser faire* would be infinitely preferable to the system of "restraint by force and fraud," or of "forced inequality of wealth,"—his way of describing the then-existing social institutions. His own account of his position, in the *Preliminary Observations*, is that he steered a middle course between the purely intellectual speculation of Godwin, and the merely mechanical philosophy of Malthus. Following on Bentham's lines, his object was to apply to social science the ascertained truths of political economy, making these and all other branches of knowledge subservient to that just distribution of wealth which tends most to human happiness.

His relation to Ricardo

"The ascertained truths of political economy" were, of course, the doctrines of the new or Ricardian School. I am more and more impressed, as I study the literature of socialism, with the far-reaching, disastrous consequences of the unfortunate colour given to economic teaching by Ricardo, and the little band of able, but somewhat hard and narrow writers who called themselves by his name. As Dr. Menger clearly shows, it was Ricardo's crude generalisations which gave modern socialism its fancied scientific basis, and provoked, if they did not justify, its revolutionary form. There are times when we are disposed to underrate the value of that drill in method which is a principal part of academic training. At such times we should think of Ricardo. Ricardo, and still more those who popularised him, may stand as an example for all time of the extreme danger which may arise from the unscientific use of hypothesis in social speculations, from the failure to appreciate the limited application to actual affairs of a highly artificial and arbitrary analysis. His ingenious, though perhaps over-elaborated reasonings became positively mischievous and misleading when they were unhesitatingly applied to determine grave practical issues without the smallest sense of the thoroughly abstract and unreal character of the assumptions on which they were founded. Thus, as Jevons has observed, Ricardo gave the whole course of English economics a wrong twist. It became unhistorical and unrealistic; it lost its scientific independence, and became the tool of a political party. At one time indeed it went very near to losing its rightful authority in legislation and affairs; nor did it regain its old position until by the greater precision of the theorists on the one side, and the broader treatment of real questions by the historical school on the other side, this elementary blunder in method was rectified. Meanwhile, by a singular irony of fate, it happened that Ricardo, by this imperfect presentation of economic doctrine, did more than any intentionally socialist writer to sap the foundations of that form of society which he was trying to explain, and which he believed to be the typical and

natural, if not, indeed, the ideal social state. William
Thompson was only one of a series of socialist writers,
culminating in Marx and Lassalle, who take the Ricardian
position as the very basis of their argument. His first
section has the familiar Ricardian ring. "Wealth is
produced by labor: no other ingredient but labor
makes any object of desire an object of wealth. Labor
is the sole universal measure, as well as the characteristic distinction of wealth." Give the word "labour"
its popular meaning, and it is merely an affair of logic
to deduce a large part of modern socialism from this
position. Whatever qualifications Ricardo may have
made upon it in his own mind, ninety-nine readers out
of a hundred took him literally, and the main impression
left by his book was that while wealth was almost
exclusively due to labour, it was mainly absorbed by
rent and other payments to the unproductive classes.
This was the text which Thompson and the English
socialists proceeded to elaborate.

and
Colquhoun.
The whole school, and especially Thompson and
Gray, were greatly impressed by the distinction be-
tween the productive and unproductive classes. Patrick
Colquhoun, in his *Treatise on the Wealth, Power, and
Resources of the British Empire*, which first appeared
in 1814, published a celebrated Table, which he describes
as " An Attempt to exhibit a General View of Society ;
and to shew how the New Property [or National Income]
. . . is *distributed* among the different Classes of the
Community." This Map of Civil Society, as Colquhoun

calls it, was the statistical foundation of the socialist movement. We meet with constant references to it, not only in the text-books of the school, but in its periodical literature. There is no doubt that the statistical detail given by Colquhoun, at a time when the nation was groaning under a crushing weight of taxation, gave quite a new vividness and realism to the formal distinction between productive and unproductive labour, and very much fostered the disposition to divide society into productive and unproductive classes. This again, under the conditions of popular agitation, inevitably tended to that narrow view of productivity which is characteristic of revolutionary socialism in all its forms. Like Hall and Gray, Thompson's view of rational consumption is somewhat narrow ; it seems to be limited to the " ordinary wants and comforts of society— food, clothing and dwellings "; what goes beyond these is due to luxury and caprice : and it was one of his chief objections to the "system of inequality " that it diverted production from the supply of the more necessary objects to "a species of industry—the least conducive to the public good." But outside all distinction between kinds of producers was the great distinction between producers and non-producers. It is upon this latter distinction, not always clearly separated from the distinction between kinds of producers, that Thompson's main argument turns.

He starts from the three *natural* laws of distribution given in the text (p. 53). Labour is to be free : His general argument : its difficulties to enjoy the whole of its products : to exchange these products voluntarily. In all three respects Thompson finds the existing system of distribution vicious. Labour is not free, either as to its direction or continuance ; there are heavy deductions from its product, in the shape of rent, profits, and taxes : exchanges are impeded by various forms of monopoly and protection. On all three heads Thompson argues at great length ; though he is not as trenchant as Gray, and he is everywhere careful to deprecate the employment of force. Godwin himself is not more profoundly attached to the voluntary principle ; it is the characteristic mark of his system. "Do we ask," he says, "whether any abstraction of the products of labour is just? The sufficient and only answer ought to be, 'Is it voluntary?'" But it is evident that no system of *laisser faire*, however perfectly realized, will ever give us equality. This brings us to a difficulty which Thompson recognizes at the outset of his inquiry, but in my opinion utterly fails to overcome. "Here," he says, " is the cruel dilemma in which mankind have been placed. Here is the important problem of moral science to be solved, ' *how to reconcile equality with security ;* how to reconcile *just distribution with continued production.*" He sees clearly enough how hard it is to retain an effective stimulus to production, and to conform to the communist ideal of distribution ; but it cannot be said that his solution is very convincing. It is of the nature of a compromise. At first indeed he contends that there is no real conflict between the principles. " It is only by an undeviating adherence to (real) equal security that any approach can be made to equality " (p. 97). Candour obliges him to abandon this position in favour of a curious evasion. "Labor should enjoy the use of the whole products of its exertions : the shares of the products of labor should be equal to all contributing, according to their capacities of mind or body, to the common stock." [1] I need not point out how completely the passage from the labourer as individual to labour in the abstract surrenders the whole contention of equity. There is less objection to the second form of his compromise, though it is obviously unpractical. "Though labor has the *right* to the whole product of its exertions, it may *voluntarily agree before production* to equality of remuneration." In any case, the supposed necessary incentive to production has vanished. The fact is that there is a radical contradiction between the equities of production and the equities of consumption. " To each according to his work," " to each according to his needs," are hopelessly inconsistent maxims, though each is plausible enough in itself. Our present happy-go-lucky system of competitive exchange makes a confessedly imperfect compromise between the two principles, but we have yet to be shown the socialistic system which would make a better one.

There is an unfortunate omission in Thompson's treatise, which deprives us of what would have been a *and drift towards communism.*

[1] *Labor Rewarded*, p. 37.

good opportunity for judging of his practical statesman-
ship. He had prepared, he says, a chapter of 100 pages,
devoted to the criticism of the then-existing institutions
of society. For the present he withholds it, in order to
prevent unnecessary irritation. It might have been
expected that William Pare, his literary trustee, would
have discovered and published this chapter in his second
edition of the book; but we are still left with only the
table of headings. We have to judge Thompson therefore as a practical reformer, by his projects for voluntary
schemes. These show the inevitable drift to communism
which must be the end of all speculations based on considerations of equity. "Would you like," he writes to
the distressed Spitalfields weavers, "to enjoy yourselves
the whole products of your labor ? You have nothing
more to do than simply to *alter the direction of your
labor*. Instead of working for you know not whom, *work
for each other*." He had said in 1824 that if any departure
is made from the principle of securing the whole product
to labour it should be in the direction of equality. At
that time he thought that such a departure "ought
scarcely ever, if ever, to occur." But after 1830 he
devoted himself, body, mind, and estate, to the advocacy
of communistic societies of the Owenite type: and the
"principle of security" seems to have been practically
abandoned in favour of the principle of equality. The
sacrifice of equity involved in this result is perhaps not
so great as even Thompson himself imagined. A careful
analysis of the real contribution of individuals to the

work of production, under modern conditions, if conducted in the spirit of Comte's philosophy, might
considerably modify our *primâ facie* impressions as to
the inequity of equal remuneration.   Still something
would undoubtedly remain.   But we. need not further
discuss the equity of arrangements so hopelessly impracticable.   Thompson's fame will not rest upon his His great
advocacy of Owenite co-operation, devoted and public- achievement.
spirited as that was ; but upon the fact that he was the
first writer to elevate the question of the just distribution
of wealth to the supreme position it has since held in
English political economy.   Up to his time, political
economy had been rather commercial than industrial ;
indeed he finds it necessary to explain the very meaning
of the term *industrial,* which he says was from the
French, and no doubt adopted from Saint - Simon.
When we get to John Stuart Mill we find production
definitely subordinated to distribution, the great and
distinguishing theme of his work.   I cannot doubt that
this change was largely due to Thompson, whose influence
on Mill is conspicuous, in more directions than one.[1]

   John Gray, the next writer who claims notice, though John Gray.
he cannot pretend to anything like the authority and
following of Thompson, was the author of a *Lecture on*

   [1] Thompson, and the English socialists generally, were all champions
of the rights of women, and the equal freedom of the sexes.   A curious
parallel might be drawn between the influence on Thompson of the
beautiful and injured Mrs. Wheeler, to whom he dedicated his *Appeal,*
and the better-known relations between Mrs. Taylor and John Stuart
Mill.

Human Happiness, which is perhaps the most striking
and effective socialist manifesto of the time.   Like
Fourier, his first experience of life was gained in trade.
Educated at Repton, he left school early to serve first as
clerk, and then as traveller in a great London wholesale
house.   The great city cast its spell over him, and raised
doubts in his mind as to the social harmonies.   London
and its myriads, he tells us, were to him for many years
an intricate problem that he could hardly venture to
hope ever to be able to solve.   At an early age, and
long before he had even heard of Owen, he became
convinced that "something was wrong . . . the commercial proceedings of mankind were at variance with
the whole system of nature."   After some reflection he
arrived at the conclusion that production instead of
being the *effect* of demand, ought to be its *cause*.   Full
of his discovery, he turned to Adam Smith, read the first
volume of the *Wealth of Nations*, and then "compiled a
violent, puerile, unintelligible, and unmendable volume,"
which he called *The National Commercial System*.   He
was dissuaded from publishing this book.   Afterwards,
advised by his brother, he read Owen's writings; and
finding in them some support to his own views, he then
(in 1825) published a fragment of the discarded work in
the shape of the famous *Lecture*, which was a favourite
text-book with English socialists for the next twenty
years.   Part of the edition was lost, and the circulation
in England was therefore restricted; but the lecture was
reprinted in Philadelphia, where a thousand copies were

rapidly sold, and it no doubt aided the growth of the American socialist group which rallied round Frances Wright, R. Dale Owen, and the *Free Enquirer*. We know, at all events, that it gave rise to one of the earliest of American socialist utterances, an *Address to the Members of Trade Societies*, written by a journeyman bootmaker; a tract which so impressed Robert Owen that he brought a copy over with him from America, and caused it to be reprinted in London in 1827. Meanwhile Gray, though differing considerably from Owen on many vital points, offered his services at Orbiston, and came to Scotland to assist; but disapproving of the plans, and not being able to make his remonstrances effective, he resolved to have nothing to do with the scheme, and wrote an article in criticism of it called *A Word of Advice to the Orbistonians.* He seems afterwards to have settled in Scotland, and embarked on various newspaper ventures, presumably with some success; for we find him later in life offering substantial prizes, and circulating his books gratuitously in large numbers.

Gray was very careful to assert his own originality, especially as against Owen. "Neither in whole nor in part," he says, "have I gathered these opinions from any man." But his independence of Owen is obvious enough. He was too revolutionary in his early work, and too individualistic throughout for Robert Owen. He owed more to Colquhoun, whose *Map of Civil Society* is the central topic and object-lesson of the *Lecture on*

His originality.

Happiness. It may have been reflection on the facts
exhibited in the *Map* which roused in Gray the biting
irony of this vigorous tract. Nothing could be more
unlike the temper and method of Robert Owen. Besides,
there is a certain continuity and individuality about all
Gray's work; it has a character of its own. From first
to last his great theme was the avoidance of dislocations
in industry by the better adjustment of production and
demand. As he advanced in years his tone became
more commercial, and we miss any trace of the revolutionary socialism which animates his first tract.
Indeed, in 1848 he goes so far as to apologize for having
used the term "Social System" in the title of his 1831
book, and to explain that the word *Social* did not then carry
with it the communistic associations it had since acquired.
He had come to identify the cause of commercial mischief
with a bullion-based currency system, and devoted the
greater part of his life to the advocacy of a scheme of
paper currency, almost as wild and impracticable as
Owen's Labour Exchange.

The
Lecture.   Looked at as a whole, Gray's career was a curious
one, and not such as would justify us in classing him
as a socialist. And yet the *Lecture on Human Happiness* is certainly one of the most remarkable of socialist
writings. How it could have been written by Gray, I
have always found hard to understand. It is a solitary
flash of lightning from an otherwise peaceful sky. The
ostensible object of the lecture is to advocate Owen's
schemes, though Gray did not really believe in the com-

munistic principle.[1] He may possibly have regarded
Owenism as a counsel of perfection; at any rate he
promises in a future lecture to propound a scheme of his
own, "quite different."

The book is so rare now, that it may be con- Analysis of
venient if, in summarizing the argument, I quote a few of its argument.
typical passages. After some general remarks intended
to meet any prejudices against Owen on account of the
novelty of his proposals, Gray inquires into the nature
of existing commercial arrangements, and gives a critical
analysis of Colquhoun's tables, laying great stress, and
much in the same way as Thompson, on the distinction between the productive and unproductive classes.
Following Colquhoun, he estimates the whole income of
the country as £430,000,000, of which he considers that
the productive classes produced £426,000,000 : "being
very nearly *fifty-four pounds a year* for each man, woman,
and child in the productive classes : of which they received about *eleven pounds*, being but a small trifle more
than ONE-FIFTH PART OF THE PRODUCE OF THEIR OWN
LABOUR !!!" "Every unproductive member of society
is a DIRECT TAX upon the productive classes." "Numbers,
even of the productive classes, are compelled by the
present system to become useless members of society."
"The persons who compose the Independent classes are
Dependent upon two things : first, upon the *industry*
of their fellow-creatures ; second, upon *injustice* which

---

[1] Cf. *The Social System*, 1831, p. 106, "I look upon all systems of
equality as unjust in principle, and quite impracticable."

enables them to command it." He denies that there
can be any just title to land. "The foundation of all
property is LABOUR, and there is no other just foundation
for it." "The interest of money is another mode of
obtaining labour without giving any equivalent for it."
"*What does the productive labourer obtain for that portion
of the produce of his industry which is annually taken
from him by incomes obtained by the lenders of money?*
He obtains NOTHING! Then, we ask, is a man the
natural proprietor of the produce of his own labour?
If he is not, what foundation is there for property at
all? . . . If he is, . . . there is no justice in requiring
interest for the use of money." Passing from the question
of right, Gray next contends (like Godwin) that there is
no real happiness in any rank under the competitive
system of society, not even among the pensioned rich; and
remarks especially upon the distressed state of Ireland.
The great cause of poverty he finds in the existence of
an unnatural limit to production, in the shape of the
principle of competition. "*The division of the interests
of men*, in their mode of employing capital, and in
the distribution of the produce of their labour, is the
tremendous engine of mischief which is the curse of the
human race, and the cause of almost every evil by which
we are surrounded." "In consequence of the ability of
the FEW to produce all that competition will allow the
MANY to consume, competition will be still further
increased." "The grand feature of *Mr. Owen's* plan . . .
is that it abolishes the circumstance which now limits

production, and gives to the producers the wealth that
they create."

Finally, he sums up in a passage which deserves to
be quoted at length. " Upon the whole, then, we have
endeavoured to exhibit society as it now is. We have
endeavoured to show by whom wealth is created, and
by whom it is consumed. We have endeavoured to
show that it is from human labour that every description
of wealth proceeds ; that the productive classes Do Now
support, not only themselves, but every unproductive
member of society ! that *they only* are productive
members of society who apply *their own hands* either to
the cultivation of the earth itself, or to the preparing
or appropriating the produce of the earth to the uses of
life ; that every individual not so employed, is a direct
tax upon those who are so employed; that (to say
nothing of the numerous and expensive class of persons
who have not even the pretension to utility in any way
whatever) all merchants, manufacturers, wholesale and
retail tradesmen, together with their clerks, assistants,
and shopmen, are either directors and superintendents
of production, or mere distributors of wealth, who are
paid by the labour of those who create it ; and that such
persons are useful only in a *sufficient number*, so as to
direct and superintend labour, and to distribute its
produce."

" We have endeavoured to show that the real income
of the country, which consists in the quantity of wealth
annually created by the labour of the people, is taken

Summary of its conclusions.

from its producers chiefly by the rent of land, by the rent of houses, by the interest of money, and by the profit obtained by persons who buy their labour from them at one price, and sell it at another; that these immense taxes of rent, interest, and profits on labour, must ever continue while the system of individual competition stands; that in the new communities ALL would be productive members of society; excepting only the persons *absolutely required* in unproductive occupations, who would also devote their time and talents to the general good, and that No ONE would be taxed either with rent, interest, or profit on his labour."

Their aggressive tone.

This is a definite programme clearly and logically expressed, and it will easily be understood how it would appeal to the Owenite societies. Some of its extravagances, such as classing as unproductive services "absolutely required" by society, the economists had already taught them to swallow; the great abuses of property then common made others sound more plausible than they do to the more critical readers of to-day. It cannot be said positively whether Gray wrote before Thompson, and in independence of him. I think he did. He makes no reference to him so far as I know. In any case, I think Gray must be regarded as the pioneer of modern militant, aggressive socialism; and his little tract must be preferred, in point of originality, terseness, and effect, to the elaborate and methodical treatise of Thompson, more notable in many other respects. Gray's convictions were less solid and matured than Thompson's, and they seem, as so often happens, to have been considerably modified by his success in life, or else by larger experience. But so far as this early writing is concerned, Gray left little for Marx to add, except in the way of incitement to the use of force. To this Gray was firmly opposed; he deprecates every form of violence, and he even says that it has been no pleasant task to him to criticize thus faithfully "the established customs of the country."

The next writer of this little group, and one of the most original, is Thomas Hodgskin. His first socialistic utterance appeared in 1825, the same year as Gray's famous lecture; but Gray's lecture, as we have seen, was really written much earlier. All Hodgskin's writing shows him to have been a man of liberal education, and some philosophic training. He quotes throughout from the best authorities on economics and social philosophy; especially from Locke, Adam Smith, and Millar. To Adam Smith he constantly refers; and he never tires of contrasting Smith's "natural system" with the "political economy" of the contemporary school. Before 1820 he travelled in North Germany, and published an account of his impressions in two volumes; and he states that he knew from personal observation the condition of the legally emancipated serfs in Austria and Prussia. John Lalor tells us[1] that Hodgskin was well known as an able and accomplished journalist; he

Thomas Hodgskin.

---

[1] Cf. *Money and Morals*, 1852, Pref. p. xxiv.

appears to have been on the staff of, or at least a frequent contributor to, the *Morning Chronicle*. At one time he was Honorary Secretary to the London Mechanics' Institution, where in 1826 he delivered four lectures, published in 1827 under the title of *Popular Political Economy*. James Mill, writing to Brougham, speaks of him as "our friend Hodgskin." Both Brougham and Mill would probably know of Hodgskin through Black and the *Chronicle*, then their great organ in the Press; and also, no doubt, through his connection with the Mechanics' Institution.[1]

His wide influence.

But, apart from personal acquaintance, there was something in Hodgskin's writing well calculated to attract the attention of those who had any real insight into the signs of the times. No member of the English socialist group seems to have been more widely read on both sides of the Atlantic, and the significance of his position was instantly recognised. He was controverted,

---

[1] Since the above was written, the appearance of Mr. Wallas's admirable *Life of Francis Place* has thrown further light on the personality of Hodgskin, and on his friendship with Place and James Mill (cf. especially, pp. 267-269). Like so many turbulent thinkers, Hodgskin seems to have been the victim of injustice. A young naval lieutenant, he was in 1813 placed on half-pay for writing a pamphlet against pressing. From this year onwards he was in intimate correspondence with Place, and once acted as travelling companion to Place's eldest son. In 1820, Hodgskin read Ricardo's *Principles*, and from this time the correspondence often related to that "Ricardian Socialism" which Hodgskin, more than any other individual, may claim to have originated. In one of the letters, according to Mr. Wallas, Hodgskin sketches a book "curiously like Marx's *Capital*," but Place dissuaded him from writing it.

amongst others, by Samuel Read in 1829, Thomas
Cooper in 1830, and Brougham in 1831. He is quoted
by Marx in the first draft for his larger work, which he
published in 1859; and Cooper speaks of his doctrines
as having influenced the New York School of socialists
and the *Free Inquirer*.

For our present purposes the two most important
works of Hodgskin are his *Labour Defended*, published
in 1825, and his *Right of Property*, which appeared in
1831. In his *Popular Political Economy*, from the circumstances in which it was prepared, Hodgskin no
doubt felt bound to subordinate his peculiar opinions,
and at any rate they are not developed with the same
freedom and originality as in the other works named.
The occasion of the first of these writings, justly described
by Marx as a "vorzügliche Schrift," will appear from
its full title:—*Labour Defended against the Claims of*
Capital; or the Unproductiveness of Capital proved with
reference to the Present Combinations amongst Journeymen.
By a Labourer. In 1824, the Combination Laws, at the
instance of Joseph Hume's Committee, had been
repealed. But there followed a great development of
trade union activity, and with it such an outburst of
strikes as to cause general alarm. This led in 1825 to
the appointment of another Committee, with a view to
the re-enactment of the old anti-combination laws. By
the tactical skill of Francis Place, however, this result
was averted, and the new Act of 1825, while imposing
certain restrictions, left the right of agreement and

*Occasion
and
argument
of Labour
Defended.*

discussion in wages questions substantially unimpaired.[1] Hodgskin's tract was intended as a theoretical contribution to the settlement of this question. "In all the debates," he says, "much stress is laid on the necessity of protecting capital. What capital performs is therefore a question of considerable importance, which the author was on this account induced to examine. As the result of that examination, it is his opinion that all the benefits attributed to capital arise from co-existing skilled labour. He feels himself, on this account, called on to deny that capital has any just claim to the large share of the national produce now bestowed on it. "This large share, he has endeavoured to show, is the cause of the poverty of the labourer; and he ventures to assert that the condition of the labourer can never be permanently improved till he can refute the theory, and is determined to oppose the practice, of giving nearly everything to capital." The thesis perhaps is rather clumsily stated, but the development of the argument is very able. There is an analysis of capital which would interest Dr. Irving Fisher and Mr. Cannan. Hodgskin insists that most of what is called capital is not so much a hoard or stock, as an income or flow estimated at a particular point of time, all of which is the product of labour. "As far as food, drink, and clothing are concerned, it is quite plain that no species of labourer depends on any previously prepared stock, for, in fact,

---

[1] Cf. the *History of Trade Unionism*, by Sidney and Beatrice Webb, 1894, pp. 85-97 ; and Wallas's *Life of Place*, ch. viii.

no such stock exists; but every species of labourer does constantly, and at all times, depend for his supplies on the co-existing labour of some other labourers" (p. 11). "All the effects usually attributed to accumulation of circulating capital are derived from the *accumulation and storing up of skilled labour.*" Fixed capital, no doubt, is stored ; but "fixed capital does not derive its utility from previous, but present labour ; and does not bring its owner a profit because it has been stored up, but because it is a means of obtaining a command over labour." The inventor deserves his reward, and so does the skilled artisan who uses the invention. "But betwixt him who makes instruments and him who uses them, in steps the capitalist, who neither makes nor uses them, and appropriates to himself the produce of both . . . he is the middleman of all the labourers." But while the middlemen of Ireland are stigmatized as oppressors, the middlemen of England are honoured as benefactors. "At least such are the doctrines of political economy."—I quote these passages, not to endorse them, but to explain Hodgskin's position, and to enable the reader to judge how far he anticipates Marx.

In one respect he was in advance both of Marx and the economists. He carefully distinguishes between the capitalist and the *entrepreneur*. "Masters, it is evident, are *labourers* as well as their journeymen. In this character their interest is precisely the same as that of their men. But they are also either capitalists or the agents of the capitalist, and in this respect their interest is decidedly opposed to the interest of their workmen" (p. 27). "The contest now appears to be between masters and journeymen, or between one species of labour and another, but it will soon be displayed in its proper characters; and will stand confessed a war of honest industry against ... idle profligacy" (p. 31). Among other points made in the argument, which is too compressed and continuous to be fairly represented by quotations, I may note that he refers to Ricardo, "not as caring much to illustrate the subtleties of that ingenious and profound writer, but because his theory confirms ... that the exactions of the capitalist cause the poverty of the labourer," and he proceeds to claim his authority for the Iron Law. He recognises that under division of labour "there is no longer anything which we can call the natural reward of individual labour." But this difficulty might be left to the "higgling of the market," if labour were perfectly free. But if he is in favour of competition as the principle by which to determine the division of labour's share between the various ranks of labourers, he is for combination against capital in order to make labour's share as large as possible. By combining, the journeymen "may reduce or destroy altogether the profit of the idle capitalist ... but they will augment the wages and rewards of industry, and will give to genius and skill their due share of the national produce."

Thus Hodgskin, while retaining an individualistic

form of society, aimed, by means of combination, at Criticized in Thompson's *Labor Rewarded*. depriving capital of any share in the produce. Thompson considered this position an impossible one. In an answer to Hodgskin published in 1827, called *Labor Rewarded*, Thompson urges that "individual competition is incompatible with equal remuneration, as it is also with securing to labor the entire products of its exertions" (p. 36). "The author of *Labour Defended* stands alone, as far as I know, amongst the advocates of Individual competition, in even *wishing* that labor should possess the whole of the products of its exertions. All other advocates of individual competition look on the notion as visionary, under the Competitive System" (p. 97). We know Thompson's solution of the difficulty. Labourers must become capitalists, and unite in communities to regulate their own labour. To ascertain for each the exact product of his own labour is impracticable. If this could be done, then justice would give each individual a property in that product. But moral considerations would force him to share that product with others. The human race could not otherwise be preserved. This voluntary distribution is best carried out under the equitable arrangements of co-operative communities, with their regulated exchanges. "It is on the regulation of exchanges," he concludes, "that the industrious classes must depend for realising the general proposition that 'the whole produce of labour should belong to the labourer'" (p. 13). We shall see later how this theme was developed by Bray.

Hodgskin as Anarchist.   While Hodgskin in his *Labour Defended* adopted a position of his own, sufficiently distinct from those of Gray and Thompson, his most characteristic and original doctrine is contained in *The Natural and Artificial Rights of Property Contrasted*. This work, published in 1832, and "practically written," he tells us, in 1829, is in form a series of letters addressed to Brougham, who in February 1828 had moved for a Commission on the State of the Law. It opposes to Brougham's demand for detail reform a drastic, radical indictment of the whole foundation of the existing property law. The vein of anarchism which is a salient feature of English socialism, and which may even be traced, thanks to Physiocratic influence, in Adam Smith himself, is nowhere more conspicuous than in Hodgskin, and especially in this his last work. It would appear that Hodgskin was mainly inspired in this attack by the teaching of the *Wealth of Nations*, for whose author he had a profound respect. Both here and in his *Popular Political Economy* he quotes Adam Smith copiously, and he is greatly impressed by Smith's well-known distinction, in Book III., between "human institutions" and "the natural order of things." "That great man," he says, "carefully distinguished the natural distribution of wealth from the distribution which is derived from our artificial right of property. His successors, on the contrary, make no such distinction, and in their writings the consequences of this right are stated to be the laws of Nature."[1]

---

[1] *Popular Political Economy*, p. xxii.

The distinction appeared to Hodgskin of the very first importance. "The contest now going on in society, the preternatural throes and heavings which frightfully convulse it from one end to the other, arise exclusively and altogether from the right of property, and can be neither understood nor relieved, but by attending to the great distinction . . . between the natural and the legal right of property" (p. i.). As he somewhat bluntly puts it, "the law of nature is that industry shall be rewarded by wealth, and idleness be punished by destitution ; the law of the land is to give wealth to idleness, and fleece industry till it be destitute" (p. 154). "To the violation of the natural right of property, effected by the law, we owe most of our social miseries" (p. 56). Among these are the exploitation of labour and industrial crises. Speaking of the "comparative pauperism and destitution" of the labouring classes, he says "it cannot be doubted . . . that the immediate and proximate cause of their poverty and destitution, seeing how much they labour, and how many people their labour nourishes in opulence, is the law which appropriates their produce, in the shape of revenue, rent, tithes, and profit" (p. 149). "To our legal right of property we are indebted for those gleams of false wealth and real panic, which within the last fifty years have so frequently shook to its centre the whole trading world" (p. 156). He was not surprised at the respect professed for the law by the Irish gentry and similar classes. "The law is the creature of their passions, and they rightly endeavour, according to their own views, to substitute it for the violence which is the offspring of the passions of other people" (p. 45, note). The Law, in short, "is a great scheme of rules, intended to preserve the power of government, secure the wealth of the landowner, the priest, and the capitalist, but never to secure his produce to the labourer. The law-maker is never a labourer [1832], and has no natural right to any wealth." However, Hodgskin did not really wish to destroy, but to reform, the law of property. "Amend the laws as to property ; for all the crimes which afflict society grow from them" (p. 179). Nor was he prepared with a scheme of reform. "Individual man does not make society, and cannot organize it. . . . I trust to that great power, call it Nature, or call it God, which has brought society forth out of the wilderness, to provide for its future welfare. When you ask me for plans and schemes, my reply is, trust in that power, do justice, and fear not" (p. 179).

The practical outcome of Hodgskin's inquiry seems tame, and, as often happens with anarchist essays, hardly in keeping with the pretensions of the critical part of the work. But at any rate it avoids the blundering absurdities into which more ambitious writers have fallen. Hodgskin was a man of affairs, and his general tone, for a socialist, was unusually practical. Much of his writing, especially in *Labour Defended*, was in advance of his time, and even now has a modern ring about it. This applies particularly to his Trades Union policy, and to his excellent economic analysis, and broad view of social philosophy. Indeed his orthodox contemporaries might have learnt much from him which was not actually incorporated in English economics till fifty years later. One distinction in any case Hodgskin can claim to have achieved. Not only did he inspire men like Marx, the founders of the modern socialist movement, but he was the first (and perhaps the last) to attract the attention of the orthodox school, and had the honour to be singled out for special attack by the great Chancellor Brougham.

John Francis Bray, the last of the six writers I have selected for special notice, seems to have been a journeyman printer, of whom little is known, except that he was the author of the remarkable book, *Labour's Wrongs and Labour's Remedy*, published at Leeds in 1839. At this time political agitation ran high, and great things were hoped from constitutional changes and Whig reforms. Bray's purpose was to recall men's attention to fundamentals, to those radical social reforms without which, in his opinion, mere political remedies would be ineffective. "There is wanted," he says, "not a mere governmental or particular remedy, but a general remedy —one which will apply to all social wrongs and evils, great and small" (p. 8). "The producers have merely to determine whether it be not possible to change *that social whole which keeps them poor*, as well as that governmental part which oppresses them because they are poor" (p. 6). "Every social and governmental

John Francis Bray. His Labour's Wrongs.

wrong owes its rise to the existing social system—*to the institution of property as it at present exists*" (p. 17). Tracing the mischief to its root, he finds it in "the principle of unequal exchanges," and the inequality of condition which results from this. This was old Vanderlint's doctrine, and Bray might have adopted his motto, "The destruction of the poor is their poverty." Robert Dale Owen, too, had arrived at a similar result in 1828. "The *present system of commercial exchange* deprives Britain's labourers, in some way or other, of $\frac{38}{45}$ths of the produce of their industry."[1] Under the present social system, "which gives to irresponsible individuals the power of grinding masses of labour between masses of capital" (p. 102), "the whole of the working class are dependent upon the capitalist or employer for the means of labour, and therefore for the means of life" (p. 52). Wealth acquired by trading is derived, by unequal exchanges, from the exertions of others. "All profit must come from labour . . . the gain of an idle class must necessarily be the loss of an industrious class" (pp. 61, 67). "Capitalists and proprietors do no more than give the working man, for his labour of one week, a part of the wealth which they obtained from him the week before" (p. 49). "Thus, view the matter as we will, there is to be seen no towering pile of wealth which has not been heaped together by rapacity" (p. 50). These passages, and I might quote many others to the same effect, will enable the reader to judge how far there was any

[1] *Co-operative Magazine*, March 1828, p. 62.

originality in Marx's famous theory of profit. Like
Gray and Thompson, Bray goes to Colquhoun's statistics
to estimate the extent of this robbery of labour. "Of six
millions of adult men, five assist in producing and distri-
buting wealth; four belong to the working class. These
last receive scarcely £200,000,000 of the £500,000,000
annually created, which averages £11 per head for the
men, women, and children comprised in this class, and
for this they toil on the average 11 hours a day" (p. 155).
As he elsewhere puts it (p. 106), the system of unequal
exchanges "robs every working man of two-thirds of his
just earnings, to keep up the supremacy and the wealth
of those who are not working men." The Whig remedies,
Free Trade, Machinery, and Emigration, are worthless.
The Trade Union movement, though sound in principle
(for Bray saw through the wage-fund theory), has failed,
and must have failed; for neither political nor trades
unions go to the root of the matter. They do not touch
the system of unequal exchanges. American experience
shows the futility of merely political reform. "Society is
upon the same principle in all countries . . . they, like ourselves, are divided into rich and poor, into capitalists and
producers, and the last are there as they are here, at the
mercy of the first" (p. 19).

A really equitable system, according to Bray, must His social
be one of Universal Labour and Equal Exchanges. He ideal,
takes as his first principle the plausible but vague
axiom on which Mr. Spencer afterwards based his
Social Statics. "Every man has a right to do what he

likes, *provided the so-doing interferes not with the* EQUAL *rights of his fellow-men*" (p. 32). He holds that this principle excludes property in land, and implies a right to the whole produce of labour (p. 33). "Equal labour of all kinds should be equally remunerated . . . inequality in the value of labour to society is no argument for inequality of reward." For this communistic principle he tries to obtain the authority of Ricardo, whose highly speculative analysis Bray and the socialists generally took too seriously. Ricardo, he says, tells us that "it is not to any one commodity, or set of commodities, but to some given *quantity of labour*, that we must refer for an unvarying standard of real value. Here is a recognition of the principle that real value is dependent upon labour; and the only inference we can draw from it is that all men who perform an equal quantity of labour ought to receive an equal remuneration" (p. 199).

and practical proposals.

These principles clearly land us in communism; and Bray's ideal system is one of community of possessions. But he recognises the extreme difficulty of establishing such a system; and therefore, as a transitional measure, he proposes a kind of National Joint-Stock Scheme. Let the whole 5,000,000 of adult producers be formed into a number of joint-stock companies, containing from 100 to 1000 men each. Each company is to be confined to one trade. They are to have in use, by hire or purchase, the land and fixed capital of the country; and to be set in motion by a circulating bank-note capital equivalent to £100 for each associated member. Their affairs are to be conducted by general and local boards of trade; the members being paid weekly wages for their labour, and receiving equal wages for equal amounts of labour. All would have a common interest, working for a common end, and deriving a common benefit from all that is produced (p. 157).

For assistance in establishing "this joint - stock modification of society," Bray looked to the Friendly Societies, with their 1,500,000 members, and the Trade Unions. Together they might bring into relation 2,000,000 producers. The finance of the scheme is original. Bray is as weak on the theory of money as socialists usually are. He thinks it quite practicable to issue paper against the whole mass of national property (p. 142). Accordingly he proposes that the working class should obtain possession of the land and capital by the issue of notes on their joint credit to the amount of 2000 millions sterling. "The past, the present, and the future transactions of Capital all depend on labour for their fulfilment. Such being the case, why should not labour itself make a purchase? Why should not the bond of *Labour*, to pay at a future time what itself only can produce, be as valuable as the bond of *Capital*, to pay what this very same Labour is to produce? . . . Is the security offered by a people of less worth than that offered by an individual?" (p. 173). In any case there must be no resort to violence. "Reason, and not force, conviction, and not compulsion, purchase, and not plunder, a systematic application of combined forces, and not an undisciplined and chaotic movement, are the proper instruments to be employed." For popular revolutions to be effectual, conviction must always precede force ; for force may establish, but it cannot always preserve " (pp. 214, 215).

Bray's scheme, it must be admitted, is more practical than the pure communism of Owen and Thompson, which he regarded as a counsel of perfection. It admits of individual property in products together with common property in productive powers, and thus combines the stimulus of private property with the equities of common interest. His companies, too, are far more practical units for industrial organisation than the self-sufficing communities of his predecessors. Indeed, if we can imagine a system of federated productive co-operation, national in its scope, and somewhat communistic in its distribution of wages, we shall have gone far towards realising what Bray seems to have intended. It might be said, indeed, that as he has foreshadowed in his financial proposals the principle of the modern labour banks, so his general conception is not without analogies in the aims of the Wholesale Co-operative Societies of our day.

Marx and Bray.

Within its limits, which though narrow are not more narrow than those of the *laissez faire* school of economists whom he was opposing, Bray's essay must be considered a closely - reasoned and philosophical piece of work. It was long a classic in the propagandist literature of the English socialists. No one can read

the work without perceiving that it had clearly anticipated many of the ideas which are supposed to be
most characteristic of Karl Marx. That Marx was
greatly impressed by the book is beyond question. In
his *Misère de la Philosophie*, 1847, when his object is to
discredit Proudhon, he quotes Bray to the extent of
nine pages, and describes his essay as a remarkable performance, little known in France, but containing the key
to all the works of Proudhon, past, present, and future
(pp. 50-62).[1] In 1859, when he had begun to develope
his own theory, the notice of Bray is limited to the
mention of his name in a footnote (*Zur Kritik*, p. 64).
Even his name does not occur in *Das Kapital*, 1867,
though the list of works quoted in that book extends to
sixteen pages, and it is here that Marx developes the
theory of profit which Bray had so vigorously put
forward in 1839. It was fortunate for Marx that in
Germany also Bray was then "little known."

[1] In this reference to Bray, Marx attributes to his influence the
foundation of the Owenite Labour Exchanges. But these were established by Robert Owen in 1832, and advocated by him as early as
1821. I do not see that Bray even notices these labour exchanges ;
his own scheme is on quite different lines. Josiah Warren of Cincinnati, who still adhered to the principle in 1863, says the suggestion
of it is "believed to have originated in England" (*True Civilisation*,
1863, p. 84). Courcelle-Seneuil, in his *Traité des Opérations de
Banque*, says the theory was first expounded, so far as he knows, in
1818, by M. Fulcrand-Mazel, who established a bank on this principle
at Paris in 1829. It is interesting to note that the system is said to
be in force in at least two existing communities : viz. the Co-operative Colony of Topolobampo, Mexican California (*Yorkshire Post*,
Sept. 18, 1896), and the Co-operative Colony of Cosme, Paraguay
(*Times*, Aug. 31, 1897).

Unde-
served
neglect of
the English
Socialists.
It must be evident from this brief survey of the writings of six principal English socialists, that the body of doctrine they advanced was of such a character as to deserve the serious attention of all who were concerned with social philosophy. It was closely reasoned, original in conception, striking at the very root of the principles on which existing society was based, and expounded in such vigorous fashion as to exert widespread influence over the mass of the people, at that time distressed and disaffected. Why did the English economists for the most part ignore ideas of such a revolutionary and far-reaching nature? We can imagine how they would have interested Adam Smith; and Malthus and Sismondi, each in his way critical of the orthodox school, might at least have been expected to see their importance. Malthus and Sismondi, however, though critical, were not radical in their criticism; both writers accepting the general social philosophy of the dominant school. Neither succeeded in founding a school of his own, or in appreciably modifying the direction impressed upon current thought by the Ricardian group. The fact seems to be that, after the appearance of Ricardo's *Principles,* the economists were largely given over to sterile logomachy and academic hair-splitting. Ricardo had adopted what was intended to be a rigorously abstract and deductive manner, but without any of those formal aids to precision and clearness which scientific, and especially mathematical, method provides. The conse-

quence was a period of indescribable confusion, remind-
ing one of that "dim, weird battle of the west,"

Where friend and foe were shadows in the mist,
And friend slew friend not knowing whom he slew.

When they concerned themselves with practical affairs,
it was mainly with those interesting to the Whig or
Radical political connections. Hence the profounder
issues raised by the socialist school were generally overlooked by the economists, although they were so largely
derived, both historically and logically, by reaction
from the teaching of their recognised leader Ricardo.

But in the case of Hodgskin at least, there were
exceptions to this general rule of neglect. James Mill
and Brougham in England, and Thomas Cooper of
Columbia, S.C., seem to have at once perceived the
significance of the new teaching. Cooper was the first
to publish any reference to the socialist school. In the
second edition of his *Political Economy*, published in
1830 (though the title-page bears the date 1829), he
added a chapter on the Distribution of Wealth, in
which he gives full consideration to the views of
"Hodgskin, Thompson, Byllesby, Messrs. Al. Ming,
Thomas Skidmore, and the mechanic Political Economists";[1] and after challenging their positions upon what

But Hodgskin noticed by Cooper,

[1] Byllesby, Alex. Ming, and Thomas Skidmore formed, with R. Dale
Owen and Frances Wright, the nucleus of a New York school of
socialists, whose organ was *The Free Enquirer*. This school well
deserves some historical notice, and I hope it may obtain one at the
hands of some American economist.

we may call common-sense grounds, he gives his own view of the measures most likely to reduce the existing inequality of conditions, which he agrees with the socialists in deploring. Cooper was a very vigorous and independent thinker, of wide experience in both old and new worlds (he was one of the many reformers who emigrated from England at the time of the Terror). A Free Trader, he rejected the theory of Natural Rights; and he anticipated Walker in the stress he lays on the value of business ability, genius and invention. His freedom from many of the narrowing dogmas of the English economists gave the greater effect to his answer to the socialists; and his arguments still remain forcible and pertinent.

By Brougham,

If Brougham, as is usually assumed, wrote the clever little defence of the existing system published in 1831 by the *Useful Knowledge Society*, under the title of *The Rights of Industry*, he must have been influenced by Cooper, who is more than once quoted in this work, and especially in those parts of it where Hodgskin is expressly attacked by name. The argument is a skilful one, lucidly expounded, and largely based on history; Bastiat and many other writers have borrowed from it illustrations which have now become classical. The book is further commendable for its fair and persuasive tone, and the general absence from its pages of the sickening cant which disfigured so much of the apologetic literature of that day. Hodgskin's immediate reply to this attack, which appeared in November, was the issue

in the December following of a second edition of his
Labour Defended, with a contemptuous prefatory note.
In his *Right of Property*, published in 1832, he may be
said to have carried the war into the enemy's country,
and attacked Brougham on his own ground.

Whether or not Brougham was the author of the
Rights of Industry, as Hodgskin supposed, the book
was certainly published under his patronage.   However,
in 1832, Brougham's attention was again called to
Hodgskin, and this time by James Mill; who in his
turn, as Mr. Wallas shows, had heard of Hodgskin's
socialistic teaching from Place.[1]   The more militant of
the Owenites had formed themselves into a National
Union of the Working Classes, somewhat resembling
the Democratic Federation, more notable for their noise
than their numbers.   Meeting at the Rotunda, they
were known as Rotundanists.   Hodgskin's doctrines
were exactly suited to their purpose, and eagerly proclaimed by them.   In October 1831, we find Mill
writing in great anxiety to Place about a deputation
"from the working classes," who had been preaching
communism to Black, the editor of the *Chronicle*.   "Their
notions about property," he writes, "look ugly."   Place
replies that "the men who called on Black were not a
deputation from the working people, but two out of
half a dozen who manage, or mismanage, the meetings of
the Rotunda. . . .   The doctrine they are now preaching is
that promulgated by Hodgskin in a tract in 1825," etc.

and by James Mill.

---

[1] *Life of Francis Place*, p. 274.

James Mill passed on the information to Brougham in the well-known letter of Sept. 3, 1832.[1] " The nonsense to which your Lordship alludes about the rights of the labourer to the whole produce of the country, wages, profits and rent, all included, is the mad nonsense of our friend Hodgkin (*sic*) which he has published as a system, and propagates with the zeal of perfect fanaticism. These opinions, if they were to spread, would be the subversion of civilised society; worse than the over-whelming deluge of Huns and Tartars." He goes on to say that he would have little fear of the propagation among the common people of any doctrines hostile to property but for two circumstances—the one the currency agitation; the other " the illicit, cheap publications, in which the doctrine of the right of the labouring people, who they say are the only producers, to all that is produced, is very generally preached. The alarming nature of this evil you will understand when I inform you that these publications are superseding the Sunday newspapers, and every other channel through which the people might get better information." [2]

James Mill, of course, could talk socialism himself when it did not go beyond the limits of his own political Radicalism. He denounced the expenditure of the State as unproductive ; speaks of the governing class as having

---

[1] *James Mill. A Biography.* By Alex. Bain, 1882, pp. 363-367.

[2] Mr. Wallas shows in his *Life of Place* (p. 371, etc.) that in 1838 the currency and socialist agitations nearly merged into one, as they have done to some extent in the modern Populist Party of the United States.

found the machinery of taxation the most commodious instrument for getting an undue share of the property of the people; and was in favour of taxing the increment of value in land. But there was nothing in these views inconsistent with a tenacious affection for the right of individual property when it took a form which he approved; while his sound instinct told him that Hodgskin's teaching struck at the very root of individual property in any form, and must, in its logical development, "subvert civilised society." He seems to have regarded the new aggressive socialism as a pestilent treason, to be suppressed rather than to be controverted; in short, much as a New York money-lender regards the modern bimetallist. Brougham, however, following Cooper's lead, made serious efforts to supply literature of a popular kind, in which the socialistic position was not unfairly stated, and was met by argument, sometimes superficial, perhaps, but cleverly enforced, conducted with temper and patience, and, as far as I can judge, widely effective for its purpose.

After James Mill and Brougham, no leading economist seems to have thought the English revolutionary socialism worth notice, and the very names of its chief writers were unknown to most of them until quite recent times. It is hard to understand how they could have been ignored by J. S. Mill. Holyoake tells us that Mill frequented the meetings of the early co-operators.[1] He must have heard of Hodgskin from his father, and

English Socialism ignored by Stuart Mill.

---

[1] *History of Co-operation*, vol. i. p. 141.

of Thompson, with whom he had much in common, from Bentham. But John Mill's favourite range of thought was the *axiomata media* of social philosophy, and he does not seem to have been quick to appreciate really original or profound conceptions, either in metaphysics or sociology. He gives no sign that he was aware of the existence of his contemporaries, Marx, Engels and Lassalle, much less of the men from whom they drew their inspiration. Socialism for him meant the romantic utopias of Fourier and Owen, or the academic industrialism of Saint-Simon and Comte. Such was the magic of his lucid style and persuasive temper, that on this, as on so many other matters, he inspired his readers with a sense of the finality of his writings. His influence, on the whole, was distinctly soporific.

And hence by his contemporaries.
After the appearance of Mill's *Principles*, English economists, for a whole generation, were men of one book ; and it must be admitted that the influence of this book did not tend to correct the distaste for historical study, and the somewhat narrow range of investigation which were already becoming traditional in the English school. Hence, half a century elapsed before the ideas of the originators of modern socialism were appreciated, or even recognised, by the official representatives of social philosophy in the country of their birth. This must always be a matter of profound regret. Perhaps it is idle to speculate on what might have resulted had their pregnant teaching been subjected at the time to searching criticism by the best English

economists of the day. But we can hardly doubt that a thorough discussion would have cleared the air of a good deal of confused and revolutionary socialism, and it would certainly have very much broadened and developed the current exposition of economic science.

Meanwhile the ideas were not dead. If they were ignored by the leaders of English thought, they remained germinating in the minds of Marx and Engels ; destined, thanks to their brilliant exposition, and the masterly advocacy of Lassalle, to develope into that social democracy which is to-day the religion of large masses of the continental working class. But they had almost equally important effects, though of a different kind, upon popular movements in England. The conditions here were most favourable to the acceptance of socialist teaching, even if its full import could not then be grasped. The people had been roused to the verge of revolution by a series of wrongs, calamities, and oppressions ; and they had been rallied by the fame, the enthusiasm, and the generosity of Robert Owen into something like a national organisation for social reform.

There is no room for more than a brief catalogue of the painful series of events which had prepared the masses for social revolt. The movement for political reform, inspired by American Independence, and under the most influential patronage, was in a fair way to a triumphant issue, when the excesses of 1793 brought with them the Reaction, and the despotic repression of the Terror. In close succession followed the crushing

But the tradition lived on in Marx and in the minds of the English masses, prepared to receive it by social wrongs.

taxation of the Great War, disastrous famines, and
unprecedented irregularity of employment. The
Apprenticeship Laws were repealed, and the rights of
the hand-worker and skilled artisan invaded without
a pretence of compensation. The old social equilibrium
was disturbed ; population increased by leaps and
bounds, and labour became politically and economically
enslaved to capital. Enclosures, and the disappearance
of the small yeomanry, whose holdings had been amalga-
mated into the large farms which were the envy of
Europe, made similar havoc with the country labourers ;
whose independence was further sapped by the abuses
of the old poor law. When the classes so gravely
injured by adverse circumstance set about them, in true
English fashion, to raise their position by united action,
they were thrust back by the rigorous combination laws,
which made it conspiracy for two men simultaneously
to ask for a higher wage. This seems to have been a
turning-point in English social history. The injustice
of the repressive policy drove all the best energy and
intelligence of England into the party of Reform. Place
and the Benthamites, Cobbett and the Radicals, the
Edinburgh Review and the Whigs, all in their various
ways began to prepare a new era. But the people still
had much to endure. The conditions of employment
were arbitrary, exhausting and insanitary in a degree
never before experienced. The revelations of the
Factory Commissioners, sickening reading even at this
distance of time, showed that the population was be-

coming enfeebled by the unnatural conditions of labour imposed by the greed of capital. The rapid growth of large towns, unprovided with effective municipal government, unpoliced and uninspected, had still further injured the masses, by degrading their homes. To measure this injury, contrast Aikin's description of Lancashire in 1795, with the Sanitary Reports of fifty years later. For this seething, undeserved misery, orthodox economy had only two remedies, and those rather of a surgical type: Restraint of Population, and the New Poor Law. The prescription was well-meant and not altogether unwholesome. But it was tendered without sympathy, and roused the bitterest resentment. After the New Poor Law, the disposition to resort to violence showed a marked increase, and the movement for political reform developed into Chartism. No wonder the gospel of socialism found a ready welcome in such times.

But I am inclined to think that the Ricardian socialism owes its vitality as much to the rise of the Owenite movement as to the social conditions of the time. The close of the first quarter of this century was certainly a critical epoch. The years 1824 and 1825 saw the decisive struggle for the right of combination. They also date the appearance of the three most notable works of the Ricardian socialists; a coincidence all the more remarkable, because, so far as we can see, these works, save for their common relation to Ricardo, were absolutely independent, alike in occasion, method and inspiration. Now it was just at this same critical

And by the Owenite crusade.

juncture that Robert Owen first began to get a hold on
the masses of the people; and the subsequent growth
and decay of the Owenite movement follows very
nearly, but at a few years' distance, the activity and
decline of Ricardian socialism.   Mr. Holyoake tells
us [1] that "it was the year 1825 which saw co-operative
views—which since 1812 had been addressed by Mr.
Owen to the upper classes—first taken up by the
working class."   Owenite literary activity was at its
zenith in 1830.   "England has never seen before or
since so many co-operative papers as 1830 saw."   In
the fifteen months preceding January 1830 there had
been a rapid growth of co-operative societies from only
4 to 100.   These were to be found in all parts of the
country; and in 1832 they were reinforced by the foundation of the Exchange Bazaars, which "spread over almost
every part of the kingdom simultaneously."   It was
these Owenite institutions, and their periodical literature, that served to propagate the doctrines of the
Ricardian socialists.   They gave resonance to teaching
which might otherwise have been but as the voice of
one crying in the wilderness, and established it firmly
in the minds of the working-class leaders.   After 1830,
the Ricardian socialism seems to have captured the
Owenite movement.   "For fourteen years now," says
Mr. Holyoake, "Co-operation has to be traced through
Socialism."   The name Socialist was of Owenite origin,
and does not seem to have been commonly applied to

[1] *History of Co-operation*, i. pp. 88, 129, 161, 175, 210.

the Owenites till May 1835. But the ideas which we associate with the term to-day came not so much from Owen as from Thompson and his school. I cannot find that this school were in any way indebted to Owen for inspiration. But the Ricardian socialism was the yeast of the Owenite movement, and the foundation of all the more able contributions to Owenite literature; while it had no small share in stimulating the political offshoot of Owenism which rallied round the Charter.

It was Ricardo, not Owen, who gave the really effective inspiration to English socialism. That inspiration was indirect and negative, but it is unmistakable. Thompson and the rest took for granted the accuracy of Ricardo's unfortunate and strained deductions, and quote him as an unquestioned authority. Finding that certain of his conclusions were abhorrent to their sense of right, and assuming that he had taken the existing conditions of society as his premises, they naturally directed all the force of their attack against these conditions. This was the real intellectual origin of revolutionary socialism, and it is for this reason I have called it Ricardian. There was plenty of revolutionary socialism in the various Owenite co-operative journals, often most ably expressed; but I am satisfied that it is directly due to the influence of Thompson, Hodgskin and Gray, and in lesser degree to Godwin and Hall, whose works they revived. The more I study the literature of English socialism, the more I feel that what in it was really pregnant with great issues was due to Ricardo, not

But the main stimulus came from Ricardo, not Owen.

Owen, though it flourished under the shelter of the Owenite movement.

Owen not revolutionary. Owen never raised claims of Right; but modern revolutionary socialism is founded on such claims. The three main subjects of his criticism were Religion, Marriage and Private Property; but he was only actively militant against the received theology and morals. In Owen the child was father to the man. Nursed in Welsh Calvinism, his doctrine throughout life always tended to be theological, and therefore an appeal to the individual, rather than to base itself on Right, and to seek for its realisation by political means. Hence his crusade against private property was platonic, resting on moral, not political considerations. This was partly due to his view of the boundless possibilities of invention and progress. In the period of his prime, 1820-35, he came very near to expounding some of the future principles of "scientific" socialism.[1] But even then his first and absorbing passion was for equitable distribution of *new* wealth. The power of production, according to his views, was so enormous, so greatly in excess of human requirements, that it was unnecessary to dwell on the negative or confiscatory aspects of socialism.[2]

---

[1] See, for instance, the highly socialistic tract, *An Address to the Members of Trade Societies*, quite in Gray's manner, which Owen caused to be reprinted in London in 1827.

[2] "It is no longer necessary, except through ignorance, that 'man should earn his bread by the sweat of his brow'; for the inventions and discoveries which have been matured, and which are now in full practice, are more than sufficient, with very light labour, under a right

To attack existing property would seem to him a gratuitous blunder. At bottom his ideas were very much of the *bourgeois* type, and his differences with the views of the ordinary British citizen were much more moral and theological than genuinely socialistic. It is the Co-operators, rather than the Social Democrats, who are the modern representatives of Robert Owen.

Upon the whole, then, it is the Owenites, rather than Owen, who are important from our present point of view. I do not underrate the interest of Owen as a figure in our social history, nor the enormous practical effects of his ceaseless energy and unflagging enthusiasm. On the contrary, the more I learn of social movements, the more highly I rate Owen's influence. I am disposed to think that it was Owen in England, and Saint-Simon in France, who brought socialism down from the study to the street, and made it a popular force. But, if we are

Scientific-ally, the Owenites more important than Owen.

direction, to supply the wants and insure the independence of all, without real injury to any.

"To understand this part of the subject, your best attention is requisite, because it is not only new to you, but it appears to be so also to legislators and political economists ; for they continue still to direct their efforts to instruct the world how to *increase* its wealth, while the real difficulty against which society has to contend is, to discover the means by which an excess of wealth, now so easily produced, can be prevented from injuring all classes, who experience from it precisely the same effects which have been heretofore engendered by poverty " (*An Address to the Agriculturists, Mechanics and Manufacturers of Great Britain*, published in the *Sphynx* Newspaper, Sept. 1827 ; and quoted in the *Birmingham Co-operative Herald*, No. 7, Oct. 1, 1829).

Owen is alluding to the effects of the crisis of 1826-27. It must be remembered that he was a cotton spinner, who lived through the age of the great inventions.

tracing the intellectual ancestry of modern socialism, Owen is less important than many of those who fought under his flag. The distinction which Dr. Menger very justly draws between Saint - Simon and the Saint - Simonians applies, I think, with even more force to Owen and the Owenites. Owen's personal fortune was of the greatest service to his movement, and still more, I think, the fact that he had made it himself. Probably nothing less than Owen's success in business would ever have brought the average Englishman to treat socialistic doctrines as anything but scatter-brained and "academic" speculations.

But Owen was certainly inferior in intellectual calibre to many of his followers, and especially to the six men who were the real leaders of aggressive socialism. These were for the most part men of liberal culture and some training in philosophy; men with a natural gift for reflection, and with far more critical insight and breadth of view than Owen. As formal and philosophic exponents of socialistic principle these men seem to stand quite apart from Owen, who is hardly in the direct line of descent from Godwin to the socialism of Marx and Lassalle. All the theoretical positions of the German writers are to be found in the writings of Owenites; few of the most characteristic of them will be found in the writings of Owen himself. Still Ricardian socialism grew up under the shelter of the Owenite movement; and, perhaps, owed to Owen its escape from the oblivion and neglect which had fallen to Godwin and Hall. It is curious how in England we neglect our social history. No figure in it is more prominent or more familiar to Englishmen than that of Robert Owen. The first serious attempt to write a history of the Owenite movement must inevitably have brought to light the important work of the Ricardian socialists. Yet until the last few years this work has been almost wholly ignored.

There were other members of the Owenite school, on both sides of the Atlantic, whose writings are full of interest from the special point of view of Dr. Menger's book, but I have only time for a bare reference to two or three of them. M'Cormac and Mackintosh on this side, and MacClure in America, not to mention a number of anonymous writers, were almost as vigorous and incisive in their defence of the labourer's right as the six chiefs of the school. M'Cormac, an eminent and public-spirited Dublin physician, was chiefly interested in practical reforms. Mackintosh was more speculative in his tendencies. He attacked Owen's doctrine of Irresponsibility, but agreed with him in the main; and some of his passages, by their anarchist tone, remind us of Hodgskin. MacClure, the partner of Owen in his New Harmony venture, was a man of considerable wealth, great part of which he devoted to the advancement of education, scientific research and socialistic communities. One of these communities was named Macluria in his honour. His characteristic theme is the distinction between producers and non-producers,

Minor Owenites : M'Cormac, Mackintosh, and MacClure.

which he expounds quite in the Saint - Simonian manner.[1]

I have already referred to the group of socialists in New York, who rallied round Robert Dale Owen and Francis Wright. This School must have been pretty active in 1829. Robert Dale Owen writes in October that *The Free Inquirer* (the official organ of the group) "had about 350 subscribers six or eight months ago,

---

[1] I quote a passage from each of these three writers, as their books are not easily accessible :—

"A single rich man, by means of his wealth, is enabled to consume the produce of the industry of thousands of labourers ; while no single labourer is permitted to use more than a portion, or its equivalent, of what he has produced, being obliged to support all the other labourers whom the rich employ in the manufacture of superfluities" (Henry M'Cormac. *An Appeal on Behalf of the Poor.* Belfast, 1830, p. 17).

"Upon an ignorant and degraded people, laws are imposed without their consent. . . . By the laws thus enacted, these slaves are hemmed in on every side ; the produce of their labour is taxed, and tythed, and rented and rated, and profited by force and fraud, until, at length, a miserable pittance remains to the slave whose toil has produced all. The poor slave, being thus reduced to a state of destitution, is compelled to let his body out by the day, to the first or highest bidder ; and thus is established a wretched and cruel system of trafficking in human flesh and blood. The difference between the system of trafficking in the *bodies* of African slaves, and the *toil* of European slaves is only nominal" (T. S. Mackintosh. *An Inquiry into the Nature of Responsibility.* Birmingham [1840], p. 87).

"Property of every denomination is produced by labor. The laborers must, therefore, in the first instance have possession of the whole property in every country, of which they are deprived by a number of artifices, laws, and regulations, both of church and state," p. 122 (William MacClure. *Opinions on Various Subjects, dedicated to the Industrious Producers.* New-Harmony, Indiana, 1831).

"Civilisation has created, maintained, and does every day continue to increase, the number and expense of that class who live on the produce of the labour of others" (p. 166).

and now has 1200." [1] Among the leading members,
besides Owen and Miss Wright, were R. L. Jennings,
L. Byllesby, Alex. Ming, Thomas Skidmore. To avoid
party names, they styled themselves the *Mechanics and
other Working Men of New York*. They seem to have
been thorough-going communists. Byllesby denied the
right of labour to superior advantages on account of
superior efficiency; Ming and Skidmore openly
advocated an equal division of property among
adults. A *Manifest*, explaining their position, was
published in the *New York Sentinel*, and is reprinted
in *The Crisis*.[2] The tone of this Manifest is studiously
moderate. It mainly attacks monopolies and the
excessive power of wealth; and demands genuine
representation of the producing classes, and an equal
system of public education. A much closer approach
to the doctrines of the celebrated Manifesto of Marx
and Engels was made by another American writer,
O. A. Brownson, editor of the *Boston Quarterly Review*.
In a tract called *The Labouring Classes*, a review of
Carlyle's *Chartism*, Brownson denounces the wage
system, privilege, and inheritance, and proclaims an
approaching war between the middle-class and the
proletariate. Wages he describes as a more successful
method of taxing labour than slavery. Our business is
to emancipate the proletaries, as the past has emancipated
the slaves. There is only one remedy, "by that most

---

[1] *London Co-operative Magazine.* Jan. 1830. Vol. iv. p. 2.
[2] Vol. i. pp. 51, 58. June 16, 23, 1832.

dreadful of all wars, the war of the poor against the rich, a war which, however long it may be delayed, will come." This is socialism of the true Marxian type, but the abundant land resources of the United States at that time provided an outlet for discontented energy, and the teaching seems to have fallen dead.[1]

The Owenite movement in its prime.

It was otherwise in England, where, as we have seen, all the conditions were favourable to socialistic agitation. Intellectually, perhaps, the Owenite movement was most brilliant and interesting in 1825 ; but it was in the full tide of its activity for nearly twenty years after that date. Owen was an excellent figurehead, and a good advertiser. He was well seconded in his missionary efforts by the enthusiasm of able followers, and by paid lecturers of no mean ability. The whole country was soon covered by a network of Owenite societies, and flooded with socialist tracts and periodical literature, some of it still of high interest. For fifteen years in succession a series of National Congresses served to focus the movement. There were seven Co-operative Congresses in the years 1830-35, in which the trade union and labour exchange elements were prominent, and fourteen Socialist Congresses, 1835 - 46, in which communistic or communitarian ideas pre-

---

[1] We find the doctrine of the New York socialists alive again in 1875. In that year the Massachusetts Labor Reform Convention adopted the following resolution :—"We affirm, as a fundamental principle, that labor, the creator of wealth, is entitled to all it creates."

vailed. During this period the Owenites were constantly before the public, and played an important part in almost every great social movement of the time.

But after the failure of the Labour Exchanges in 1834, the influence of Owen seems to have been steadily on the decline. The narrowness and limitations of his culture began to produce their natural consequences; and these were aggravated by his almost total lack of any sense of humour, and any knowledge of the larger world. Even in his prime, Owen always inclined to ethical and theological, rather than to political activity. With advancing years this tendency increased, while he became more and more barren in practical suggestion. At length his tedious persistence in the iteration of dogmas antagonistic to the received theology and morals had the effect of alienating the sympathies of many of the most earnest of his followers, and especially of Wesleyans and others who were foremost in the Factory agitation and many other social movements. As Owen's personal influence declined, the movement began to disintegrate. The diverse elements which had found a common rallying-point in the Owenite flag, began to follow independent and natural lines of divergence, and the great socialist camp gradually broke up.

Causes of its decline.

Those among the Owenites who were most in harmony with their master's later activities, drifted into moral and theological controversy, and devoted

Its offshoots

themselves mainly to a secularist crusade.[1] The more
politically minded, goaded by the severities of the
New Poor Law, by industrial tyranny, and social
oppression, became more or less political revolutionaries,
physical force men, or Chartists ; and abandoned Owen's
voluntary communism for social democracy.   Other
groups, avoiding heroics, speculative or political, recurred
to some of those more business-like measures which
Owen's visions of New Moral Worlds had rather thrown
into the shade.   Co-operation, in both its forms, made a
fresh start.   The Rochdale Pioneers in 1844 laid the
foundations of the great distributive movement; and
the Christian Socialists, a few years later, gave what
has proved to be an enduring impulse to the still
greater enterprise of productive co-operation.   Last, but
not least, the Trade Unionists gradually broke away
from the Owenite connection.   They had gained from it
inspiration and enlarged aims, but very little else.   The
great flare-up of 1834 was quickly followed by reaction
and discouragement;   but when they dropped Owen's
pretentious schemes, and resumed the old and tried
methods which Place in 1815 had praised as "the
perfection of wisdom," they made solid progress; and
when 1852 arrived, they were ready to take advantage
of the great expansion of trade which brought them
in 1874 to the high-water mark of their power and
prosperity.

---

[1] The secularist movement perhaps owed more to Bentham and
Place than to Owen.   Cf. Holyoake, *Life of Carlyle*, 1849.

Of these developments, the Chartist agitation, and
especially the teaching of such men as Bronterre
O'Brien, has the closest affinity to the doctrines which
are the subject of Professor Menger's work. This will
be seen from O'Brien's programme. It includes nationalisation of land at the decease of existing owners (with
full pecuniary compensation to their heirs and assigns);
security of the tenants' right to improvements; cessa-
tion of further national loans; the quarter of wheat to
be the standard of value; paper money to be a Government monopoly, and to be issued "against every
description of exchangeable wealth"; equitable exchange bazaars, and district banks (somewhat of the
Proudhon type), to enable industrious men to stock
farms, and to manufacture on their own account.[1] But
it is not part of my present purpose to consider these
later outgrowths of Owenism. They have been ex-
cellently dealt with by authoritative writers. Mr.
Holyoake's well-known works are a mine of valuable
material for the History of Co-operation and for the
personnel of Owenism in all its forms; the History of
Trade Unionism has been admirably written by Mr.
and Mrs. Sidney Webb; Mr. Graham Wallas's *Life of
Place*, and Gammage's *History of Chartism*, throw
invaluable light on the political side of the movement.

To the outside observer in 1850, the great Owenite

---

[1] Cf. the *National Reformer*. New Series. No. 1, Oct. 3, 1846;
and No. 16, Jan. 16, 1847; also O'Brien's posthumous book, *The Rise,
Progress and Phases of Human Slavery*, 1885.

movement must have appeared a complete failure.
The communities were wrecked, the societies had broken
up, and the remarkable doctrines which inspired them
seemed to have been forgotten. Yet it would be
difficult to exaggerate the importance of the results
which followed, directly, or indirectly, from the twenty-
five years' campaign. It gave resonance to all voices that
were raised in the cause of social amelioration. Popular
education, trade - unionism, co - operation, allotments,
factory legislation, and sanitary reform, in short, almost
all the great measures which have proved most effective
in raising the condition of the people, either originated
in, or were powerfully reinforced by, the Owenite agitation. This, too, at a time when all these measures,
except the first and last, were frowned upon by the
economists, and before they had been taken up by
either of the great political parties. These were great
services ; but for the most valuable legacy of Owenism
we must look deeper than these merely institutional
reforms, useful as they were, It left the English
people saturated with a faith in progress and a tradition
of social perfectibility which are still fresh and vigorous,
and which are a never-failing source of inspiration to
popular social effort, and the most effective of antiseptics
against political cynicism and commercial corruption.
It is tempting to speculate on what might have
happened if Owen's energies had been directed into a
political channel, after the fashion of contemporary
socialists. I am inclined to think that the immediate

material results would have been greater, but the moral influences less; and, upon the whole, I should doubt whether the Owenite movement would have had the same historical significance. As it was, it made a profound and abiding impression not merely on English social institutions, but on the English character; and it gave asylum to ideas which may prove to be the germs of wider and more fundamental change.

There are, of course, many writers not directly con-nected with the Owenites or the principal School, who would certainly require careful notice in any formal history of English socialism. I hope the Bibliography appended to this volume may serve to remind the reader of some of these. I can only here refer briefly to the two who seem to me most important, viz. Thomas Spence and William Cobbett; two singular characters, agreeing in their originality and independence, and perhaps in little else. Spence was the first to agitate for the public ownership of land. The Corporation of Newcastle, his native town, had been enclosing certain common lands, but were defeated in an action brought against them by some of the freemen in defence of the commoners' rights. It would seem that it was the stir of this contest which first set Spence thinking on the land question; and there is no doubt that the mischiefs and injuries resulting from the enclosures greatly aided his agitation. His particular proposal, first made in a lecture, in 1775, was "to administer the Landed Estate of the Nation as a Joint-Stock Property, in Parochial

Thomas Spence.

Partnerships, by dividing the Rent." At one time he
had a considerable following, and during the period of
war-rents and the great scarcities he seems to have
caused alarm to the Government. But the discussion
of his views was considerably impeded by the repressive
measures which followed the events of 1793 ; and when,
in 1817, the Government took special powers for dealing
with the alleged "Spencean Conspiracy," the harmless
Society of Spencean Philanthropists received a shock
from which it never rallied. Their feeble agitation
must, in any case, have been soon overshadowed by the
superior pretentions and popularity of Robert Owen
and William Cobbett, then at the zenith of their
fame.

William
Cobbett.

William Cobbett, the greatest popular leader who
ever sprang from the ranks of the English peasantry,
was rather a politician than a socialist. The very
antipodes in this respect of his contemporary Robert
Owen, he attacked persons and classes rather than
principles, measures rather than institutions. But he
often verges on the socialist creed, especially in his
assertion of the rights of the producers ; and no one
did more to make labour politically self-conscious, or to
bring the "Condition of the People Question" to the
front. He was a master in the craft of the agitator.
No man ever commanded a style more apt for his
purpose, or so thoroughly understood the labourers to
whom and for whom he appealed. There is a delightful
breezy freshness about his writings, like the sea air

blowing over his native chalk downs ; and a thoroughly
sound, healthy, robust, and old-world tone about the
instincts which inspire them. Both man and style
have an unmistakable out-door quality about them, and
smack of the field and the plough. Cobbett's earlier
activity was financial; and in his celebrated *Political
Register* and *Paper against Gold* his attacks are mainly
directed against the war-finance with its heavy taxation,
and the paper money, which he regarded as its chief
support. "The misery, the degradation of Englishmen
by means of paper money," he writes in 1821, "has been
the ruling passion of my mind." But as he saw the condition of the labourer steadily decline, until his hardest
exertions did not enable him to secure the dietary of a
convicted felon, Cobbett's resentment was roused, and
his language becomes more socialistic. For practical
purposes, the teaching of the *Poor Man's Friend, Two-
Penny Trash*, and the *Legacy to Labourers* was perhaps
more socialistic in its tendency than Robert Owen's.
It was certainly more calculated to rouse the masses
to revolt ; and the general belief that it was Cobbett's
influence which prompted the rick-burning exploits of
"Captain Swing" and his associates was not altogether
unfounded. One or two quotations may serve to show
how nearly Cobbett approached the doctrine of the
Thompson school. In *Paper against Gold* he had
written—"Taxes create drones, who devour the earnings
of the laborious." [1] This does not greatly differ from

[1] Letter iii. Sept. 11, 1810.

the view of James Mill and the Ricardians. In *Two-Penny Trash* the emphasis is stronger. "Here is the whole affair. Here it is *all*. The food and the drink and the raiment are *taken away from those who labour, and given to those who do not labour.*"[1] "Now men may talk, and do whatever else they please, and as long as they please, they will never persuade the labourers of England *that a living out of the land is not their right in exchange for the labour which they yield or tender.* This being the case, the thing to be aimed at is, to give them employment; and this employment is to be given them in sufficient quantity only by putting a stop to the transfer of the product of labour to the mouths of those *who do not labour;* and this stop is to be put in no way but that of taking off the taxes."[2] This last passage shows exactly where and how Cobbett falls short of the true socialistic doctrine. Up to the final clause it might have been written by Gray or Hodgskin; but the disparity of the remedy shows that Cobbett did not see the full significance of the language he used. He was a bit of a *bourgeois* at bottom; and when he attacked the propertied classes, it was not because he denied the right to property, but because he considered that the owners neglected its duties. In *Paper against Gold* he once said expressly that landlords "do not live upon the earnings of others"[3]; and if the tone of much of his later writing is not quite consistent with this admission, yet there was nothing revolutionary in his mind.

[1] Vol. i. p. 131.   [2] *Ib.* p. 138.   [3] Letter iii. Sept. 11, 1810.

There is no reason to think that he ever came under socialistic influences. Typical Englishman as he was, he had in view merely certain specific reforms, directed to a simple unpretentious end. His homely ideal for his favourite labourers is well known. Beer, bread, bacon, and cheese, enjoyed as far as possible from the " Great Wen," in the wholesome conditions of a country life,— this was his conception of the labourer's right. To secure these comforts to the class from which he sprang was the main purpose of Cobbett's untiring activity. "Before the day shall come," he says, "when my labours shall cease, I shall have mended the meals of millions." [1] This is not precisely "scientific" socialism, either in method or aim : but Cobbett's influence certainly contributed in no small degree to promote socialism in others, and he must always have a place in the history of the English School. He was a typical example of the combination of feudal sentiment with socialistic sympathies ; and may be regarded as the father of the conservative socialism which we more often connect with the names of Kingsley and Disraeli.

I have said nothing of foreign socialism in this brief French and German influences. sketch because I do not consider that it essentially modified the spontaneous development of the English School. Owenism in its earlier stages may have gained a certain reinforcement from the imported influences of Saint-Simon and Fourier, as it certainly did in the later period from the more congenial inspiration of

[1] *Rural Rides*, 1830 ed. p. 584.

Marx and Engels, and of the men of 1848.   But, on the whole, its evolution was independent and self-contained. There was for many years a group of English Fourierites, who had a journal of their own, the *London Phalanx*, and even, one may say, a literature; but the really vital doctrines of Fourier never took hold of his English followers.   They were impressed with the externals of his system, the *abracadabra* of his luxuriant terminology; but seem to have failed to catch the inspiration of his really profound and luminous suggestions.   It is curious that the far more practical Saint-Simon, whose methods were eminently English, had even less influence in this country.   There is just a trace of his spirit in Thompson and Stuart Mill; but his teaching had no important following here until the tradition came to us at the hands of the brilliant English disciples of Auguste Comte.   German communism was first introduced to English readers by Engels, in a series of contributions to the *New Moral World* in 1843 and 1844.[1]   A notice of Wilhelm Weitling appeared in English in 1844; and finally, in 1850, G. Julian Harney published a translation of the Communist Manifesto in his paper, the *Red Republican*.[2]   The revolutionary tone of Marx, and especially his summons to a class war, may have been

---

[1] Cf. his articles on *The Progress of Social Reform on the Continent*, Nov. 4, and 18, 1843; and his letter "*The Times*" on German Communism, Jan. 20, 1844.

[2] Cf. Nos. 21-24; Nov. 9-30, 1850.   Harney was one of the most able and courageous of the Chartist leaders, and our last link with the men of that time.   He died only last December (Dec. 9, 1897), at Richmond, aged eighty.

relished by militant Chartists of the Harney type; but the average Englishman was too deficient in philosophic training to appreciate the methods of German and Marxist socialism. Hence these brief notices of it were almost wholly ignored, alike by the economists and the common people. Far deeper, at least for the time, was the impression made on English minds by the events of 1848. Our insularity was not proof against the wave of revolt which swept over Europe in this year. The ferment of thought and the dramatic course of events in France stirred the minds and roused the hopes of our social reformers. French influences gave us a literature on the Right to Employment, and undoubtedly helped to bring the Chartist rising to a head. But any weight which the doctrines of 1848 might have had in the abstract was heavily discounted by their failure when put into execution. The collapse of the National Workshops in Paris, and the fiasco of the Physical Force men in London were object-lessons not easily forgotten. Thus in the end the Revolution of 1848 did more to depress than to stimulate contemporary social movements. Not until the lapse of another generation did foreign influences leave any permanent impression on socialism in England.

Upon the whole, then, English socialism was too insular to gain much stimulus from other countries; and when, in 1848, it was most nearly in sympathy with the foreign movement, the complete failure of the Revolution reacted heavily on this side of the Channel,

English socialism declines with the growth of prosperity after 1852.

and did much to dishearten the English socialist leaders. A less obvious, but in the long run a far more effective check resulted from the famous gold discoveries of this period. The abundant supply of precious metal which set in after 1852 put a term to the period of contraction and industrial depression which had followed the Peace of 1815. The next twenty years were years of rising prices and unprecedented prosperity. Trade advanced "by leaps and by bounds," employment was abundant, and the condition of the people rapidly improved. The rise of prices was as fatal to revolutionary socialism as it was favourable to the more pacific and commercial methods of co-operation and trade-unionism. How co-operation advanced we all know. Mr. and Mrs. Webb tell us that trade-unionism reached its high-water mark in 1874. But the general activity of production took the wind out of the sails of the socialist movement. So far as its more revolutionary forms are concerned, there was a complete collapse, as prices and trade expanded; and the very literature, never more vigorous than in 1848-50, vanishes after 1853, not to revive again until the serious check to prosperity, a generation later, in 1884. When the next period of depression set in, the revived socialism in England was a purely exotic growth. It seemed to have altogether lost touch with the parent school of Thompson and his contemporaries; and, except for such slight countenance as it derived from the teaching of John Stuart Mill, was entirely inspired from foreign sources, and especially by

Modern revivals.

the writings of Marx and Lassalle, and the crusade of Henry George.[1] Of late years, the authority of Marx and George has greatly waned in this country. The current forms of socialism are once more of native origin, and like most really English movements, have gradually purged themselves of the revolutionary temper. The Fabian Society, in particular, though genuinely socialistic in its ulterior aims, appears from its latest manifesto to have adopted a policy of gradual and detailed reform, so practical and opportunist that it can hardly be called socialistic in the sense here given to that term.

THE APPENDICES

I must now close a sketch which, though far from complete, already fills too large a part of this little volume. Those who may wish to pursue the subject further will find in the two appendices to the book some assistance in their inquiries. The first appendix contains a translation of the Preface to the now rare first instalment of Marx's *Kapital*, printed in 1859. This is instructive as enabling us to compare Marx's own account of the development of his views with the account given by Dr. Menger of their derivation from the socialists of the English School. The complete

The 1859 Preface.

---

[1] George adopted the English doctrine of the Right to the Whole Produce of Labour, though it is clearly inconsistent with his scheme for the confiscation of property in land. It is indeed inconsistent with any scheme of equality, unless efficiency and industry are equal, as they notoriously are not.

absence of any reference to the English School in this preface is remarkable, and contrasts significantly with the full quotations which appeared in Marx's attack on Proudhon, twelve years before. After what I have written above, I need hardly say that Dr. Menger's contention seems to me abundantly justified.

The Biblio-graphy. In the second appendix will be found a bibliography of the English School; arranged chronologically, because its main purpose is to facilitate the historical study of the English Socialist movement. Any such list must necessarily be a somewhat arbitrary one, and I do not propose to attempt to justify the particular selection I have made. No two compilers would probably make quite the same choice of entries. I may, however, explain that it is not a general bibliography, even of English socialism, but is concerned mainly with what I have here called the English School. It does not pre-tend to deal with foreign socialism, nor with the later English socialism developed under French and German influences; though I have occasionally noted translations from foreign socialists which may have influenced the native school. The chief aim has been first to give a list of the writings of the English School themselves, and secondly to indicate some of the principal non-social-istic works against which their writings were directed, or in which they were controverted. Here and there an entry has been made in order to mark contemporary and closely-connected movements, such as the Factory and Chartist agitations. Such references, however, are only incidental. The Trade Union movement already has a bibliography of its own; the Factory and Chartist movements deserve one. I have not dealt with either here, except in so far as they may have some point of intrusion into the main subject. At the end will be found a list of a few histories and biographies which may serve as general manuals for the student. I have taken special pains to give an accurate account of the periodical publications of the School. All socialistic literature is troublesome to catalogue. It is obscure and irregular, and the bibliographical indications, where they are present, are often incorrect and confusing. Worst of all in these respects are the periodical issues. But some of them are of great historic value, and well deserve, as far as is now possible, to be placed on record. That, in spite of all care, the list now offered is defective, no one knows better than the compiler. But I hope it is sufficiently complete to be representative; and I look with some confidence to those who have ever made similar attempts for an indulgent judgment on its imperfections.

Conclusion

My object in this introduction has been to expound, not to criticise, the doctrines of the English Socialists. Dr. Menger's searching examination leaves little mcre to be said by way of criticism, at all events from the juristic standpoint which he has chosen; and it would

Critical results.

be out of place here to enter upon a more strictly economic scrutiny of their teaching. Otherwise it might be interesting to analyse with some rigour the nebulous phrases "product of one's labour," and " unearned income." I find it very difficult, for instance, to conceive any economic definition of a right to the product of labour which does not carry with it a right to what comes within some meanings of the term "unearned income." It might appear, too, on a close investigation, that this latter term is full of ambiguities, and that a rigorous definition of earnings would not be altogether favourable to revolutionary claims of right. Doctrines of abstract right are apt to be double-edged, and have been appealed to by the defenders, as well as by the enemies, of the existing social order.

But the economic solidarity of modern society makes all claims of individual right, whether or not sound at law, more or less defective in equity. This applies alike to the ridiculous brag of the so-called " self-made " capitalist, and to the revolutionary claim of the socialist labourer. No one, in a modern society, can possibly say what the produce of an individual's labour really is. We know what the law allows him to acquire; we cannot say what he has equitably "earned." Social obligation is involved in every acquisition ; at every moment he depends on tradition from his ancestors, on co-operation from his contemporaries, and even on expectation from his successors. In short the modern fact of economic solidarity seems to me to have cut

away the foundation from the individualistic socialism
of abstract right. The conflict between the two tendencies of thought constitutes the inner contradiction
of modern socialism, but the issue of the conflict hardly
admits of question. No doubt the claim of Labour in
general to the whole product of industry is better
justified than the claim of any individual labourer to his
own product. But all doctrine founded on equity alone
irresistibly gravitates towards pure communism. This
appears to me to be the most important result of Dr.
Menger's criticism; and it is one in which I fully
concur. The lessons of history, even more than the
results of analysis, make the conclusion inevitable.
The doctrine of abstract right seems to have had its day.
It has been proved to have great revolutionary power
and consequent political significance; but it has always
tended to a certain confusion of issues, and its effects
have been mainly, if not wholly, destructive. For
substantial guidance in that work of social reorganisation
which will be the true business of the next century, and
is the real aim to-day alike of socialists and economists,
we must look rather to a conception of social ends than
of individual rights.

Dr. Menger's practical conclusions, on which he does *Practical*
not insist at length, may perhaps not find such general *conclusions.*
acceptance here as his criticism. They seem to have
too exclusively in view the political situation in
Austria - Hungary. The strong anti - Agrarian tone
which prevails throughout the book will hardly be

intelligible to English readers familiar with the present conditions of our rural economy. This political standpoint may have partly affected Dr. Menger's judgment on some particular questions : for instance, his strong condemnation of State assistance to facilitate redemption of mortgages, which takes no account of the changes, whether political, fiscal, or monetary, that often form the main justification of such measures. But his broad conclusion rests on perfectly general grounds. Whatever direction social development may take, he holds that it must not be imperilled by revolution ; and in order to avert this peril, the State must observe a strong policy in reference to unearned income. There must be no legislative increase, and no legislative transfer, of this kind of income. This will be a hard saying to many of us, whether individualists or socialists. If capital is wisely borrowed, the consequent creation of unearned income represents a benefit to the borrower. Is the State, whose credit stands so high, to be debarred from using this advantage for the benefit of those it represents ? If so, how are its functions to be enlarged, as socialists desire ? We are not justified in tacitly assuming that unearned income is an evil, even if we grant that it is politically invidious. Men are not always earning, nor always earning most when their wants are greatest. Hence it will always be a convenience, and to all classes, to have the means of redistributing earnings according to wants, which is provided by the institution of investment and interest. The perception of this convenience will increase with civilisation; and this will require and justify the increase of unearned income. It thus appears equally necessary from the point of view of borrower and lender, and the question who pays for the convenience must be merely one of demand and supply, and does not seem to involve a reference to equity.

Nor is the legislative transfer of unearned income always to be accounted an evil. There may be historical circumstances, as in Ireland, and economic changes, like the recent change in the value of money, which make such a transfer not only expedient but just. The various legislative acts which have developed peasant properties, and the usury acts which have sheltered the small proprietor from the extreme exactions of the creditor, are cases in point. In short, if it is possible, by well-advised and cautious legislation, to promote a more equitable and more secure distribution of unearned income, such legislation will be the reverse of revolutionary in its results. We may agree with Dr. Menger that it is a form of social surgery not lightly to be used; we must still hold that in certain morbid conditions it may often be the best, and sometimes the only available, remedy.

None the less it remains true, as Dr. Menger warns us, that you cannot long attack one form of "unearned" income without ultimately endangering the whole. It may suit party exigencies to throw the Jews to the wolves in one country, or the landlords in another; but the policy is logically rotten and politically perilous. The various kinds of economic income are so inextricably involved and combined in actual life that we cannot deal with them justly or effectively by the clumsy and partial method of class legislation. Where the existing ownership of wealth offends against the social equities, the wrong can best be redressed, so far as it admits of legislative redress at all, by a wise and equal scheme of taxation. But the duty of the State does not end here. It is far more important, and far more practicable, to take care that the acquisition of new wealth proceeds justly, than to attempt to redistribute wealth already acquired. In a form of society where the distribution of wealth is left to depend upon contract or bargain, it is obviously of the first consequence that the general economic conditions should be favourable to fairness and equality in bargaining. Great progress has been made in this direction during the last fifty years, by agencies of all kinds, legislative and other. But still more remains to be done; and one need not be a socialist to feel that in the last resort the chief responsibility in the matter must rest with the State. "Proudhon," says an American writer, "has declared that Property is Theft. It is for a wise Government to see that Theft shall not be Property."

PREFACE TO THE SECOND GERMAN EDITION

SINCE the appearance of the first edition of this book, a great deal of material for the history of socialist ideas has come to me from all sides. As the book has won for itself a wide circle of readers mainly by its shortness and conciseness, I can only avail myself of a limited selection of this new matter. It was my endeavour in the first edition to refer the socialist theories in all cases to their first originator and advocate. I am fully aware that this, in my opinion, truly scientific work has wounded the feelings of very influential circles. But to men who, at a time when socialist ideas aroused so little interest, bore in their lives, besides other persecutions, the grief of being unappreciated and forgotten, there is at least due the tardy justice of immortality in the memory of their fellowmen, as the originators of world-moving thoughts.

ANTON MENGER.

VIENNA, *May* 1891.

PREFACE TO THE FIRST GERMAN EDITION

THE object of the present essay is to work out the main ideas of Socialism from a legal standpoint. It is a fragment of a larger work, in which I am attempting a synthesis of Socialism as a body of legal rules. Not until socialist theories are laid down as bare legal conceptions, denuded of the endless economic and philanthropic disquisitions which form the main contents of socialist literature, can practical statesmen recognise how far our present legal system may be modified in the interests of the suffering masses of the people. Such a juridical elaboration of Socialism appears to me the most important task of modern jurisprudence, the right accomplishment of which will materially assist the peaceful reform of our social conditions.

I had great difficulty in tracing through socialist

literature the gradual development of the right to the whole produce of labour from the French Revolution to the present time.   It may be said without exaggeration that the historical study of Socialism is in a condition which does anything but honour to German science.   The older historical researches of Stein and Marlo are based on a study of original authorities, however superficial and incomplete.   But the modern historians of Socialism have been content to give extracts from, or even absolutely copy, Reybaud, Stein, and Marlo, without going back to the works of French and English socialists, although in them we find the starting-point of the modern social movement.   Naturally enough, a method so subversive of all the rules of historical research has resulted in a constantly increasing dead weight of errors and misconceptions, which has to be dragged along by our history of Socialism, so that many works, although they bear names of great learning, absolutely give the impression of a caricature of the matter of which they treat.   In the following account of the development of one of the most fundamental socialist ideas, I have always gone direct to the original authorities, except where the contrary is expressly stated.

This almost complete ignorance of English and French Socialism, especially of the older period, has contributed not a little to the disproportionate esteem which the writings of Marx and Rodbertus now enjoy in Germany. If, thirty years after the publication of Adam Smith's *Wealth of Nations,* some one had again "discovered" the theory of the division of labour, or if to-day an author were to publish Darwin's theory of evolution as his own intellectual property, he would be regarded as an ignoramus or a charlatan. Successful attempts of this kind are only conceivable in the domain of social science, which still almost completely lacks a historical tradition. I shall show in this book that Marx and Rodbertus borrowed their most important theories without any acknowledgment from English and French theorists. Indeed, I do not scruple to assert that Marx and Rodbertus, whom many people would fain regard as the creators of scientific Socialism, are really far excelled in depth and thoroughness by their predecessors.

No one knows better than myself how faulty is the historical and dogmatic portion of this essay. The juridical elaboration of Socialism, whose stage is the whole world, and whose organs are countless writers, parties, and sects, is indeed a task far transcending the powers of an individual, and I shall be quite content with the modest result of having given an incitement and a beginning to the great task.   For the true solution of the problem can only be attained by the co-operation of men of science from all civilised nations.

THE AUTHOR.

VIENNA, *September* 1886.

CONTENTS

THE RIGHT TO THE WHOLE
PRODUCE OF LABOUR

§ 1. INTRODUCTION

THE RIGHT (*a*) TO THE WHOLE PRODUCE OF LABOUR.
      (*b*) TO SUBSISTENCE.
      (*c*) TO LABOUR (*droit au travail*).

THE social aspirations of our time aim essentially at a reorganisation of the economic life of mankind. They start, it is true, from a searching criticism of our existing economic conditions ; but this criticism leads to certain juridical postulates which involve an organic reconstruction of our actual rights of property (laws of things, obligations, and succession, *Sachen-Obligationen-und Erbrecht*). Many socialistic systems, indeed, go much further than this, and aim at a reorganisation of sexual relations, the abolition of the State and of religion, and so on; but it is only the demand for a thorough reconstruction of our traditional law of property, which can be regarded as the common programme of all socialist schools.

If we look at the economic life by which we are surrounded, we find its main purport to be that men labour for the satisfaction of their wants, that all labour aims at a return, every want at satisfaction. Labour and the produce of labour, wants and satisfactions, are in fact the two sequences in which the economic life of mankind fulfils itself. The ideal law of property, from the economic point of view, would therefore be attained in a system which ensured to every labourer the whole produce of his labour, and to every want as complete satisfaction as the means at disposal would allow.

Our actual law of property, which rests almost entirely on traditional political conditions, does not even attempt the attainment of these economic ends. Originally, the occupation of most countries was effected by conquest and settlement, and since then the sword has sufficiently often modified the existing distribution of property. When the State began to legislate as to rights of possession, it was generally content to sanction actual relations with a few unimportant alterations; so that it is easy to see how our property law, being the outcome of quite other than economic conceptions, seeks neither to secure to the labourer the full produce of his labour, nor to guarantee to existing wants the greatest feasible satisfaction.

Our present law of property, which centres in private possession, does not, in the first place, guarantee to the labourer the whole product of his labour. By assigning the existing objects of wealth, and especially the instruments of production, to individuals to use at their pleasure, our law of property invests such individuals with an ascendency, by virtue of which without any labour of their own, they draw an unearned income which they can apply to the satisfaction of their wants. This income, for which the legally-favoured recipients return no personal equivalent to society, has been called rent (*Rente*) by the Saint-Simonians and the followers of Buchez and Rodbertus; by Thompson and Marx, surplus value (*Mehrwert*); I intend to call it unearned income (*arbeitsloses Einkommen*). The legally recognised existence of unearned income proves in itself that our law of property does not even aim at obtaining for the labourer the whole product of his industry.

The character of unearned income may be most clearly discerned in the case of rent for land and buildings and interest on loans, where the activity of the owner is confined to its collection from tenants and debtors. But even the landlord who farms his own land, and the capitalist who himself engages in industry or trade, still of necessity obtain unearned income in the forms of rent and profit respectively. The amount of this can be estimated in any particular case by merely subtracting from the entire returns of the undertaking the sum which the owner must expend to replace his own activity by a deputy.

Neither does our actual law of property—and this is the second point—set itself the task of providing for every want a satisfaction proportionate to the available means. Our codes of private law (*Privatrecht*) do not contain a single clause which assigns to the individual even such goods and services as are indispensable to the maintenance of his existence. So far as our private law is concerned, the situation is somewhat brutally but very rightly expressed by Malthus in a passage which by its very frankness has attained a certain fame.

" A man who is born into a world already possessed, if he cannot get subsistence from his parents on whom he has a just demand, and if the society do not want his labour, has no claim of *right* to the smallest portion of food, and, in fact, has no business to be where he is. At Nature's mighty feast there is no vacant cover for him. She tells him to be gone, and will quickly execute her own orders." [1]   What Malthus says here of food applies to the satisfaction of all other wants.

It is true that this deficiency of our private law is to some extent made good by a public institution— namely, the poor law; but a long experience has shown the inadequacy of the remedy. Quite lately Germany and Austria have been engaged in at any rate partially recognising the legal right of every member of society to the satisfaction of his urgent needs, by comprehensive legislation as to insurance against illness, accident, infirmity, and old age. We shall come back to this again (§ 14).

[1] Malthus, *An Essay on the Principle of Population*, 2nd ed., 4º 1803, p. 531. This famous passage, which is so often quoted in socialist literature, was omitted by Malthus in the third edition of 1806, and in the later editions of the Essay.

The scheme of law postulated by Socialism is in energetic contradiction to our present law. Every socialist organisation of property, however much the opinions of the different schools may vary, aims either at guaranteeing to the working-classes the whole produce of their labour, or at reducing to just proportions individual needs and existing means of satisfaction; in other words, socialists would discard a distribution based on political conditions in favour of a system of property adapted to the realisation of economic aims.

Now it is clear that no socialistic organisation of property, however Utopian its assumptions, can hope to attain completely both of these fundamental objects at the same time; because it stands to reason that labour and wants will never absolutely coincide in any constitution of society. Any attempt to carry to a logical conclusion the idea of the labourer's right to the whole produce of his labour is immediately confronted with the numerous persons who are incapable of work (children, the aged and invalids, etc.), and who must depend for the satisfaction of their wants on unearned income. On the other hand, it were well to reflect seriously before making individual requirements the sole measure of distribution, independently of the labour which creates the very means of satisfaction. So that most socialist systems strive to reconcile two principles leading to such widely different results with as few contradictions as may be.

The attainment of these two objects is the aim of

the socialist movement, which since the end of the last century has maintained a steadily increasing hold on civilised nations. As the objects of the political agitations of the seventeenth and eighteeeth centuries may be summarised in certain constitutional postulates called fundamental political rights, so we may characterise the ultimate aims of socialism as economic rights. I am quite aware that an exaggerated importance has been attached to the recognition of political rights, which is in striking disproportion to their scanty practical effect; nevertheless, the formulation of such rights is not without value, as they crystallise into a password the chief aims of political and social movements.

The recognition of the justifiable claim of the labourer to that which his labour has produced gives the first fundamental economic right, *the right to the whole produce of labour*. While to postulate the responsibility of the law to provide for every need a satisfaction in proportion to existing means defines the second economic right, *the right to subsistence*. These two fundamental rights mark the limits within which every logical socialistic or communistic system must work. To these should be added a third economic right, *the right to labour*, which is only a peculiar modification of the right to subsistence, and which has attained considerable historical importance as a means of transition to a socialistic organisation. I will now proceed to the discussion of the chief characteristics of these three economic rights of Socialism.

(a) The Right to the whole Produce of Labour

Numerous socialist systems advocate the opinion that every member of society can claim of right that the law should assign to him the entire produce of his labour.[1] A commodity should belong only to the individual by whose labour it was produced. If, however, it be the result of the contemporary or successive co-operation of many persons, as is the preponderating rule under a system of division of labour, each worker should receive such a share of its exchange value as was contributed by his work. Seeing that such a system of distribution divides the entire produce between the labourers, unearned income (rent and interest) and its legal cause, private property, are impossible under its domination.

But on what principle is the exchange value of a commodity produced by the co-operation of many workers to be divided amongst the assistants?

It is in itself quite conceivable that the traditional prices of labour should be retained even in a socialistically ordered society, being merely increased by a given amount in consequence of the abolition of unearned income. For, indeed, a completely new settlement of prices which left all traditional rates out of account,

---

[1] Cf. below, § 4 (Charles Hall); § 5 (William Thompson); § 8 (Rodbertus)—see also Kautsky, *Die Vertheilung des Arbeitsertrages im socialistischen Staat*, in Richter's *Jahrbuch für Socialwissenschaft*, second year of issue, 1881, pp. 88-89.

and was merely the result of a general principle,
would disturb society almost more profoundly than the
introduction of a socialist organisation. Unconcerned
by this, Rodbertus, who is one of the chief supporters
of the right to the whole produce of labour, proposes to
replace our metallic money by a currency of labour-
hours, every workman who co-operates in the production
of a commodity receiving as many hours of its value as
an average workman would require for his share of the
work. This principle of distribution therefore assumes
the equation of the labour-hours, or at any rate of the
labour-days, of all workmen, in so far as in them the
average work has been performed.[1]

(b) The Right to Subsistence

Many socialist systems recognise not labour, but
wants, as the standard of distribution.[2] Now, although
the direct consequence of this view is the principle that
every commodity shall belong to him who has the most
urgent need of it, only a few socialists have really drawn
this deduction, amongst them being Godwin, whose

---

[1] Cf. below, §§ 8 and 13.

[2] Cf. for instance Morelly, *Naufrage des isles flottantes ou Basiliade*,
vol. i., 1753, pp. 2-7.   Brissot, *Sur la propriété et sur le vol*, 1780, sect. 2.
Cabet, *Voyage en Icarie*, 5th edition 1848, on the title-page ; "*A chacun
suivant ses besoins*, de chacun suivant ses forces."   Louis Blanc, *Nouveau
Monde*, 16th July 1850, p. 4.   (*Questions d'aujourd'hui et de demain*,
vol. iii., 1880, p. 225).   "De chacun selon ses facultés, *à chacun selon ses
besoins*," and so on.   Cf. Schramm in the *Zukunft*, 1878, pp. 497-507.

views will be discussed further on (§ 3). Nor can it be denied that individual wants are far too indefinite, subjective, and variable to form a basis for what is the most important of the consequences of a system of law—namely, the distribution of wealth. Such a principle can only be carried out in a small association united by the closest ties of mutual inclination (for instance, the family).

Now, when so many communists speak of an *equal* distribution of wealth in a communistic state, it is this distribution in proportion to wants and existing means of satisfaction to which they refer. For no one could seriously strive for a really equal distribution in the face of the enormous differences in wants due to age, sex, and individual character.

Those wants, on the satisfaction of which depends the maintenance of life itself, and which are therefore called absolute necessities, stand out by their practical importance from other less pressing needs,[1] and being of a general and more objective character might certainly serve as a standard of distribution, though it must not be forgotten that they vary considerably according to time and place. The necessities of life form the basis of the right to subsistence which plays so great a part in the socialist systems of all periods, and which may be characterised as recognising the claim of every member of society to the commodities and services

---

[1] Cf. as to this Carl Menger, *Grundsätze der Volkswirthschaftslehre*, 1871, p. 88.

necessary to support existence, in preference to the satisfaction of the less pressing wants of others.

In socialist systems, and in the practical trials of a communistic state of society which have been made hitherto, the extent of the right to subsistence varies with the age of the claimant. In the case of minors it allows education and support; for grown persons mere necessaries, in return for which the claimant is bound to perform an equivalent amount of labour; while for those who by reason of age, illness, or other infirmity are unable to work it allows support.[1] In a logical socialist organisation the right to subsistence would represent the interests of the individual against the community, thus replacing the rights of property in our present legal system.

Whereas a logical realisation of the right to the whole produce of labour renders all unearned income and private property impossible, the maintenance of both side by side with the recognition of the right to subsistence is quite conceivable. The right of all citizens to the satisfaction of their absolute needs may in such a case be regarded as a form of mortgage on the national income having a first claim before the unearned income of favoured individuals. And, indeed, as we shall

---

[1] As to the form of the right to existence in the American socialist communities, cf. below, p. 166, notes 1-3. In the *Code de la nature*, Morelly defines the right to existence as follows: "Tout citoyen sera homme public, sustenté, entretenu et occupé aux dépens du public" (p. 152 of Villegardelle's edition of the code, 1841). Cf. also the English poor law of 1601, p. 13, note 1 below.

see in the course of our inquiries, the social aspirations of our time aim at the realisation, to a certain
extent, of the right to subsistence on the one hand, and
on the other at the maintenance of the fabric of our
system of private property (§ 14). But a complete
realisation of the right would absorb so large a portion
of the unearned income which property now bestows
on landowners and capitalists, and deprive private
wealth of so much of its social value that it would
soon be converted into common property.

On the other hand, the right to subsistence is equally
compatible with the socialist opposite of property, the
right to the whole produce of labour. Even under a
system which had abolished unearned income, it would
be quite practicable to force every citizen to labour a
certain number of hours per day to earn his absolute
subsistence, leaving the entire return of the remaining
hours at his own disposal within certain limits. And
indeed such a combination of the rights to existence
and to the whole produce of labour, uniting as it does
self-seeking and public spirit, freedom and compulsion,
might be advisable in a time of transition, when socialist
institutions would have to work with a population
educated in an individualistic atmosphere.

(c) THE RIGHT TO LABOUR

An infinite number of compromises are conceivable
between the actual right of private possession and the

distribution of wealth according to wants or the produce
of labour which constitutes the ultimate goal of the
socialist movement. Such a compromise is the so-called
right to labour to which the events of 1848, and latterly
an utterance of Prince Bismarck's [1] in the German Im-

[1] In a sitting of the Imperial Parliament on 9th May 1884, during
the discussion on the extension of the law against the social democratic movement as dangerous to the State (passed on 21st October 1878),
Prince Bismarck as Imperial Chancellor made the following declaration :
" To sum up my position, *give the labourer the right to labour as long as
he is in health,* give him work as long as he is in health, *ensure him care
when he is ill, and ensure him a provision when he is old.* If you will do
this and not spare the price, and not cry state-socialism at the first
mention of old age pensions, if the State shows a little more Christian
care for the working class, then I believe that the authors of the Wydener
programme will pipe to the workman in vain, that their following will
greatly diminish as soon as he sees that the government and the legislature
are in earnest in their care for his well-being " (*Report of the Proceedings
of the Imperial Parliament,* Session 1884, vol. i. p. 481). In the further
course of the same debate Prince Bismarck replied as follows to a speech
of Eugen Richter's : "I will first answer the first question upon which he
(Richter) touched, the 'Right to Labour.' Yes, I recognise uncondition-
ally a right to labour, and shall advocate it as long as I am in this place.
And in doing so I stand on the ground, not of that socialism which is said
to have begun with the Bismarck ministry, but of the Prussian civil code "
(quoting the *Preussisches Landrecht,* ii., tit. 19, §§ 1 and 2, the paragraphs
are given below, p. 14, note 1 ; the reading of § 1 was met by cries of " Poor
law ! "). " Well, gentlemen, what of the inarticulate cries of scorn of a
few moments ago ? Was not the right to labour openly declared at the
time of the publication of the civil code ? Do not our whole moral relations demand that the man who says to his fellow citizens, 'I am healthy
and willing to work but can find no work,' should have the right to say
'find me work,' and that the State should be bound to find him work ?
The first speaker said that the State would have to father very large
undertakings. Yes, as it has done before in times of distress, as in '48,
when the ebullition occasioned by the progressive movement caused great
want of work and scarcity of money. Who does not remember the
' Rehbergers,' with their red feathers and top-boots ? Then the State considered it a duty to find work for those men, vagabonds most of them,

perial Parliament, have given a considerable historical
importance. It is an offshoot of the right to subsistence
which is to be grafted on to our present system of
private property.

The idea which lies at the root of the right to labour
appears to have been suggested by certain fundamental
clauses of a State poor law which occur almost identi-
cally in the legislature of various countries. The
English poor law of 1601,[1] the French constitution of
1791 and 1793,[2] and the Prussian civil code of 5th

though there were a few honest men amongst them, who really did not
know how to get a living. If such a scarcity should recur, then I hold
the State still under the same obligation, and the State is engaged in
undertakings of such magnitude that it can well fulfil its duty of finding
work for those of its citizens who cannot find it for themselves. The
State carries out many schemes which would otherwise be left undone
owing to financial scruples ; for instance, the making of canals and analogous works, and a number of other useful undertakings " (Report as
above, p. 500).

[1] Act for the Relief of the Poor, 43 Elizabeth, c. 2, 1601, sect. 1 :
" They (the poor law guardians) shall take order from time to time . . .
for setting to work the children of all such parents who shall not . . .
be thought able to keep and maintain their children ; and also for setting
to work all such persons, married or unmarried, having no means to
maintain them, who use no ordinary and daily trade of life to get their
living by ; and also to raise, weekly or otherwise, . . . in the said parish,
in such competent sum and sums of money as they shall think fit, a
convenient stock of flax, hemp, wool, thread, iron, and other necessary
ware and stuff to set the poor on work, and also competent sums of money
for and towards the necessary relief of the lame, impotent, old, blind,
and such other among them, being poor and not able to work, and also
for the putting out of such children to be apprentices, to be gathered out
of the same parish, according to the ability of the same parish." Cf.
Aschrott, *Das englische Armenwesen*, 1886, p. 10.

[2] *Constitution de la République Française* of the 24*th June* 1793. *Déclaration des droits de l'homme et du citoyen*, art. 21 : " Les secours

February 1794 [1] all agree in the declaration that the State or the local authorities (commune, parish, etc.) are bound to support the poor, or to provide them with work. But the right to labour must be distinguished from the right to relief, even when this is given in the form of work; for the right to labour, as understood by socialists, is of the nature of a right to any other property, and is neither founded in liberality on the part of the State, nor implies indigence on the part of the claimant, so that it must not assume the humiliating form of poor relief.[2]

Again, the right to labour must be clearly differ-

---

publics sont une dette sacrée. La société doit la subsistence aux citoyens malheureux, soit en leur procurant du travail, soit en assurant les moyens d'exister à ceux qui sont hors d'état de travailler." Cf. also the French Constitution of 3rd September 1793, tit. 1.

[1] *Preussisches Landrecht*, part ii. tit. 19, §§ 1, 2 : "It is the duty of the State to provide for the food and support of those citizens who cannot obtain a living for themselves, and can also not receive it from other people bound by particular laws to provide for them. Those who lack only the means and the opportunity to work for their support and that of their family should be given work suited to their powers and strength." These declarations, which by their wording would seem very comprehensive, really contemplate only poor relief.

[2] The discussion of the Right to Labour held in the French National Assembly on 12th to 16th September, and 2nd November 1848, turned upon the question whether the right to relief only, or also the right to labour should be recognised. Thiers spoke in favour of the former, but against the latter. (Girardin, *Le droit au travail au Luxembourg et à l'Assemblée Nationale*, 1849, vol. ii. p. 231, and the *Constitution of 4th November 1848*, did in fact recognise only the right to relief ("droit à l'assistance") in accordance with the constitution of 1793. Joseph Garnier, in his *Le droit au travail à l'Assemblée Nationale*, 1848, p. 385, and a few other writers are therefore certainly incorrect in attempting to identify the two rights.

entiated from the right to search for labour with more
or less chance of success.   In the famous edict of
12th March 1776, which attempted the introduction
of free industry into France, Louis XVI., or rather
Turgot, speaks of a right to labour, the exertion of
which ought not to be restricted by the guild system.[1]
The advocates of the guilds regard, on the contrary, the
right to labour as the right of a guild member to work
at his trade to the exclusion of outsiders.[2]   Both views
are equally incorrect.   The right to labour confers on
every citizen the right not to seek work, but to find it.

In so far as any definite result may be obtained
from the varying and obscure theory and practice, the
true conception of the right to labour would appear to
be that by virtue of this right every capable citizen
who cannot find work with a private employer may
claim that the State or the local authorities (county or
corporation) shall provide him with common day labour
at the customary wage.

The right to labour therefore differs from the right
to the whole produce of labour, in that the worker can

---

[1] French edict of February 1776 in the *Recueil général des anciennes
lois françaises*, by Jourdan, Decrusy, and Isambert, vol. xxiii. p. 370
(cf. the *Lit de Justice* for the registration of this law of 12th March
1776, same vol. p. 398): "Dieu en donnant à l'homme des besoins, en
lui rendant nécessaire la ressource du travail, a fait du *droit de travailler*
la propriété de tout homme, et cette propriété est la première, la plus
sacrée et la plus imprescriptible de toutes." Cf. also the *Recueil*, same
vol. pp. 374 and 375.

[2] Cf. for instance Marlo, *Untersuchungen über die Organisation der
Arbeit*, 2nd edit. 1884, vol. ii. p. 314.

only claim a wage (not the entire product of his work), while the instruments of production are merely lent him to use on behalf of the State. It was therefore incorrectly that many speakers in the French National Assembly (p. 14, note 2), during the debate on the right to labour, assumed it to involve the right to capital.[1] On the contrary, the right to labour is essentially complementary to our existing law of property, and actually assumes the existence of private ownership of land and capital.

It is this subsidiary character which also principally distinguishes the right to labour from the right to subsistence. The latter is an immediate claim on the State or the local authorities, from whom the claimant may demand in return for his work the direct satisfaction of his necessities ; but the right to labour can only be enforced when it is proved that the claimant has failed to find work under a private employer. Moreover, the right to subsistence extends to minors and to the infirm, while the right to labour applies only to able-bodied citizens.

How far this specification of the idea of the right to labour is correct may be seen in the following account of the historical development of the right.

The right to labour in its present sense was first advocated amongst socialists by Fourier, who seems to

---

[1] Cf. Émile de Girardin, *Le droit au travail au Luxembourg et à l'Assemblée Nationale* (Speeches of Barthe and Dufaure), 1849, vol. ii. pp. 139, 321.

have been unacquainted with Fichte's, on many points, analogous elaboration (§ 2). In his most comprehensive work, the *Traité de l'Association domestique-agricole*, Fourier [1] enters into a violent polemic against the theory of natural rights (droits de l'homme) in the merely political sense given it by the revolution and the parliamentary doctrinairism of the restoration; and he shows of how little value to the interests of the suffering masses are the political doctrines of the sovereignty of the people, of freedom, equality, and fraternity, in spite of the blood which has been shed for them in wars and revolutions.

Fourier proceeds to assert economic rights in opposition to these political rights. In a state of nature the savage has the right to hunt and fish, to gather fruits, and to pasture his cattle at his pleasure. [2] But in a state of society in which natural resources are already appropriated, the exercise of these four economic rights is hardly feasible, and they must be replaced by an equivalent which Fourier sometimes calls the right to

---

[1] Fourier, *Traité de l'association domestique-agricole*, vol. i., 1822, pp. 116-143 ; *Œuvres complètes*, vol. iii. 1841, pp. 151-187. Moreover, the "droit au travail" is mentioned by Fourier in his first work : *Théorie des quatre mouvements et des destinées générales*, 1808, p. 270 (*Œuvres complètes*, 3rd edit. 1846, vol. i. p. 193).

[2] With that eccentricity which Fourier so often unites with the deepest thoughts, he proceeds to add to the natural rights of man in a state of nature the right to congregate in tribes, to steal outside the tribe and live happily, taking no thought for the morrow (Fourier, *Traité de l'association*, 1822, vol. i. pp. 126-129) Considérant, in his pamphlet on the right to labour (note 6, p. 18), has naturally not adopted these "rights," but recognises only the "Droit de chasse, de pêche, de cueillette et de pâture."

labour,[1] and sometimes the right to a minimum of subsistence,[2] ignoring the difference between the two.[3] But, according to Fourier, even this equivalent cannot be obtained under existing conditions, nor will be so until the institution of his proposed social organisation.[4]

These ideas of Fourier's were elaborated by his school in numerous pamphlets and articles ;[5] and I should like to call attention particularly to Considérant's pamphlet on the right to labour, which, thanks to its avoidance of all exaggeration, exercised a marked influence on the events of 1848.[6]

Considérant differs from his master in that he would not wait for the recognition of the right to labour

[1] Fourier, *Traité*, pp. 137, 143.

[2] Fourier, pp. 126 and 135. In his chief work, *Le nouveau monde industriel et sociétaire*, 1829, so far as I can see, he only speaks of the right to the minimum of subsistence. Cf. *Nouveau monde*, pp. 4, 12, 38, 42, 74, 185, 328, 333, 373, 420, 430.

[3] Fourier describes the "Droit au travail" in the *Traité*, vol. i. p. 138, by making a poor member of a "phalanstère" thus address his fellows : "Je suis né sur cette terre ; je réclame l'admission à tous les travaux qui s'y excercent, la garantie du fruit de mon labeur ; je réclame l'avance des instruments nécessaires à exercer ce travail, et de la subsistance en compensation du droit de vol (note 2, p. 17) que m'a donné la simple nature."

[4] Fourier as above, pp. 135, and 143 note.

[5] Cf. Paget's article in the *Phalange* of 20th Oct. 1836, p. 337 (*Droit au travail*), Considérant in the *Phalange*, 1st Nov. 1836, pp. 379 and 380, Cantagrel also in the *Phalange : revue de la science sociale*, vol. ii. 1845, pp. 261-291 ; vol. v., 1847, pp. 152-180. *Du droit au travail et de son organisation pratique.*

[6] Cf. Considérant, *Théorie du droit de propriété et du droit au travail*, 3rd edit. Paris, 1848 (appeared first as an article in the *Phalange* of 1st June 1839, p. 584). Franz Stromeyer has published a German version, *Organisation der Arbeit*, 1844, pp. 75-104.

until the establishment of the Fourierist system, but actually considers it to be an indispensable complement to our present conditions, and the only means by which to retain private property intact.[1] He assumes, on the one hand, that to the human race belongs the common participation in the fruits of the earth in their original form (*capital primitif*), while, on the other hand, that which has been produced by human labour, improvements of land and capital (*capital créé*), belongs as private property by an indisputable title to these producers and their legal heirs.[2] By virtue of that right of participation in the common natural fund, man in a state of nature could exert his four economic rights (note 2, p. 17) of hunting, fishing, harvest, and pasture; but in our present conditions, Considérant submits, following Fourier, that this right of participation must be replaced by an equivalent—the right to labour.[3] And this he defines, by no means juridically, as conferring on the proletarian who exerts it the right to receive in return for his work at least so much of the means of subsistence as he could have obtained for himself by the exertion of his four original economic rights.[4]

A model of brevity and clearness, Considérant's

---

[1] Considérant, as above, p. 23 ff.   [2] *Ibid.* p. 17 ff.

[3] *Ibid.* p. 15 ff.

[4] *Ibid.* p. 24 : "La condition sine qua non pour la légitimité de la propriété est donc que la société reconnaisse au prolétaire le *droit au travail* et qu'elle lui *assure* au moins autant de moyens de subsistance pour un exercise d'activité donné que cet exercice *eut pu* lui en procurer dans l'état primitif."

pamphlet had a great success ; if we except Louis Blanc's cry of the organisation of labour, which he borrowed from the Saint-Simonians and propagated in his famous work, there is hardly a question so often discussed in the socialist papers and pamphlets of the Forties as this of the right to labour. So that when after the revolution of February the proletariate became for the moment the determining factor, it immediately extorted from the provisional government the proclamation of 4th February 1848, recognising the right to labour, which was afterwards incorporated in the French legal code.[1] This proclamation, coming into being as it did under the direct pressure of an excited populace,[2] is very badly drafted, but it states practically that the provisional government of the French republic assures to the labourer subsistence by his labour, and pledges itself to guarantee work to all citizens.[3]

---

[1] See Carrey, *Recueil complet des actes du gouvernement provisoire,* vol. i., 1848, No. 18. The proclamation is reprinted in the *Bulletin des Lois* of 29th February 1848, No. 18.

[2] Cf. the account of the conception of this decree given by its author Louis Blanc in his *Histoire de la Révolution de* 1848, vol. i. ch. 7.

[3] The text of this famous proclamation which for the first time recognised an economic right in the interest of the proletariate, runs as follows :

PROCLAMATION PAR LAQUELLE LE GOUVERNEMENT PROVISOIRE S'ENGAGE À FOURNIR DU TRAVAIL À TOUS LES CITOYENS.

PARIS, 25 *Février*, 1848.

République Française.

Le Gouvernement provisoire de la République française s'engage à garantir l'existence de l'ouvrier par le travail ; Il s'engage à garantir du travail à tous les citoyens ; Il reconnait que les ouvriers doivent

For the practical realisation of the right to labour a decree of the provisional government, dated 28th February 1848,[1] ordered the establishment of national workshops in France, a measure which a further decree of 27th April[2] extended to the French colonies; but in reality they were only founded in Paris and its neighbourhood.[3] The director of the Paris workshops, Émile Thomas, in his history of these institutions, confesses that the erection of the workshops was not a serious experiment, that the Government never supplied him with sufficient work to occupy his applicants, and that the entire arrangement had in the eyes of the Government no other object than the *reductio ad absurdum* of the socialist theories.[4]

Details of the organisation of the national workshops would be out of place here, and I will only note that Thomas organised them according to Saint Simonian doctrines on a strictly hierarchical basis, so that they partook more of the nature of a labour army than of industrial establishments.[5] The workmen were admitted by the mayors of arrondissements without any examin-

s'associer entre eux pour jouir du bénéfice (légitime) de leur travail. Le gouvernement provisoire rend aux ouvriers auxquels il appartient le million qui va échoir de la liste civile.

[1] Carrey, vol. i. No. 30 (*Bulletin des Lois*, 29th February 1848, No 24).

[2] *Ibid.* No. 290 (*Bulletin des Lois*, 14th May 1848, No. 305).

[3] *Arrêté du ministre des travaux publics portant organisation des ateliers nationaux ordonnés par le décret du 27 Février* 1848, dated 7th March 1848, Art. 1. (Carrey, vol. ii. No. 78).

[4] Émile Thomas, *Histoire des Ateliers nationaux*, 1848, pp. 142, 144-145, 244 ; cf. below, § 10, p. 121, note 1.

[5] Thomas, as above, pp. 35, 38.

ation of the particular circumstances of each case, so that by 19th May 1848 the number of workmen received into the workshops had already reached the enormous figure of 87,942 persons.[1] The most important controversy which arose during the short time before the abolition of the right to labour, turned upon the question whether it guaranteed to the citizen only ordinary day labour, or whether he might demand an occupation suited to his previous training.   Now, in the national workshops, those labourers who were occupied at all, were all, without respect to their callings, put to work at earthworks.   But Thomas did set up a few special workshops (for cartwrights, shoemakers, and tailors) which gave very satisfactory results.[2]   Nevertheless, and not without reason, this extension of the right to labour was one of the main arguments brought by the opponents of Socialism against the recognition of the right in the French constitution.[3]   For were the State bound to find employment in his own trade[4] for

---

[1] Thomas, as above, pp. 29, 378, *Arrêté du ministre des travaux publics* of 7th March 1848, Art. 3.

[2] Thomas, as above, pp. 177, 234.

[3] Cf. Barthe's speech in Girardin, vol. ii. p. 136, and Dufaure's, p. 321.

[4] Proudhon accepts the right to labour in this sense in his pamphlet *Le droit au travail et le droit de propriété*.   "Le droit au travail est le droit qu'a chaque citoyen, de quelque métier ou profession qu'il soit, d'être occupé *dans son industrie*, moyennant un salaire fixé non pas arbitrairement et au hasard, mais d'après le cours actuel et normal des salaires."   See Proudhon *Le droit au travail et le droit de propriété*, 1850, p. 13.   (*Œuvres*, vol. vii. p. 198.)   The whole pamphlet is directed against the right to labour in this sense.

every workman who fails to obtain work under a private
master, its economic activity would reach such huge
dimensions that our actual social system could never
exist by its side.[1] Unless we contemplate, therefore, the
substitution of a purely socialistic state for the present
organisation of society, and the replacement of the right
to labour by the right to subsistence, it is impossible to
recognise in the right to labour—according to the
definition I have given—more than the claim to be
provided with ordinary day labour at the rate of the
usual daily wage.[2]

The practical realisation of the right to labour brings
us face to face with the question, of great moment in a
socialist society, as to what authority should undertake
the discharge of the resulting obligations. Does this
function rest with the State, the country, or the
municipality?[3] Although the funds for the maintenance of the national workshops were, at any rate
in an overwhelming proportion, certainly provided by
the State,[4] their founders seem, nevertheless, to have

[1] Cf. Léon Faucher in Joseph Garnier's *Le droit au travail à
l'Assemblée Nationale*, 1848, p. 350.

[2] In the same sense Thiers in Girardin, as above, vol ii. p. 233, and in
his paper *De la Propriété*, 1848, p. 322. On the contrary, Louis Blanc
in *Le Socialisme. Droit au travail*, 1848, pp. 80, 81, logically from his
position (§ 10), defends trade workshops and the right to obtain work in a
particular trade. Cf. Proudhon's definition in note 4, p. 22.

[3] Cf. on this point Dufaure's speech, Girardin, as above, vol. ii. p. 319.

[4] Cf. Thomas, p. 146. Decree of the provisional government, 24th
March 1848 (*Bulletin des Lois* of 1st April 1848, No. 188), by which, of the
expenses of the national workshops in Belleville, one-third is borne by the
State, one-third by the town of Paris, and only one-third by Belleville itself.

regarded them as municipal institutions, for only work-men resident in Paris were admitted to the Paris shops. At first no specified period of residence was required,[1] but later on, when the dissolution of the workshops was already decided upon (21st June 1848), a residence of six months became a necessary qualification for admittance. But in contradiction to this municipal conception of the national workshops, the Government, by the decree of 21st June, reserved to itself the right of occupying the Paris labourers at earthworks in the departments.[2] And in fact this clause was the signal for the fearful risings of June (23rd to 26th June 1848), which ended in the complete defeat of Socialism.

The defeat of the socialist parties in the June risings naturally reacted on the acceptance of the right to labour. Just before the June revolt (on 20th June 1848), Marrast laid before the Committee of the National Assembly appointed to draft the Constitution a scheme [3] which placed the right to labour and relief under the same constitutional sanctions as property, and which also contained some detailed suggestions for its enforcement.[4] In consequence of the result of the June revolt

---

[1] Decree of 7th March 1848 (above note 3, p. 21), Art. 2 and 3.

[2] Thomas, as above, pp. 271, 343.

[3] The scheme is reprinted in the Parisian newspapers of 21st June (for instance in Proudhon's *Représentant du Peuple*, No. 81), and the decisive clauses in Garnier, p. 2.

[4] Cf. Art. 2 of the scheme, " La constitution garantit à tous les citoyens : La liberté, l'égalité, la sureté, *l'instruction, le travail*, la propriété, l'assistance " ; Art. 7, " Le droit au travail est celui qu'a tout homme de vivre en travaillant. La société doit par les moyens productifs

a new draft was submitted on 29th August, which no longer recognised the right to labour, but only the right to relief.[1] Mathieu thereupon moved an amendment to the draft expressly guaranteeing to every citizen the right to education, labour, and relief,[2] and this amendment was modified, but only immaterially, on a motion of Glais-Bizoin's. The debates on these proposals form, in connection with Fourier's writings and those of his school, the main sources for the history of the right to labour. On a division, Glais-Bizoin's amendment was defeated by 596 votes against 187,[3] and the National Assembly confirmed this decision when Felix Pyat moved a similar amendment to the second reading of the draft constitution (2nd November 1848).[4] Since then French Socialism has abandoned the right to labour.

et généraux dont elle dispose, et qui seront organisés ultérieurement, *fournir du travail aux hommes valides qui ne peuvent pas s'en procurer autrement.*" Art. 132, "Les garanties essentielles du droit au travail sont : la liberté même du travail, l'association volontaire, l'égalité des rapports entre le patron et l'ouvrier, l'enseignement gratuit, l'éducation profession-nelle, les institutions de prévoyance et de crédit, et *l'établissement par l'État de grands travaux d'utilité publique, destinés à employer, en cas de chômage, les bras inoccupés.*"

[1] Art. 8 (Girardin, vol. ii. p. 1), "La République doit *l'assistance aux citoyens nécessiteux,* soit en leur procurant du travail dans les limites de ses ressources, soit en donnant, à défaut de famille, les moyens d'exister à ceux qui sont hors d'état de travailler."

[2] La République reconnaît le droit de tous les citoyens à l'instruction, *au travail* et à l'assistance (Girardin, vol. ii. p. 2). In the course of the debate this resolution was replaced by Glais-Bizoin's amendment, which replaced the words "au travail" by "à l'existence par le travail."

[3] See Garnier, p. 439.

[4] *Ibid.* p. 429.

The right to labour came before the Frankfort National Assembly also, during the discussion of a German national constitution. During the second debate on the constitutional rights of the people, which (Art. VIII. § 30),[1] declare in the usual manner the inviolability of property, Nauwerk[2] and Ludwig Simon[3] submitted amendments aiming at the recognition of the right to labour. But they were defeated at the sitting of 9th February by 317 votes against 114, without any close debate on the right to labour, and that because the support of infirm paupers was held to be a matter of settlement laws, municipal affairs, and poor law.[4]   Marlo, as we shall see, supported the right to labour at about the same time (1850), but since then the whole question has been dropped in Germany too, until quite lately some German authors, amongst them

[1] Cf. the *Proceedings of the German National Assembly in Frankfurt a. M.*, 1848-1849, vol. ii. p. 678.

[2] Nauwerk's amendment to § 30 of the rights (*Proceedings*, vol. vi. p. 210) :—"Every German has a right to subsistence. A man who is idle against his will, and cannot get help from his relations or companions, should be provided with the means of subsistence, as far as possible, by being set to work by the State or the local authority." Cf. also the *Protokoll der 160. Sitzung* of 8th February 1849 (*Proceedings*, vol. i. p. 706).

[3] During the sitting of 8th February 1849 (*Proceedings*, vol. i. p. 705), L. Simon moved the amendment :—" (3) The support of indigent and infirm persons is the duty of the State or the local authority ; (4) The State or the local authority should provide work for those who are idle against their will."

[4] Cf. the *Proceedings*, vol. i. p. 710, and the essay *Die Arbeiterfrage im Frankfurter Parlament* in the *Neue Zeit*, vol. i. 1883, pp. 38-46.

Stöpel,[1] Hitze,[2] and Hahn,[3] have recognised the right of the citizen to labour. But these writers, not even excepting Stöpel, lack insight into the connection and historical development of socialist theories, to which, of course, the right to labour belongs, so that they are not in a position to obtain a clear conception of the right itself.

Having specified the meaning of the three fundamental socialist rights, I shall proceed to trace the gradual historical development of the right to the whole produce of labour in socialist systems since the middle of the last century. These alone stand in unbroken historical connection with the modern social movement, and I have therefore excluded the socialism of an earlier time, especially the very copious Utopian literature. For the same reason I can only include those systems which centre in the right to the whole produce of labour, reserving for a future volume an account of those writers who aim rather at a realisation of the right to subsistence. It was, indeed, no easy task to carry out this classification, as most socialist systems seek a compromise between the two principles; so that

[1] Franz Stöpel, *Die freie Gesellschaft*, 1881, pp. 263-299, and *Sociale Reform*, 3rd number, 1884, *Das Recht auf Arbeit*, pp. 6, 7, 13, 25 (the best German work on the right to labour).

[2] Franz Hitze, *Kapital und Arbeit und die Reorganisation der Gesellschaft*, 1881, pp. 145-196, and also v. Hertling, *Reden and Aufsätze*, 1881, p. 30.

[3] Otto Hahn, *Das Recht auf Arbeit*, 1885 (a confused and quite worthless book). Just as worthless is Haun, *Das Recht auf Arbeit*, 1889, a work whose historical information, quotations not excepted, are for the greater part copied from this book without acknowledgment.

I can hardly escape the blame of drawing somewhat arbitrary distinctions. My treatment of German jurisprudence (§ 2) will be particularly open to such criticism, because German legal theory, so far as it recognises socialist ideas at all, tends rather towards the right to subsistence. Still I consider it not merely interesting but indispensable to my subject to review the position of German jurisprudence with regard to the problem of the fundamental economic rights.

It may seem hardly worth while to discriminate between different socialist systems from this point of view, seeing that they one and all strive for essentially the same object, the amelioration of the working classes. But it must not be forgotten that they rely on the action of quite opposite springs of human nature for the attainment of their common end. Every socialist system which centres in the right to the whole produce of labour is founded in self interest, and that to a more advanced degree than our present organisation; for under such a system every one works for himself alone, while under present conditions he works partly for himself and partly for another's unearned income. But such social systems, on the other hand, as strive for the recognition of the right to existence must depend on neighbourly love and a sense of brotherhood. Thus although the systems of both groups belong to Socialism in its traditional sense, there is yet between them a sharp and essential contrast which demands separate treatment and classification.

§ 2. GERMAN JURISPRUDENCE

MODERN jurisprudence distinguishes between inherent, or natural, and acquired rights ; the former appertaining to every individual by virtue of his existence, while the latter must have in every case a special foundation in contract, inheritance, or some other legal fact. The right to the whole produce of labour (and equally the right to subsistence) can of course only be sought amongst the rights of the first order.

Now, has jurisprudential doctrine recognised an inborn right of every individual either to the whole produce of labour or to subsistence? The question may be answered by an absolute negative, at any rate with regard to the great majority of legal theorists. The generally accepted position of jurisprudence allows to every man an original right, the so-called " Urrecht," founded in his human nature and directed to the satisfaction of its most fundamental necessities. The exact nature of this " Urrecht" has been widely disputed ; Stahl defines it as entitling to that which is necessary to the existence of the personality, namely, integrity (protection for life and limb), freedom, honour, legal

capacity, and protection of acquired rights.[1]   Many
authorities add equality [2] to these elements of the original
right, while others repudiate various items—for instance,
the right to honour.[3]   I may pass over these matters
of dispute as in no way connected with the present
subject.

[1] Stahl, *Philosophie des Rechts*, 3rd ed. vol. ii. p. 312.   Ahrens,
Naturrecht, vol. i. § 47 ; vol. ii. § 56 ff.   Against the theory of natural
rights, cf. Lasson, *System der Rechtsphilosophie*, 1882, p. 258.

[2] Cf. for instance the *Déclaration des droits de l'homme et du citoyen*
of the Constituent Assembly, 26th Aug.–3rd Nov. 1789, Art. 1, "Les
hommes naissent et demeurent libres et *égaux en droits* . . . " Art. 2, "Le
but de toute association politique est la conservation *des droits naturels et
imprescriptibles de l'homme*.   Ces droits sont la liberté, *la propriété*, la
sûreté et la résistance à l'oppression."   The declaration of human rights
thus enacts on the one hand the equality of mankind in respect of
their rights, and on the other hand declares property, the most important
source of all inequality, to be a natural and imprescriptible right.   As the
same contradiction occurs in many succeeding constitutions, not excepting
that of 24th June 1793, Arts. 1-3, the absurd conception of "equality
before the law," Art. 3 *cit.*, has sprung up in modern constitutional
doctrine meaning equality only before the less important parts of
law (criminal law and procedure and civil procedure), but inequality
before the most important branch of civil law—the law of property.
Robespierre wished to extend equality before the law to the law of
property during the discussion of the constitution of 1793, but his
efforts were not successful.   Cf. Robespierre's speech in the sitting of the
Convention of 24th April 1793, and his sketch of a declaration of the
rights of man in the *Œuvres de Robespierre*, published by Vermorel, 1866,
pp. 268-274, also Saint-Just, *Fragments sur les institutions républicaines*,
pp. 34, 58, 70, 71 (original edition).   The communist, Francois Boissel,
submitted a declaration of the rights of man, which had quite a socialist
character, to the sitting of the Jacobin Club of 22nd April 1793, but
this was rejected even by the Jacobins, cf. Buchez, *Histoire parlementaire*, vol. xxvi. p. 107, and for Boissel's life and doctrines, Grünberg's
essay in the *Zeitschrift für die gesammte Staatswissenschaft*, 1891, pp.
207-252.

[3] Cf. for instance Anton Bauer, *Lehrbuch vom Naturrecht*, 3rd edition,
1825, §§ 86-88, and the literature to which he there refers.

For it is clear even from this short sketch that the theory of natural rights has been developed mainly from the point of view of the propertied classes. This is more especially shown by the fact that the legal doctrine of natural rights recognises no right of the individual to avail himself of the natural resources round him, or in other words, the accepted view of the original right has no economic foundation. Moreover, modern jurisprudence recognises neither the right to the whole produce of labour nor that to subsistence.

It stands to reason that many glaring contradictions must arise from this position. The original right, according to the prevailing conception, confers a claim to protection for life and limb, but none to extraneous necessities of existence, though life cannot be maintained for any length of time without food, shelter, and clothing. A man's original right, according to our jurisprudence, protects such artificial interests as his honour and freedom of thought, but does not confer on him the attainment of the most important of all individual aims, to lead a life worthy of his humanity. In short, however self-evident the theory of original right may appear at first sight, it contains essentially nothing beyond the claims made on the law by the educated middle classes of our own day.

Instead of an inborn right to a joint participation in surrounding natural resources and material means of existence, the prevailing doctrine only asserts the abstract capability of man to acquire rights in general and rights of appropriation in particular (*die Rechts-fähigkeit, das Zueignungsrecht*). So that each individual can only acquire even such things as are indispensàble to prolong his existence by contract, inheritance, or some other legally recognised process. Thus the methods of acquiring property in nearly all forms of wealth are so constituted by legal theory and practice alike as to render them available to no more than a comparative minority of citizens, thereby restricting the natural rights of the majority to mere legal capacity, and, as it were, ratifying the harsh contrast of wealth and poverty with all its consequences.

Abstract capacity to acquire property, and concrete right to a joint use of surrounding nature— the whole social question lies hidden in the folds of this contradiction. It is the reproach of theoretical jurisprudence, that, though free from the trammels of historical tradition which hem in the positive science of law at every step, it has, even in this most important of all questions, confined itself to a mere registration of prevailing legal conditions. Our modern jurists do not, indeed, go so far as Christian v. Wolff, who in his *Natural Law* had the bad taste to assert and demonstrate mathematically both feudal law and the law of exchange; but who can deny that in all fundamental points they cling with the utmost caution to that famous saying of Hegel's, " What is reasonable is real, and what is real is reasonable,"[1] which brought upon the philosopher so many unjust attacks?[2]

The immanent contradiction which lies in the whole conception has not, indeed, escaped all writers on jurisprudence. Chronologically, the famous jurist, Hugo, should be mentioned first, who in his *Text-book of Natural Right* violently attacks private property as an unjust and pernicious institution,[3] using here, as in his defence of slavery,[4] many of the party cries of later socialist literature. Still Hugo's position is essentially negative, and he gives no clear idea of the institution by which he would replace the private property he attacks.

Fichte goes much further than Hugo in his *Closed Mercantile State* (1800),[5] the main lines of which he drew from the government of the French Republic during the Terror (1792-1794) with its *assignats* and its *maximum,* and perhaps also from the plans of the Babeuf conspiracy (1796). Fichte is no collectivist ; on the contrary, he retains private property and individualistic production in his State according to Reason (*Vernunftstaat*) ;[6] moreover, he advocates the most energetic

[1] Hegel, *Grundlinien der Philosophie des Rechtes,* 3rd edition, 1854, p. 17.

[2] Cf. also the preface to the above by Gans, p. 9.

[3] Hugo, *Lehrbuch des Naturrechts als einer Philosophie des positiven Rechts* (2nd volume of the *Lehrbuch eines civilistischen Kursus*), 2nd edition, 1799, §§ 209-218 ; edition 1819, §§ 100-105.

[4] Hugo, as above, §§ 141-146 ; edition 1819, §§ 186-195.

[5] Reprinted in Johann Gottlieb Fichte's collected works, vol. iii., 1845, pp. 387-513.

[6] Fichte pp. 406, 407, 446, 497, 506. Cf. also p. 442.

government interference in economic relations, so that
his ideal state, far from being communistic or socialistic,
is rather the reign of economic compulsion and police.

Fichte considers as the province of the State, not
only the protection of existing rights, but what is to
him far more important, first to give to every one that
which is his, to put him into possession of his property,
and then to maintain him in it.[1] And Fichte answers
the question, what in the ideal state appertains to a
man, what is his, by a straightforward recognition of
the right to subsistence. " The aim of all human activity
is to live, and to this possibility of living all who have
been placed in life by nature have of right an equal
claim. The division, therefore, must in the first place
be so made that all can exist. Live and let live!"[2]
Indeed, Fichte even goes so far as to recommend as a
reasonable solution of the problem an equal division
of the wealth produced amongst the members of the
closed mercantile state.[3]

The practical proposals which Fichte makes in the
further course of his sketch are, it is true, not adapted
to even approximately realise these radically communistic principles. Their main purport is that the
State should only admit to the pursuit of industry and
commerce such a number of persons as the existing

---

[1] Fichte, pp. 399, 420, 445, 453.

[2] *Ibid.* p. 402.   Cf. also his *Grundlage des Naturrechts nach
Principien der Wissenschaftslehre*, 1796, § 18.   *Collected Works*, vol. iii.
p. 210.

[3] *Ibid.* pp. 402, 403.

agriculturists can supply with food;[1] agriculturists, manufacturers, and traders having at the same time an exclusive right to the pursuit of their particular calling.[2] The State, moreover, should fix all prices in terms of the most indispensable food-stuff (rye or wheat).[3] I omit the rather rough and unpractical methods by which this standard of value is applied to fix the prices of all commodities,[4] noting however, that the State would issue a national currency (*Landesgeld*) with a forced circulation, based on this standard,[5] abolish metallic money,[6] and assume the control and authorisation of foreign trade.[7]

It may be asserted, without exaggeration, that these proposals of Fichte's combine the most conflicting elements—on the one hand, State control of the profession of every citizen and the prices of all goods, and on the other, the maintenance of an individualist system of production and of private property. We shall see further on, when discussing the schemes of Rodbertus (§ 8), that such a combination is practically unrealisable. I would only remark here that the distribution of the citizens

---

[1] Fichte, pp. 408, 409.   [2] *Ibid.* pp. 446, 447, 406, 407.
[3] *Ibid.* p. 416.   [4] Cf. *Ibid.* p. 416 ff.
[5] *Ibid.* pp. 431, 454, 485 and 509. Ludwig Gall, the first German socialist, also proposes a cereal currency, without forced circulation however, which would approximate to our present *Lagerscheine*. *Was könnte helfen? Immerwährende Getreidelagerung, um jeden Not des Mangels u. des Ueberflusses auf immer zu begegnen, u. Kreditscheine, durch die Getreidevorräte verbürgt, um der Alleinherrschaft des Geldes ein Ende zu machen*, 1825, pp. 103, 131. See also Adam Smith, *Wealth of Nations*, vol. i. chap. v.
[6] *Ibid.* p. 485.   [7] *Ibid.* p. 497.

amongst different trades with fixed and exclusive spheres of operation, and the State settlement of prices are far from adequate to ensure to the members even a minimum of subsistence. For, private ownership of land and capital being maintained, the man of property and the empty-handed proletarian would then as now stand face to face within each trade.

In conclusion, Marlo should be mentioned here, whose chief work[1] has, it is true, mainly an economic character, but contains at the same time comprehensive juridical discussions, and so can hardly be reckoned amongst the strictly socialist literature treated of in §§ 3-12. In the case of Marlo, too, we may remark that his practical proposals fall far short of his very radical principles.

Marlo recognises candidly that man's original right involves the right to a joint use of surrounding nature. "Every man has an inherent and inalienable right to such a share of the forces of nature as is equivalent to his powers of work, and can dispose at will of the produce created by their means."[2] Of the two possible forms which this inherent right of participation in the forces of nature may assume, namely, the right to the whole produce of labour and the right to subsistence, he

---

[1] Karl Marlo (Pseudonym for Karl Georg Winkelblech), *Untersuchungen über die Organisation der Arbeit oder System der Weltökonomie*, 3 vols. 1850-57. I quote from the 2nd completed edition, which appeared in 4 vols., 1885-86. See also the detailed account of Marlo's views in Schäffle's *Kapitalismus und Socialismus*, 1870, Tenth lecture.

[2] *Ibid.* vol. i. p. 307. Cf. also pp. 313, 330.

seems to prefer the first.[1] But beyond this, Marlo lays
down as a complement to the right to the whole produce of labour a special right to labour, by virtue of
which society is bound to provide all persons who
cannot find work under private employers with un-
skilled labour on public works (roads, waterworks, and
railways), paying them for an average expenditure of
strength such a wage as will suffice for the supply of
the necessaries of life.[2]

While Marlo, as follows from this description,
advocates principles as radical as the most advanced of
socialists, he vies in the weakness and half-heartedness
of his practical schemes with the liberal statesmen whom
he so hates and depreciates.   Marlo contemplates in his
ideal state the retention of heritable property, individualist production, and free competition.[3] All undertakings
for private profit are to be carried on by guilds, which,
however, are open (perhaps by examination) to every
citizen.[4] The business undertaken must not exceed
a certain amount, fixed for the agricultural guilds in
proportion to their land, in other cases according to the
number of persons employed.[5] This organisation is
supported by a system of credit, which places such
capital as the rich burghers cannot use in their under-

---

[1] Marlo, vol. i. pp. 302, 309, 314, note 2 ; vol. ii. p. 314.   Cf. also
iii. p. 775.
[2] *Ibid.* vol. i. p. 321 ; vol. iii. pp. 766, 755.
[3] *Ibid.* vol. i. pp. 329, 324.
[4] *Ibid.* vol. i. p 321 ; vol. iv. p. 306.
[5] *Ibid.* vol. i. p. 321 ; vol. iv. pp. 308, 309.

takings at the disposal of the poor who lack the necessary means to render fruitful their powers of production. Loans, however, are the only instruments of credit permissible; the letting of the means of production and the mortgaging of objects of exchange being legally prohibited.[1]

These, and numerous other projects of Marlo's, have manifestly the object of enabling every citizen to carry on a trade on his own account ; for since private property and individual production are to be maintained, the right to the whole produce of labour can neither be realised, nor unearned income abolished, as indeed Marlo himself clearly recognises.[2]

In fact, Marlo's ideal state (*Föderalismus*) can only be regarded as a somewhat disconnected aggregation of well-meant economic police regulations, the effects of which are in glaring discrepancy with his radically socialist principles.   However, a conclusive judgment of Marlo's projects is not possible, as his work was interrupted just as he was beginning to elaborate the details of his labour organisation.[3]

It appears, therefore, that the right to the whole product of labour and the right to subsistence are not even recognised by the great majority of jurisprudential systems ; while even the minority of writers who express themselves in favour of these rights, propose wholly inadequate measures for their realisation.   For although

---

[1] Marlo, vol. i. p. 322.   [2] *Ibid.* vol. ii. p. 322.
[3] *Ibid.* vol. iv. pp. 254, 255.

the axioms of legal theory may appear to be deduced
from first principles, jurisprudence is in its essence
nothing more than a ratification of traditional legal
conditions. As such, it shares the one-sidedness which
earned for modern economics the title given it by the
socialists of *bourgeois* political economy, and might be
called a *bourgeois* jurisprudence. In the course of the
last century the proletariat discovered in Socialism a
jurisprudence of the non-possessing, which now stands
opposed to the *bourgeois* jurisprudence of the propertied
classes. From the middle of the eighteenth century till
Ricardo Socialism was actually, not only in essence but
in form, a philosophical jurisprudence ; and it only
assumed an economic character and a mainly polemical
tendency when Ricardo's harsh and one-sided development of *bourgeois* economics laid them so peculiarly
open to the socialist attack. But this notwithstanding,
the jurisprudential element remains to-day the real
kernel of Socialism, in spite of the economic garb,
of which the modern socialists, more especially in
Germany (Rodbertus, Marx, Lassalle), make so much.
It remains for us to examine at greater length the
attitude of this popular jurisprudence towards the right
to the whole produce of labour.

[1] Ricardo's chief work, *Principles of Political Economy and Taxation*,
whose theory of value exerted so profound an influence on later socialists
(see for instance § 5, notes 7 and 8), appeared in 1817.

§ 3. WILLIAM GODWIN

THE first scientific advocate of the right to the whole produce of labour, known to me, is William Godwin (1756-1836), whose *Enquiry concerning Political Justice* appeared first in 1793,[1] and afterwards in several editions.[2] In fact, Godwin may be regarded as the first scientific socialist of modern times, possessed of the seeds of all the ideas of recent Socialism and Anarchism. He exerted a very marked influence on Hall, Owen, and Thompson, and through them on the development of Socialism.

Godwin distinguishes three degrees of property, or as we should more correctly express it, three modes of distribution of wealth. They correspond in principle

---

[1] William Godwin, *An Enquiry concerning Political Justice, and its Influence on General Virtue and Happiness*, 2 vols. 4to., London 1793. The 2nd and 3rd editions of this important work appeared each in 2 vols. 8vo, in 1796 and 1798. A new reprint of the 8th book, which contains most of Godwin's socialistic theories, was published in London in 1890, by H. S. Salt, under the title, *Godwin's Political Justice: a Reprint of the Essay on Property, from the Original Edition*. The most important reply to it is Malthus's *Essay on the Principle of Population*, especially book iii., chaps. ii. iii. For Godwin's life and teachings, compare C. Kegan Paul, *W. Godwin, his Friends and Contemporaries*, 2 vols., London, 1876; and Held, *Zwei Bücher zur socialen Geschichte Englands*, 1881, p. 89 ff.

[2] I have made use here of the third edition, which, especially with regard to the subject of this book, varies materially from the original edition.

to the three economic rights which I summarised before (§ 1): the right to subsistence, the right to the whole produce of labour, and the private property of our present legal system.

Godwin states the first degree of property to be that every man has a permanent right to those things, the exclusive possession of which being awarded to him, a greater sum of benefit or pleasure will result than could have arisen by their being otherwise appropriated. In other words, he who has the best use for things shall possess them.[1] This principle of distribution may appear a chimera to us, brought up in the school of the Roman law of private property ; but, nevertheless, it is put in practice in every family in which right feeling prevails, and on a larger scale in the American communistic associations. Godwin, moreover, is quite aware that the application of this principle must be preceded by a complete revolution in the intellectual and moral conditions of mankind.[2] More than ten years before, indeed, Brissot, afterwards a leader of the Girondins, in his work, *Sur la Propriété et le Vol*, upheld the same view, that the standard of possession should be the wants of the individual, and that every one who accumulates property disproportionately to his needs is guilty of an injustice to his fellow-men.[3]

---

[1] Godwin's *Political Justice*, 1798, vol. ii. p. 432.

[2] *Ibid.* p. 480.

[3] Cf. J. P. Brissot de Warville, *Sur la Propriété et le Vol*, 1780, pp. 62, 63, 66, 69, 93, 95, 96 of the Brussels reprint of 1872, and the other writers mentioned in § 1, p. 8, note 2.

The principle that wants shall be the measure of property entails as its first and most important consequence the right to subsistence (see above, § 1). Even when thirty years later, in his answer to Malthus, Godwin upheld our existing legal system,[1] he still maintained the right of the poor to public support.[2]

The second degree of property according to Godwin consists in the empire to which every man is entitled over the produce of his own industry.[3] Of course this principle does not lead to the same results as the first mentioned; on the contrary, it may very well happen that a thing is my property as the product of my labour, of which some one else may have a far more pressing need than I.[4] It is the same contradiction between the right to the whole produce of labour and the right to subsistence that we discussed before (§ 1). For this reason the second degree of property appears to Godwin himself less natural than the first; as, indeed, it is impossible not to recognise in it a transition to the actual system of private property.

The third form of distribution which Godwin distinguishes is the right of property based on individual possession as it exists everywhere in the civilised states

---

[1] W. Godwin, *An Enquiry concerning the Power of Increase in the Number of Mankind. Being an Answer to Mr. Malthus's Essay on that Subject*, 1820, p. x.

[2] *Ibid.* book vi. chap. iv.

[3] Godwin, *Political Justice*, vol. ii. p. 433. Scattered suggestions of the right to the whole produce of labour are to be found in Locke, *Two Treatises of Government*, ii., § 27. Cf. also Adam Smith, *Wealth of Nations*, book i. beginning of chap. viii.   [4] *Ibid.* p. 739.

of Europe. The essence of this system, in his opinion, is the right bestowed by law upon certain classes of society to dispose of the produce of other men's industry, or in other words to draw an unearned income.[1]

According to Godwin, men deceive themselves grossly when they speak of the property left them by their ancestors. Property, or, as we should now say, income, is produced by the labour of actually living men. All that their ancestors bequeathed to them was a mouldy patent, which they use to extort from their neighbours what the labour of these neighbours has produced. Thus riches, and especially inherited riches, are nothing but a sinecure of which the labourers pay the salary which the owner squanders in luxury and idleness.[2]

Of the proportion borne by wages to unearned income, as of that between the working and idle classes of society, Godwin entertains a very unfavourable estimate which cannot be acquitted of exaggeration. He believes that in England only the twentieth part of the inhabitants is seriously employed in the labours of agriculture, and that this number could, in the leisure enforced by their agricultural occupation, accomplish all necessary industrial work. So that the twentieth part of the population suffices to supply the whole with the absolute necessaries of life, or what comes to the same thing,

---

[1] Godwin, *Political Justice*, vol. ii. pp. 434, 435.

[2] *Ibid.* vol. ii. pp. 435, 458, 459. *The Enquirer: Reflections on Education, Manners, and Literature*, 1796, p. 177. "What is misnamed wealth, is merely a power vested in certain individuals by the institutions of society to compel others to labour for their benefit."

reckoning a working day of ten hours, each individual would need to devote only one half hour daily to mechanical work.[1]

The practical measures by which Godwin proposes to carry into effect the principles on which the law of property must be based in a socialistic society are as unsatisfactory as his grasp of these principles is clear. He rejects the whole apparatus of the communistic state, government control of production and consumption, common labour, common meals, common magazines for the storage of useful commodities.[2] On the contrary, he would retain an individualistic social and industrial organisation, and private property, the latter however being equally divided amongst the members;[3] but this condition could only be rendered permanent by a complete transformation of human character, for every associate must be willing to make over to another any part of his property which in the hands of this other would satisfy a more pressing need.[4] In other words, this ideal condition of perfect equality can only be inaugurated and maintained when the right to subsistence has attained general and practicable recognition as the principle of distribution.

Assuredly no one can fail to recognise the chimerical nature of these premises.   Godwin was obliged to refuse all State aid towards the accomplishment of his main

---

[1] Godwin, *Political Justice*, pp. 482-484.   *Enquirer*, pp. 163, 214.
[2] *Ibid.* pp. 497, 498, 502.   *Enquirer*, p. 168.
[3] *Ibid.* pp. 499, 431.   [4] *Ibid.* p. 474.

principle of distribution, because in all important relations he assumes the position of modern anarchists. He aims at the dissolution of the historical State into separate parishes, doing away with every executive or legislative central authority, and only allowing the meeting of national assemblies in cases of extraordinary emergency. The present State, which reigns over its members as a superior power, would then naturally cease to be, and the activity of the parishes would be limited to administration. Of the apparatus of our modern government he would retain only trial by jury in criminal and civil cases, while any coercive power whatsoever would only appertain provisionally to the courts and to the national and parish councils, whose functions would eventually be restricted to inviting the members of the community to co-operate in a certain way to the common advantage. As such an advising and admonishing authority would not be a government at all in the modern constitutional sense, Godwin is logically obliged to point to the dissolution of Government as the ultimate aim of all political efforts at reform.[1] And indeed his political ideal is a social organisation reduced to the simplest elements, without government, without penal or coercive power, in which goods are equally divided between the members, but in which every one voluntarily relinquishes his property in favour of another's more urgent need.[2]

[1] *Political Justice*, book v. chaps. xxi.-xxiv.
[2] *Ibid.* book viii. chap. i. Cf. vol. ii. p. 856 of the first edition, and above, p. 44, note 4.

Godwin's anarchical ideas had no direct influence on the development of Socialism ; it was two generations later before Anarchism—as it would appear unconnected with Godwin—was revived by Proudhon, Stirner, and Bakunin.   On the other hand, the effect of his theories on a new principle of property is already clearly to be seen in the next social writer of importance, Charles Hall.

§ 4. CHARLES HALL

IN the year 1805 there appeared under the title, *On the Effects of Civilisation on the People in European States*,[1] a work by Charles Hall, which had a great influence on the older English socialists, and through them indirectly on the socialist movement of our own day. Hall examines in this essay the results of the progress of civilisation on the social condition of the mass of the working-class, and finds these results to be, on the one hand, a constant increase of the wealth and power of the idle rich, and on the other, the greater poverty and subjection of the labouring poor.[2] So great, indeed, has the disproportion between wealth and labour become in England, that the working-classes, which Hall estimates at four-fifths of the entire population, only receive and enjoy one-eighth part of the produce of their labour, the remainder being appropriated by the rich as rent

---

[1] I quote from the reprint of Hall's essay, published in London in 1850 (in the Phoenix Library). Some notes on the life of this remarkable man, who died at a great age in a debtor's prison, because he would not allow his friends to pay a claim which he considered unfounded, may be found in John Minter Morgan's *Hampden in the Nineteenth Century*, vol. i., 1834, pp. 20, 21.   [2] Hall, § 13.

and interest on capital.[1] Out of an eight hours' day, therefore, the poor man works but one hour for himself, the return of the other seven being, under our present system, the property of the rich.[2]

It is Hall's view that these inequitable conditions must be altered, and as a basis for their reform, he lays down two fundamental principles: firstly, every man shall labour so much only as is necessary for his family ; secondly, he shall enjoy the whole fruits of his labour.[3] Hall may therefore be regarded as the first socalist who saw in rent and interest unjust appropriations of the return of labour, and who explicitly claimed for the worker the undiminished product of his industry.

To carry out these principles he, in the first instance, proposes the abolition of the English law of primogeniture, which is certainly peculiarly adapted to concentrate great wealth in the hands of a few favoured heirs, and by this means disproportionately to increase the unearned income of particular individuals. At the same time he would forbid, or at least heavily tax, the manufacture of luxuries (refined manufactures) in order to confine the work of the poor to the production of the necessaries of life.[4]

It is sufficiently clear that sumptuary laws and the equal division of property amongst the children of a family do not avail to ensure to every man the whole fruits of his labour, seeing that these measures have

---

[1] Hall, § 16. Cf. also § 33.   [2] *Ibid.* § 6.
[3] *Ibid.* § 37.   [4] *Ibid.* § 30.

existed at various times and in many countries without
the attainment of any such result. Nor does Hall fail
to devise a more effectual means. He proposes that
the State shall possess itself of the whole land of the
nation, and parcel it out in allotments to the different
families in proportion to their numbers; these allotments being indefeasible, until on the extinction of the
family they revert to the State.[1] As families increase
at different rates a redistribution shall from time to
time be taken in hand.[2] In this way Hall proposes to
combine community of property with an individualistic
system of production and family life. The land is the
property of the whole nation, and is by it assigned in
allotments to the various families, who cultivate it on
their own account (common property, separate usance).
Among later socialists, Colins[3] proposes a similar combination, but Hall differs from the majority of modern
collectivists, who favour community of production as
well as of possession. He justifies his position by a
comparison with the agrarian systems of the Spartans,
the Jews, and of the Jesuits in Paraguay,[4] which are
based on much the same principles; and we may further
instance the Russian village communities (see below,

[1] Hall, § 37.

[2] *Ibid.* § 38. A lively attack on this proposal is contained in the first
English socialist newspaper which appeared under Owen's influence, *The
Economist*, vol. i., 1821, p. 49.

[3] Cf. for instance Colins, *Qu'est-ce que la science sociale?* vol. ii., 1853,
pp. 261-372.

[4] As to the conditions in Paraguay, cf. Gothein, *Der christlich-sociale
Staat in Paraguay*, 1883, p. 33.

p. 161) in which this union of common property with separate usance is most clearly developed.[1]

Hall's discrimination fixed on the one system of property which can even approximately realise the right to the whole produce of labour. Collective ownership with separate usance is not, in truth, perfect Socialism, but we shall see later on that every system which aims at community both of possession and of production must inevitably end in an infringement of the labourer's right to the undiminished fruits of his labour.

[1] Haxthausen, *Studien über Russland*, vol. iii., 1852, p. 124. Keussler, *Geschichte u. Kritik des bäuerlichen Gemeindebesitzes in Russland*, vol. i., 1876, p. 224.

§ 5. WILLIAM THOMPSON

So much of the socialist philosophy as centres in the right to the whole produce of labour is completely expounded in the writings of William Thompson. From his works the later socialists, the Saint-Simonians, Proudhon, and above all, Marx and Rodbertus, have directly or indirectly drawn their opinions. And yet modern historical works take but little notice of a writer who is the most eminent founder of scientific Socialism.[1]

William Thompson,[2] by birth an Irishman, was

[1] Held, *Zwei Bücher zur socialen Geschichte Englands*, 1881, pp. 379-385, certainly mentions William Thompson, but without recognising the importance of the man for the development of scientific Socialism. Compare also Henry Soetbeer, *Die Stellung der Socialisten zur Malthusischen Bevölkerungslehre*, 1886, p. 21. [Supplement to the 2nd edition: "By these references, which are taken verbatim from the 1st edition, I made it clear to every one at the very beginning of the chapter on Thompson, that this writer was known in Germany before me. If, then, Gustav Cohn (of Göttingen), in a tone which proves his bad taste, reproaches me with having appropriated the merit of discovering Thompson (cf. Cohn in Schmoller's *Jahrbüchern*, 1889, p. 14), I may complacently leave the public to judge of his love of truth."]

[2] Cf. the biographical notes in Pare's second edition of Thompson's *Inquiry into the Principles of Distribution of Wealth*, pp. xvi.-xxvii. ; *Hampden in the Nineteenth Century* (John Minter Morgan), vol. ii., 1834, pp. 294, 295. Holyoake, *History of Co-operation in England*, vol. i., 1875, p. 109.

among the chief advocates of the co-operative system, in favour of which Robert Owen led a brisk agitation in England during the second and third decades of this century.   He was a pupil of Bentham, whose views were not without influence in many directions on his works; though whereas Bentham never overstepped the limits of political radicalism, and was, especially, an energetic opponent of communism, Thompson takes his stand from the first on a very advanced Socialism.   His most important work, *An Inquiry into the Principles of the Distribution of Wealth most conducive to human Happiness; applied to the newly-proposed System*[1] *of voluntary Equality of Wealth,* appeared in 1824 and survived two more editions,[2] while, besides this, Thompson

---

[1] "The newly-proposed system" refers to Owen's scheme.

[2] The 2nd edition (an extract made by Pare which omits many of the most important passages) appeared in 1850, the 3rd edition in 1869.   It is characteristic of Marx and Engels that they have for forty years misquoted this fundamental work of English Socialism, placing its first publication in 1827.   Cf. Marx, *Misère de la Philosophie,* 1847, p. 50 ; also his *Zur Kritik der Politischen Oekonomie,* 1859, p. 64, note : Engels in the German translation of the *Misère de la Philosophie* (p. 49 of the translation), also in his preface to Marx's *Kapital,* vol. ii., 1885, p. xvi. In one or two of the above passages (Marx's *Misère,* pp. 49, 50 ; Engels in the German translation of this work, p. viii.) Marx and Engels mention Hopkins (pseudonym for Mrs. Marcet) as a socialist, while in point of fact she was one of the most violent, as well as one of the best known, opponents of Socialism.   Cf. John Hopkins's *Notions on Political Economy,* 1833, pp. 1-10, and *passim.*   It is only in the preface to the 2nd volume of Marx's *Kapital* that Engels replaces the imaginary socialist Hopkins by the right name of Hodgskin.   I only mention these surprising blunders, because Engels reproaches German professors (in the preface to *Kapital,* vol. ii. p. xvii.) with absolute ignorance of English anti-capitalistic literature of the Twenties and Thirties, and wishes himself to pose as an authority in this field, as I think quite unduly.

published several smaller works, also intended to further the diffusion of socialistic ideas.[1] He died on 28th March 1833.

Thompson starts from three general principles which might be subscribed to by the most ardent of " Manchester" economists, but to which he naturally gives quite a different meaning from that attached to them by the classical school. These three natural laws of distribution are—(1) All labour ought to be free and *voluntary*, as to its direction and continuance; (2) all the products of labour ought to be secured to the producers of them; (3) all exchanges of these products ought to be free and *voluntary*.[2]

It is a surprising circumstance that the English political economists and Thompson draw from identical propositions such opposite conclusions; but the reason may be found in the fact that, while the former look upon our present system of private property, and particularly private property in land and capital, as the limits within which these emancipating principles are to be carried out, Thompson, on the contrary, considers a reconstruction of our actual system to be an essential preliminary to their realisation.

[1] *An Appeal of one Half the Human Race, Women, against the Pretensions of the other Half, Men, to retain them in Political, and thence in Civil and Domestic Slavery*, London, 1825. *Labour rewarded, the Claims of Labour and Capital conciliated : or how to secure to Labour the whole Products of its Exertions*, London, 1827. *Practical Directions for the speedy and economical Establishment of Communities*, etc., London, 1830. I was only able to make use of the last of these papers for the present essay.

[2] Cf. Thompson, *Distribution of Wealth*, 1824, p. 6 ; 2nd ed. p. 3.

Like so many English economists, especially Ricardo,[1] Thompson bases his argument on the assumption that all value in exchange is derived from labour alone.[2] From this economic postulate he draws the juridical inference —and with this proposition Socialism leaves Ricardo and the classical school far behind—that to him who has wrought to produce the value, should belong the undiminished reward of his effort ; or, in other words, that to the producer should be secured the free use of whatever his labour has produced.[3] In our present organisation of society the labourers certainly do not receive the full produce of their labour, but only the smallest possible remuneration compatible with existence (Lassalle's iron law of wages, *Ehernes Lohngesetz*),[4] the remainder of the value they create falling to the share of the landowners and capitalists in the form of rent and interest.

Thompson does not fail to see that under our present system, in which private possession of land and capital exists, the workman is bound to yield to the owners a portion of the return of labour in payment of the use of

[1] Ricardo, *Principles of Political Economy and Taxation*, 1817, chap. i. In the complete edition of his works by M'Culloch, 1881, p. 71. Cf. also Adam Smith, *Wealth of Nations*, book i. chap. vi.

[2] Thompson, *Distribution of Wealth*, 1824, pp. 6, 95 ; 2nd ed., pp. 5, 73.

[3] *Ibid.* p. 95 ; 2nd ed. p. 73.

[4] *Ibid.* p. 171 ; 2nd ed. p. 133. "The productive labourers stript of all capital, of tools, houses, and materials to make their labour productive, toil from want, from the necessity of existence, their remuneration being kept at the lowest compatible with the existence of industrious habits."

buildings, machines, tools, and raw materials.   But this
limitation of the right to the whole produce of labour
should go no further than is absolutely necessary.   On
the one hand, the worker should indemnify the owner
of land and capital for wear and tear, while the latter
might claim such a share of the produce of all the
labourers he employed as would yield him an income
equal to that of the best paid workman.[1]

But, according to Thompson's view, this just standard
of distribution is very far from application under our
present social conditions.   Capitalists, who have all
legislation in their own hands, rather look upon the
difference between the absolute necessities of the
labourer and the increased produce of his labour, due to
the use of machinery or other capital, in the light of a
surplus value which belongs of right to the owner of
land or capital.[2]   So that rent and interest are nothing
but forced abstractions from the entire produce of labour
made, to the prejudice of the labourer,[3] by landowner and

[1] Thompson, *Distribution of Wealth*, p. 167 ; 2nd ed. p. 128.
[2] *Ibid.*   " The measure of the capitalist, on the contrary, would be the
additional value produced by the same quantity of labour in consequence
of the use of machinery or other capital ; *the whole of such surplus
value to be enjoyed by the capitalist for his superior intelligence and
skill in accumulating and advancing to the labourers his capital or the
use of it.*"   Sismondi, who has evidently materially influenced Thompson
in this and other directions, himself uses the term " mieux-value " for
the unearned income, without, however, looking upon it as an injustice.
Cf. *Nouveaux Principes d'Économie Politique*, vol. i., 1st ed. 1819, pp. 88,
102.
[3] *Ibid.* pp. 40, 67, 164, 165, 181, 394 ; 2nd ed. pp. 31, 53, 54, 125,
126, 143, 281, 282.

capitalist in virtue of their monopoly of political power. We recognise at once, in these opinions of Thompson's, the train of thought, and even the mode of expression, which reappear later on in the works of so many socialists, especially of Marx and Rodbertus. This view, held by Thompson and many other socialists, that rent and interest are deductions made by the owners of land and capital from the full produce of labour, is by no means peculiar to socialists, for many representatives of the classical school, for instance Adam Smith,[1] start from the same idea. Thompson and his followers are only original in so far as they consider rent and interest to be *unjust* deductions, which violate the right of the labourer to the whole produce of labour. So that here, again (see above, p. 54), the difference between the two views is rather juridical than economic.

How, then, is a condition of things to be obviated, which, as conceived by the socialist, accords to the rich a life of idle luxury, while it condemns the poor to incessant, hopeless toil?

Thompson is as cautious in his proposals for reform as he is searching in his criticism of existing social conditions. It is only in a negative direction that he consents to interference by State legislation, demanding, in agreement with the Liberal programme, the abolition of all restraints on the freedom of trade, especially of all impediments to the free disposal of land by landowners, all wages-assessments, monopolies,

---

[1] Adam Smith, *Wealth of Nations*, vol. i. chaps. vi., viii.

etc.;[1] but he looks to the voluntary formation of socialist communities as the positive means for the removal of the disadvantages accruing to the labourer from the existence of rent and interest. In all important points, Thompson[2] follows, as to the details of these communities, the schemes which Robert Owen had for so many years put forward in writing and before public meetings.[3]

Owen proposes that a number of individuals (500 to 2000 or more), whose mutual co-operation can, according to circumstances, produce the most important necessaries of human existence, shall voluntarily associate together to produce these means of enjoyment by their united labour, with all the aids of science and art, thus keeping supply and demand always commensurate to each other. In all cases these communities shall cultivate so much land as will provide for their own wants; the surplus labour of the members being applied to the production of industrial objects either for their own use or for

[1] Thompson, *Distribution of Wealth*, p. 600; 2nd ed. pp. 455 456.

[2] *Ibid.* p. 386; 2nd ed. p. 274. He gives a very detailed plan for the founding of such communities in the *Practical Directions*. (Cf. p. 53, note 1.)

[3] Robert Owen, *Report to the Committee of the Association for the Relief of the Manufacturing and Labouring Poor*, 1817; printed in *A New View of Society*, 1818, and in *Life of Robert Owen*, vol. I.A, 1858, p. 49. *Report of the Proceedings at several Public Meetings held in Dublin*, by Robert Owen, Esq., Dublin, 1823; also reprinted in the *New Existence of Man on the Earth*, vol. iv., 1854, p. liv. (the best summary of Owen's plans). Of a later date: Robert Owen, *Revolution in the Mind and Practice of the Human Race*, 1849, pp. 61, 62. John Bellers made similar suggestions long before Owen: *Proposals for Raising a Colledge of Industry*, London, 1696; reprinted in Owen's *Life*, vol. I.A, pp. 158, 159.

purposes of exchange. Wherever it is practicable, the necessary land, buildings, and stock shall be purchased; but when the members of the community are not sufficiently rich to do this, the land may be rented and the required capital borrowed.

The most important question, from the legal point of view, is naturally that which is concerned with the distribution amongst the members of the commodities produced by the socialist communities. As Thompson lays special stress on the right to the whole produce of labour (p. 54, note 3), it might be supposed that such a share of the produce would be assigned to each member as coincided, according to some fixed standard, with the product of his work. It is true, as we have already seen (§ 1), and as will be still more clearly shown in the course of this work (§ 13), that this standard may vary considerably; it may be either the time work of each member, or the average work, or it might be the traditional prices of labour plus the increment due to the abolition of unearned income. But in every socialistic system which carries out logically the right to the whole produce of labour, the goods allotted to the individual must be in proportion to the work performed by him, at any rate as regards those capable of labour.

In reality Thompson bases the distribution on the second of the two principles we distinguished (§ 1), namely, distribution according to needs, corresponding to the right to subsistence. All members of the socialist communities are to be fed, clad, and housed out of the general store, the children being educated in common.[1] Thompson endeavours to reconcile this contradiction by his proposal that while in the socialist communities goods are to be equally distributed, that is according to individual requirements, on the other hand every member who can labour would be forced to perform the same amount of work, measured, it would seem,[2] by the time devoted to it. That the right to the whole produce of labour, logically carried out, leads to quite other results will sufficiently appear in the further course of this work. Thompson's object, like that of so many other socialists, was to prove the injustice of unearned income and private property by the assertion of this economic right; but the communistic tendencies which he borrowed from Owen prevented him from drawing its positive consequences.

The idea that the unearned income (*Mehrwerth, Rente*) drawn by the capitalist classes, as rent and interest without work, is an unjust appropriation of the produce of labour made solely by virtue of their political ascendency, was repeatedly expressed in more modern English socialist literature, although the term "surplus value" does not appear to be used by the later writers.

It is impossible to mention separately the innumerable papers and articles which elaborated the ideas

---

[1] Thompson, *Distribution of Wealth*, pp. 388, 389.

[2] *Practical Directions*, p. 7. "The time employed must be the measure of exertion."

discovered by Godwin, Hall, and Thompson, and I must
confine myself to noticing those points which are of
greatest theoretical importance.

The position we have described is defended with
great decision by John Gray, in a pamphlet [1] which
appeared in 1825, and whose searching criticism reminds
one of Proudhon, who, however, was nearly half a
generation younger. Practical proposals for the reform
of the evils of our present social system were made by
Gray in a number of later works; [2] and we must
also mention Edmonds, who formulated the opposition between earned and unearned income more
clearly than any of his predecessors; [3] while to a

---

[1] John Gray, *A Lecture on Human Happiness,* 1825. This very little
known work is of the greatest importance in the development of scientific
Socialism. [As this book is very rare,—even the British Museum does not
possess a copy,—it is well to quote the extracts especially referred to by
Prof. Menger.

"The whole income of the country is produced by the productive
classes—gives very nearly fifty-four pounds a year for each man, woman,
and child—in the productive classes of which they receive about eleven
pounds ; being but a trifle more than *one-fifth part of the produce of their
own labour ! ! ! !*" p. 20.

"*What does the productive labourer obtain for that portion of the produce of his industry which is annually taken from him by incomes obtained
by the lenders of money ?* He obtains NOTHING ! Then, we ask, is a
man the natural proprietor of the produce of his own labour ? If he is
not, what foundation is there for property at all ? . . . Either a man *is
not* the *JUST* proprietor of the produce of his own labour, or there is no
JUSTICE in requiring interest for the use of money," p. 39.—Trans.]

[2] John Gray, *The Social System,* 1831. *An Efficient Remedy for the
Distress of Nations,* 1842. *Lectures on the Nature and Use of Money,*
1848.

[3] T. R. Edmonds, *Practical, Moral, and Political Economy,* 1828, pp.
114-122.

later time belong the writings of John[1] and Charles Bray.[2]

[1] J. F. Bray, *Labour's Wrongs and Labour's Remedy : or the Age of Might and the Age of Right*, 1839 (especially pp. 33, 37, 58, 59).

[2] Charles Bray, *The Philosophy of Necessity, or the Law of Consequences ; as applicable to Mental, Moral, and Social Science*, 2 vols. 1841 (especially vol. ii. pp. 301, 303, 389, 390).

§ 6. SAINT-SIMONIANISM

THE right to the whole produce of labour is completely ignored by the French socialists of the eighteenth century. For although Meslier, Morelly, and Mably all vigorously attack property, their polemic is based on the idea that as a legal institution it is the source of many vices, more especially of pride and selfishness.[1]

That private property confers on its owner an ascendency which enables him to draw an unearned income from his neighbours' industry, that such an unearned income is an injustice, and that every one possesses a right to the whole produce of his labour,

---

[1] Jean Meslier (died 1729 or 1733), *Le Testament*, first complete edition published by Rudolf Charles in three vols. (Amsterdam, 1864), vol. ii. pp. 168, 169. Morelly, *Code de la Nature*, 1755, pp. 29, 30. Mably, *Doutes proposés aux philosophes-économistes sur l'ordre naturel et essentiel des sociétés politiques*, 1768, pp. 12, 13. *Principes de la législation*, 1776, livre i. chap. iii. For Meslier, who may be regarded as the first theorist of revolutionary Socialism, cf. the excellent essay by Grünberg in *Die neue Zeit*, 1888, pp. 337-350. Rousseau, too, has occasional half socialistic remarks of a similar tendency, which, however, are hardly in agreement with other passages in which he declares property to be the most sacred of rights. Cf. for instance, *Discours sur l'origine et sur les fondements de l'inégalité parmi les hommes*, 1755, 2nd part at the beginning ; and the *Contrat Social*, 1762, book i. 9 note, with his article in the Encyclopedia, *Économie politique*.

—these ideas which recur so often in later socialist systems, are foreign to older French Socialism.

Neither do I find these views expressed in the writings of Babeuf, whose conspiracy (1796) must be regarded as the starting-point of the present social movement. As Babeuf himself admits in his speech for his defence,[1] which has lately appeared for the first time in a complete form, he was under the influence of Mably, Helvetius, Diderot (correctly Morelly[2]), and Rousseau—an assertion which is confirmed by the contents of the newspaper (*Tribun du Peuple*) which he edited before and during the conspiracy, as well as by the papers which were found in his possession. In the *Tribun du Peuple*,[3] Babeuf attacks property most vehemently in so far as it exceeds the needs of the individual, and calls such disproportionate possession,

[1] Cf. Victor Advielle, *Histoire de Gracchus Babeuf et du Babouvisme*, vol. ii., 1884, pp. 43, 51, 58. Only a small fragment of Babeuf's concluding speech is given in the official report of his trial before the Vendôme court, which the Directory published in 4 vols. Cf. *Discours des accusateurs nationaux, défenses des accusés et de leurs défenseurs, faisant suite aux débats du procès instruit contre Drouet, Babeuf et autres*, vol. iv. p. 362.

[2] The *Code de la Nature*, which appeared anonymously in 1755, was for a long time wrongly attributed to Diderot, and even included in a collection of his works published during his lifetime in 1773. Cf. Villegardelle in his edition of the *Code de la Nature*, 1841, p. 6. Babeuf, who in his speech quotes several passages from the *Code de la Nature*, also regarded Diderot as the author.

[3] The *Tribun du Peuple* is a continuation of the *Journal de la liberté de la presse*, also edited by Babeuf (together they reached forty-three numbers). The *Tribun* only assumes a socialist character in its thirty-fourth number. Complete sets of this first socialist newspaper are among the greatest rarities of socialist literature.

as Brissot[1] did before him, theft from fellow-citizens.[2]
But, from Babeuf's point of view, the distribution of
goods should be proportioned, not to labour performed,
but to individual needs ; or, in other words, he takes his
stand on the second of the two rights we distinguished
in Chapter I., which corresponds, generally speaking, with
the right to subsistence.[3] This is comprehensible, if we
remember that the main object of the Babeuf conspiracy
was to inaugurate economic by the side of political
equality (*égalité réelle, égalité de fait*). Now there
could be no question of complete economic equality
between the citizens of a socialist state which recognised
the right to the whole produce of labour. The papers
of the conspiracy, which were partly discovered at
Babeuf's, partly published later on by Buonarroti, are
in complete agreement with the opinions expressed in
the *Tribun du Peuple*.[4]

---

[1] Cf. § 7, "Proudhon," p. 75, note 2.

[2] Babeuf says in the *Tribun du Peuple*, No. 35 (17 Brumaire an IV.), p.
102, "que . . . tout ce qu'un membre du corps social a *audessus* de la
suffisance de ses besoins de toute espèce et de tous les jours, est le résultat
d'un vol fait aux autres co-associés, qui en prive nécessairement un nombre
plus ou moins grand, de sa cote-part dans les biens communs."

[3] Babeuf in the *Tribun*, No. 36 of the 20 Frimaire an IV. p. 112,
mentions approvingly the expression, "En parlant sans cesse du droit de
propriété, ils nous ont ravi *celui d'exister*."

[4] Cf. Buonarroti, *Conspiration pour l'égalité dite de Babeuf*, vol. i.,
1828, pp. 208, 209 ; also the *Manifeste des Égaux*, drawn up by Sylvain
Maréchal, but refused because of one or two passages by the secret
directory of the conspiracy, in *Copie des pièces saisies dans le local que
Babeuf occupait lors de son arrestation*, vol. i. (an V.) p. 154; and Buonarroti
as above, vol. ii. p. 130, as well as vol. i. p. 115, note ; also the fragment
of a *Décret économique*, in Buonarroti, vol ii. p. 305 art. 9, and so on·

Neither do the social systems of Saint-Simon and Fourier, which belong to the first decades of the nineteenth century, recognise the right to the whole produce of labour.

Saint - Simon's most important social works were written during the Restoration, that is, at a time when there was some danger that the feudo-clerical government might push entirely into the background the bourgeois society which had developed itself during the Revolution and under Napoleon's rule. This conflict, which belongs rather to Liberalism than to Socialism, forms the centre of the polemic which Saint-Simon directed against existing conditions. As a type of Saint-Simon's views we may take an essay which he first published in the *Organisateur* (1819), and which afterwards became so famous under the title of Saint-Simon's Parable.[1] Saint-Simon imagines in this parable that France, in the first place, suddenly loses her most distinguished philosophers, artists, agriculturists, manufacturers, merchants, and bankers. By such a loss,

---

That Condorcet, who was in no sense a socialist, should have declared just before his death (1794) that he held the equality of all men in education and wealth to be the last aim of all political efforts (dernier but de l'art social), shows how natural at that time seemed the application of the principle of equality to economic questions. Cf. Condorcet, *Esquisse d'un tableau historique des progrès de l'esprit humain*, 2nd ed. (an III.) p. 329. Sylvain Maréchal took this passage of Condorcet's as the motto of his *Manifeste des Égaux*.

[1] Saint-Simon, *L'Organisateur*, part i., 3rd ed. 1819, pp. 9-20. Under the title *Parabole de Saint-Simon*, this essay appeared in the first collected works of Saint-Simon, edited by Olinde Rodrigues in 1832, pp. 71-80, and later several times (ed. 1841, pp. 71-80).

France, according to Saint-Simon's view, would be instantly converted into a soulless mass (corps sans âme), and would remain in a condition of inferiority to rival nations until there had grown up in new generations the necessary amount of distinguished ability in science, art, and industry.

Saint-Simon next supposes, on the other hand, that the royal family, the highest officials of Court and State, all the higher clergy, and ten thousand of the richest inhabitants of France suddenly die. He believes that this loss would entail no disadvantageous results whatever for France (il n'en résulterait aucun mal politique pour l'État), as people in plenty would be found to fill the vacant places quite as ably as the original occupants.

These views, which recur in all Saint-Simon's contemporary and later writings in a hundred variations,[1] are manifestly rather radical than socialist in the modern sense. For Saint-Simon counts amongst the specially useful members of society the most distinguished *entrepreneurs* in the fields of industry, commerce, and finance, the very men whom modern Socialism reproaches with deriving their riches mainly from the produce of other men's labour.

Still less than Saint-Simon could Fourier, from the

---

[1] Cf. for instance, Saint-Simon's two pamphlets, *Le parti national ou industriel comparé au parti anti-national*, and *Sur la querelle des abeilles et frelons*, appeared first in the *Politique*, 10th and 11th numbers, 1819. *Du système industriel*, 1821, pp. iv., v., and *Catéchisme des industriels*, 1st number, 1823, p. 1, and so on, *Œuvres*, p. 1.

whole tendency of his system, attain to any recognition of the right to the whole produce of labour. In Fourier's socialist communities (phalanstères) the entire product of labour is divided between capital, labour, and talent, in the proportion of $\frac{4}{12}$ to capital, $\frac{5}{12}$ to labour, and $\frac{3}{12}$ to talent.[1] From which it would appear that he was far from intending to abolish unearned income; in fact he expressly asserts the necessity of a considerable inequality of fortune to his proposed organisation of society.[2] His school always held to this mode of distribution, and to the unearned income of owners of capital in particular.[3]

Saint-Simon's school, on the other hand, went far beyond their master, who in his numerous writings was content to point out the contrast between the unproductive nobility and clergy and the productive classes (agricultural, industrial, and commercial). Enfantin and his nearest friends may be regarded as the chief promoters of this new departure, which first gave Saint-Simonianism a distinctly socialist character in our present sense of the word. In the *Producteur*, as early as 1825-

---

[1] Fourier, *Le Nouveau Monde industriel et sociétaire*, 1829, pp. 364, 365.

[2] *Ibid.* pp. 7, 135.

[3] Considérant, *Destinée sociale*, vol. i., 2nd edition, 1847, pp. 250, 270 ; vol. ii., 2nd edition 1849, p. 390. Hippolyte Renaud, *Solidarité*, 5th edition 1877, p. 90. Gatti de Gamond, *Réalisation d'une commune sociétaire d'après la théorie de Charles Fourier*, 1841-42, p. 180. S. R. Schneider, *Das Problem der Zeit und dessen Lösung durch die Association*, 1834, pp. 17, 18, 47, 48. Albert Brisbane, *Social Destiny of Man: or Association and Reorganisation of Industry*, 1840, pp. 345-361.

1826, Enfantin had published articles emphasising as of the greatest importance the difference between those who live by their own industry and those who depend on the labour of others (travailleurs et oisifs).[1] These articles express the view that rent and interest are a tax paid by the labourers to landlords and capitalists to obtain from them the disposal of the instruments of production (*Producteur*, vol. i. p. 243; vol. ii. p. 411). This enslavement by capital will eventually disappear, just as human slavery disappeared, although somewhat later (vol. i. p. 249); but this will be brought about not by the confiscation of the instruments of production (vol. i. p. 564), but by the progress of public opinion tending to recognise more and more clearly the injustice of a life of idleness led at the expense of other men, and also by the gradual development of associated labour (vol. iv. pp. 204; vol. i. pp. 247, 561).

It is easy to see how nearly these views of Enfantin's coincide with those of contemporary English socialists. Whether Enfantin was acquainted with the works of Godwin, Hall, and especially Thompson, whose chief work had lately appeared (1824), cannot be decided from his essays, as in them he mentions only Ricardo, Malthus, and other members of the classical

---

[1] Enfantin's most important papers are : *Considérations sur la baisse progressive du loyer des objets mobiliers et immobiliers, Producteur*, vol. i., 1825, pp. 241-254, 555-567 ; *Conversion morale d'un rentier*, vol. ii., 1826, pp. 401-411 ; vol. iv., 1826, pp. 213-243 ; *Considérations sur l'organisation féodale et industrielle*, vol. iii., 1826, pp. 66-85.

school of economists. But Sismondi's chief work, in which he sets forth the theory of surplus value and unearned income (§ 5, p. 55, note 2), was certainly known to Enfantin, as he published a criticism of the book in the *Producteur* (vol. v. pp. 94-98).

In the lectures on the Saint-Simonian teachings, delivered between 1828 and 1830 by Bazard for the chief Saint-Simonian Council, and under its supervision, Enfantin's position is maintained and still more sharply accentuated. So far as I can see, these lectures contain no express recognition of the right to the whole produce of labour, such as occurs so often in the writings of the English socialists, but the germ of the theory is certainly comprised in that famous principle of the Saint-Simonians, that in a just social state every one would be occupied according to his capacity and rewarded according to his performance.[1] And Bazard at once draws from this principle the conclusion that our present form of property must be abolished and replaced by other institutions, because it allows the exploitation of the labouring classes by idle landowners and capitalists. In fact these lectures, which are amongst the most important landmarks of Socialism,

---

[1] *Doctrine de Saint-Simon, Exposition,* 1st year, 1828-29, seventh sitting, 11th March 1829. " Si . . . l'humanité s'achemine vers un état où tous les individus seront classés en raison de leur capacité et rétribués suivant leurs œuvres, il est évident que la propriété, telle qu'elle existe, doit être aboli, puis qu'en donnant à une certaine classe d'hommes la faculté de vivre du travail des autres, et dans une complète oisiveté, elle entretient l'exploitation d'une partie de la population la plus utile, celle qui travaille et produit, au profit de celle qui ne sait que détruire."

contain all the modern socialist shibboleths (see particularly lectures 6-8), and later socialists could add but little to the criticism there given by Bazard and Enfantin of a social organisation based on private property.[1]

The principles expressed in these lectures on the Saint-Simonian doctrines were maintained in innumerable newspaper articles by the Saint-Simonians during the whole public activity of the school. I will only call attention here to one short article from the chief organ of Saint-Simonianism, the *Globe* of 9th February 1831, because it contains precisely the essence of the Saint-Simonian tenets, and was much noticed and discussed in the socialist papers of that date.[2] The *Constitutionnel*, at that time, with the *Journal des Débats*, the most important liberal daily paper in Paris, had mentioned with a touch of irony the "mystic" followers of Saint-Simonianism, whereupon the *Globe* formulated in this article the programme of Saint-Simonianism as follows :—

"Nous voulons l'abolition de tous les privilèges héréditaires sans exception ; nous voulons l'émancipation des travailleurs et la déchéance de l'oisiveté qui les ronge et les flétrit ; nous voulons qu'il n'y ait

---

[1] According to Fournel, *Bibliographie Saint-Simonienne*, 1833, pp. 66-70, the sixth and seventh lectures are by Bazard, the eighth by Enfantin.

[2] Cf. for instance, Fourier's article in the *Réforme industrielle*, 22nd November 1832, p. 222 ; also Abel Transon in the same, pp. 209, 212.

honneur, considération et abondance que pour les
hommes qui nourissent les nations, qui les éclairent,
qui les animent de leur inspirations, c'est-à-dire pour
les industriels, les savants et les artistes ; nous voulons
que celui qui sème récolte ; que les fruits du travail des
classes laborieuses ne soient pas dévorés par les classes
oisives qui ne font rien, qui ne savent rien, qui n'aiment
qu'elles-mêmes ; nous voulons un ordre social complète-
ment basé sur le principe : A chacun selon sa capacité,
à chaque capacité selon ses œuvres ; nous voulons,
ceci est clair, *la suppression graduelle de tous les
tributs que le travail paie à l'oisiveté sous les noms
divers de fermage des terres, loyer des usines et des
capitaux.*"

The right to the whole product of labour is not
expressed in words in this programme, which was
doubtless conceived under the preponderating influence
of Enfantin, but all the consequences which that right
implies are clearly and concisely formulated. A few
weeks later (in the *Globe* of 7th March 1831) an essay
by Enfantin appeared under the title, *Les oisifs et les
travailleurs: Fermages, loyers, intérêts, salaires,* which
treats in greater detail of the contrast between the
propertied and labouring classes in the direction marked
out by the programme.[1] And this essay was followed
by a number of newspaper articles and pamphlets by

---

[1] Enfantin's articles in the *Globe*, belonging to the period from 28th
November 1830 to 18th June 1831, were published afterwards as a
pamphlet, *Économie politique et Politique*, in three editions.

various authors, all illustrating this subject, some of them from very opposite points of view.[1]

By what practical measures do the Saint-Simonians propose to emancipate the working-classes from the tax which they pay to the idle rich as rent of land and buildings and interest on capital ? Their ideal consists in a universal association for the purpose of peaceful labour,[2] within which the autonomy of separate nations shall remain unimpaired. The individual right of inheritance acknowledged by our law is to be abolished in favour of the State, which must be stripped of its present bureaucratic and military form, and converted into a society of labourers.[3] By the State-right of inheritance, all instruments of production and all useful commodities will gradually and peaceably become the property of the State; and the State government, which, according to the Saint-Simonians, should have a theocratic tone, will appoint a central department (banque unitaire, directrice) with the necessary branches, which will have the control of all wealth and all instruments of production.[4] It will

---

[1] Cf. for instance, Fournel, *L'Oisif antique et l'Oisif moderne*, in the *Globe*, 21st March 1831 ; also his *Questions sur le droit d'hérédité*, *Globe*, 26th June, 26th August, and 27th September 1831. Isaac Pereire, *Leçons sur l'industrie et les finances* in the third lecture, *Globe*, 16th and 27th September 1831, p. 38 of the reprint, which appeared in 1832. Michel Chevalier, *Politique industrielles*, *Globe*, 30th March 1832, and p. 29 of the reprint of 1832.

[2] See the *Exposition* in the collected works of Saint-Simon and En-fantin, vol. xli., 1877, pp. 180, 220, 221.

[3] *Ibid.* p. 343.

[4] *Ibid.* pp. 252-271.

delegate these latter to the most capable persons for use in production ;[1] the producer, however, not working on his own account, but claiming only a fixed salary.[2]

So that Saint-Simonianism would attain the realisation of its first principle, the occupation of every one according to his capabilities, and his reward in proportion to his achievement, by means of unrestricted, theocratic State Socialism.

A number of writings made the Saint-Simonian teachings known in Germany soon after their publication. I only mention the works of Carové,[3] Bretschneider,[4] and Moritz Veit,[5] in which the views of the Saint-Simonians as to the right of the whole produce of labour, which I have just discussed, are briefly described.[6] It may therefore be assumed that those German writers who afterwards recapitulated without any material variations the Saint-Simonian theories (Rodbertus !) did not discover them independently, but borrowed them from their predecessors.

[1] *Exposition*, pp. 303, 329.   [2] *Ibid.* p. 274.

[3] Wilhelm Carové, *Der Saint-Simonismus und die neuere französische Philosophie*, Leipzig, 1831.

[4] K. G. Bretschneider, *Der Saint-Simonismus und das Christenthum*, Leipzig, 1831.

[5] Moritz Veit, *Saint-Simon und der Saint-Simonismus. Allgemeiner Völkerbund und ewiger Frieden*, 1834.

[6] Carové, p. 139 ; Bretschneider, p. 35 ; Veit, pp. 156-178.

§ 7. PROUDHON [1]

PROUDHON, too, maintained the fundamental principle of the Saint-Simonians, that all unearned income, whether it be drawn in the form of rent or interest, is a wrong to the working-classes; but his criticism of existing conditions is more forcible, and his expressions more uncompromising, than theirs. The tone of his writings strikes one at once as likely to find a powerful resonator in masses of discontented labourers. The practical measures by which he proposes to abolish unearned income are more original than his criticism, though his scheme of a social exchange, which will be discussed further on, probably owes something to Owen's Labour Exchange in London (see below, § 8), and Mazel's Exchange in Marseilles (1829-45).[2]

Quite at the beginning of his chief work on property [3]

---

[1] Cf. as to Proudhon, the recent work of Karl Diehl; *P. J. Proudhon: Seine Lehre u. sein Leben*, books i., ii., 1888-1890, particularly ii. pp. 35, 176. Also Arthur Mülberger, *Studien über Proudhon*, 1891.

[2] Cf. Engländer, *Geschichte der französischen Arbeiterassociationen*, vol. iv., 1864, pp. 62, 76; and Mazel, *Code social*, 1843, pp. 59, 106.

[3] P. J. Proudhon, *Qu'est-ce que la propriété? ou recherches sur la*

Proudhon answers the question, What is property? by
the famous proposition, Property is theft (La propriété
c'est le vol);[1] a view similar to that which had already
been expressed by Brissot, afterwards one of the leaders
of the Girondins, in his work on property and theft, and
also by Babeuf in the *Tribun du Peuple*.[2] Proudhon
explains in great detail the wrong which, according to
him, is involved in the existence of property, which he
calls murderous and tyrannical, and therefore declares
to be *impossible*.[3] The right of the labourer to the
whole product of his industry—the positive side of
this vigorous criticism of private property—is also more
clearly expressed by Proudhon than by the Saint-
Simonians. Proudhon declares—and believes himself
to be original in so declaring—that the worker, even
after he has received his wage, still has a natural right

principe du droit et du gouvernement, 1840 ; also *Lettre à M. Blanqui
sur la propriété. Deuxième mémoire*, 1841. *Avertissement aux pro-
priétaires, ou lettre à M. Considérant*, etc., 1841. The two first papers
form the first volume of the collected works published by Lacroix.

[1] Proudhon, *Œuvres complètes*, vol. i. p. 13.

[2] Brissot, *Sur la propriété et sur le vol*, p. 63 of the Brussels reprint
(§ 3, p. 41, note 3) : "Si quarante écus sont suffisants pour conserver notre
existence, posséder 200 mille écus est un vol évident . . .," p. 64. "Cette
propriété exclusive est un délit véritable contre la nature . . .," p. 108.
"Le voleur dans l'état de nature est le riche, c'est celui qui a du superflu ;
dans la société, le voleur est celui qui dérobe à ce riche." In the same
way Babeuf in the *Tribun du Peuple*, vol. ii. p. 102 (an IV.) : "Que . . .
tout ce qu'un membre du corps social a *audessus* de la suffisance de ses
besoins de toute espèce et de tous les jours, est le résultat d'un vol fait aux
autres co-associés, qui en prive nécessairement un nombre plus ou moins
grand de sa cote-part dans les biens communs." There is a perfectly similar
passage in Locke's *Two Treatises of Government*, ii. 46.

[3] Proudhon, *Qu'est-ce que la propriété ?* chap. iv.

of property in the objects he has produced.[1] Allowing
for the absence of legal terms, which is marked in many
of Proudhon's writings, the right of the labourers to the
whole produce of labour is thus clearly asserted in his
first important work.

As a natural consequence of his position, Proudhon,
in his paper on a labour bank[2] (1849), declares all
unearned income to be an injustice, regarding it as
nothing more than a payment made by the working-
classes, for the mere permission to engage in productive
labour;[3] landlords and capitalists being able to levy
this tax solely by virtue of their political ascendency,
and not in return for any personal effort on their part.
He does not wish in this work to repeat the dangerous
formula, *la propriété c'est le vol,* which he laid down
nearly ten years before,[4] but he nevertheless makes a
formal protest against property and all its consequences.[5]

But though Proudhon is a violent opponent of private
property in its present form, he nevertheless regards as

---

[1] Proudhon, vol. i. p. 91. "Voici ma proposition : Le travailleur
conserve, même après avoir reçu son salaire, un droit naturel de propriété
sur la chose qu'il a produite."

[2] Proudhon, *Résumé de la question sociale, banque d'échange,* 1849 ;
reprinted in vol. vi. of the collected works.

[3] Proudhon, *Œuvres,* vol. vi. p. 174. "La Propriété . . . est le
veto mis sur la circulation par les détenteurs de capitaux et d'instruments
de travail. Pour faire lever ce *veto* et obtenir passage, le consommateur
producteur paie à la propriété un droit qui, suivant la circonstance et
l'objet, prend tour-à-tour les noms de rente, fermage, loyer, intérêt de
l'argent, bénéfice, agio, escompte, commission, privilège monopole, prime,
cumul, sinécure, pot-de-vin," etc.

[4] *Ibid.* p. 148.   [5] *Ibid.* p. 174.

Utopian and undesirable every form of communism, in which, according to him, Socialism must eventually result;[1] so that he prefers the retention of individualistic production and free competition.[2] And credit is the means by which he proposes to reconcile these apparently contradictory views.

As early as his *Système des Contradictions économiques* (1846),[3] Proudhon had promised—somewhat obscurely, it is true—a new solution of the social problems on the lines thus indicated. The events of 1848 compelled him to submit his scheme to the public in the form of pamphlets and newspaper articles,[4] whereas he had

---

[1] *Système des Contradictions économiques, ou philosophie de la Misère*, vol. ii., 1846, chap. xii. *Œuvres*, vol. v. p. 258.

[2] *Système*, vol. i., 1846, chap. v. *Œuvres*, vol. iv. p. 174. Also the passage in the *Œuvres*, vol. vi. p. 92.

[3] *Ibid.* vol. v. p. 414 (vol. ii. p. 527 of the original edition of the *Système*, 1846).

[4] Proudhon's three chief writings on the solution of the social question are : *Organisation du crédit et de la circulation et solution du problème social*, 1848. *Résumé de la question sociale, banque d'échange* (appeared first in the *Représentant du Peuple*, 26th April 1848, and as a pamphlet, 1849). *Banque du peuple, suivie du rapport de la commission de délégués du Luxembourg*, 1849. These pamphlets are reprinted in the sixth volume of Proudhon's collected works, but a thorough comprehension of his plans can only be obtained by a study of the papers to which he contributed from 1848-50 (*Le Représentant du Peuple. Le Peuple. La Voix du Peuple. Le Peuple* of 1850). Besides these, cf. the famous discussion between Proudhon and Bastiat on gratuitous credit, which appeared originally in the *Voix du Peuple* from 22nd October 1849 onwards, and then in two reprints got up by Bastiat and Proudhon under the title, *Intérêt et principal*, 1850, and *Gratuité du crédit*, 1850. At the present time this correspondence is included in Proudhon's *Œuvres complètes*, vol. xix., and more completely in Bastiat's *Œuvres complètes*, vol. v. In his *Idée générale de la Révolution au XIXᵉ siècle*, 1851, 5th study, Proudhon

originally intended publishing a scientific exposition of
his proposals in one work, under the title *Programme
de l'association progressive, solution du problème du
prolétariat.*[1]

In principle his scheme is to found a national bank
or exchange (*Banque d'échange*, afterwards *banque du
peuple*) which will be able to give gratuitous credit.
The inevitable result of this gratuitous credit would be,
as Proudhon rightly claims, the disappearance of rent
and interest;[2] for who will pay such taxes to the
owners of land and capital, when this freedom of credit
enables him to provide himself by means of a loan,
free of interest, with land, houses, and factories at will?
In other words, once realise by any combination the
gratuitousness of credit, and unearned income is thereby
done away with, and the social problem solved in this way,
leaving private property and individual production intact.

makes essentially different proposals for the solution of the social question,
especially for the abolition of unearned income.

[1] Darimon in the *Œuvres complètes*, vol. vi. p. 136.

[2] Cf. Proudhon's ninth letter to Bastiat (21st December 1849) in Bastiat's
Gratuité du Crédit, 1850, p. 149 ; and Proudhon's *Intérêt et principal*,
1850, p. 109. "Si donc l'intérêt, après être tombé pour le numéraire, à
trois quarts pour cent, c'est-à-dire à zéro, puisque trois quarts pour cent
ne représentent plus que le service de la Banque, tombait encore à zéro
pour les marchandises ; par l'analogie des principes et des faits, il tombe-
rait encore à zéro pour les meubles ; le fermage et le loyer finiraient par se
confondre avec l'amortissement." Cf. also Proudhon in *Le droit au travail et
le droit de propriéte*, 1848, *Œuvres complètes*, vol. vii. p. 208. This tendency
to gratuitous credit is a capital distinction between Proudhon's proposals
and Owen's and Mazel's Labour Exchanges, which are only intended to
effect the direct exchange (without the intervention of money) of wares and
services. Cf. Proudhon, *Les Confessions d'un révolutionnaire*, 3rd edition
1851, p. 240.

But how does Proudhon propose to bring about a result of such incalculably far-reaching influence? By a very simple method! The gratuitousness of credit is to be effected by means of a paper currency issued by the bank, to be called "Bons de circulation," and which all members of the bank association shall be bound to accept as payment. The bank is under no obligation to convert these *bons* into coin, the *bon* being merely an order on the members of the bank association (sociétaires et adhérents) to deliver to the holder goods and services to a specified amount.[1] So that they do not differ appreciably from inconvertible bank or State notes with forced circulation, except that the legal enforcement is replaced by a voluntary undertaking amongst the members to accept the *bons*.

The criterion of the system is, of course, the conditions and amount of issue of such *bons* to the members of the bank. Proudhon fixes no limit to the issue; on the contrary, he is of opinion that it would increase indefinitely.[2] But as to the conditions under which the *bons* are to be issued to the members, the bank statutes are hardly in accordance with Proudhon's theoretical expositions. In the pamphlet in which he first recommended the bank[3] he was far

---

[1] The main purport of such a *bon* is as follows: "A vue, payez au porteur, contre le présent ordre, en marchandises, produits ou services de votre industrie, la somme de cinq francs, valeur reçue à la Banque du Peuple. A tous les adhérents de la Banque du Peuple." (Cf. the specimen in Proudhon, vol. vi. p. 309.)   [2] *Œuvres complètes*, vol. vi. p. 120.
[3] *Organisation du crédit et de la circulation, et solution du problème social* (see above, p. 77, note 4) in the *Œuvres complètes*, vol. vi. p. 89.

from sparing of his promises; he declares that his
scheme will place credit on so comprehensive a basis
that no calls will be able to exhaust it, while a demand
will be created with which production will never keep
pace.[1] The abolition of metallic money, of taxes,
customs, national debts, and mortgages, were to be
amongst the first consequences of the new credit
system.[2] That the issue of an enormous quantity of
bons would be required for the accomplishment of these
aims stands to reason. In what other way could Proudhon expect the bank to attain the gratuitousness of credit,
and the abolition of unearned income (p. 78, note 2)?

But, according to the bank statutes, the notes were to
be issued at first only against ready money, or as dis-
count on sound commercial bills.[3] Later on the bank
was, it is true, to be less strict; still, however, observing
when discounting claims the usual banker's precautions.[4]
Now every one knows that the first of these precautions
looks to the solvency of the holder, which means that
he must belong to the propertied classes.

Nor did the statutes of the bank realise the
gratuitousness of credit. It was indeed laid down as a

---

[1] Proudhon (vol. vi. p. 90) gives as the object of his proposals:
"Doubler, tripler, augmenter à l'infini le travail et par conséquent le produit. Donner au crédit une base si large, qu'aucune demande ne l'épuise,"
etc.   [2] *Ibid.* p. 120.

[3] Statutes of the *Banque du Peuple*, 31st January 1849, articles 31,
32.

[4] ". . . L'escompte . . . sera fait dans une proportion de plus en plus
large, sauf les précautions ordinaires prises par les banquiers, et fixées par
le règlement de la banque" (art. 32 of the statutes).

principle that the loans made by the bank should not bear interest;[1] but provisionally the notes were only to be issued at a rate of 2 per cent, and although eventually the rate was to be lowered, it was not to fall below one-quarter per cent, which represented the charge for the services of the bank.[2]

Proudhon's bank was never established, for the capital required (50,000 frs.) was never subscribed, and he himself could not assume the management of the institution owing to his sentence to a long term of imprisonment.[3] But had it come into existence it would certainly never have fulfilled the hopes of its founder. For if the management issued the notes in large quantities, and without regard to the solvency of the holders, an unlimited depreciation of the paper was inevitable. While if the bank discounted only the claims of solvent persons,—and this seems in fact, according to the bank statutes, to have been eventually Proudhon's intention,—the circulation of the *bons* must have remained a very limited one, the gratuitousness of credit, and still less the abolition of unearned income, could never result, and indeed the economic ascendency

---

[1] Statute of the Bank, art. 34 : "D'après le principe et le but de son institution, qui est la gratuité absolue du crédit, la Banque du Peuple remplaçant dans une proportion toujours croissante la garantie du numéraire par la garantie qui résulte de l'acceptation réciproque et préalable de son papier par tous ses adhérents, peut et doit opérer l'escompte, et donner crédit moyennant un intérêt toujours moindre."

[2] Statute of the Bank, arts. 34, 35.

[3] Cf. Proudhon's announcement in his paper *Le Peuple*, No. 144, of 12th April 1849.

of the solvent, that is of the wealthy classes, must have been absolutely increased by the exchange bank (as by all other banks).

Thus, instead of the communistic Utopias he so vigorously attacked, Proudhon himself erected an individualist Utopia of the crassest and most signal impracticability.   No one pointed out more clearly than Proudhon that the unearned income drawn by landowners and capitalists is only a result of the political ascendency allowed them by the law.   But as long as this ascendency lasts—and Proudhon contemplates no change in this direction—no organisation of credit, however ingeniously devised, can ever abolish unearned income.

§ 8. RODBERTUS

A LIVELY dispute has arisen of late between the respective followers of Marx and Rodbertus as to the originality of the socialist principles of the two writers. Rodbertus himself, in one of his letters to Dr. Rudolf Meyer, declared "that he sees himself plundered without his name being even mentioned by Schäffle and Marx."[1] And in another letter[2] he says : " In my third economic letter I traced the origin of the capitalist's profit broadly on the same lines as Marx, only much more concisely and clearly." On the other hand, Engels, in a paper authorised by Marx himself, assures us that the latter made the "great discovery " of surplus value, whereby for the first time Socialism became a science.[3] Since then the question which of the two writers borrowed his most important ideas from the other has been often discussed.[4] The truth is, that both Rodbertus and Marx

[1] Dr. Rudolf Meyer, *Briefe und socialpolitische Aufsätze von Dr. Rodbertus-Jagetzow*, vol. i. p. 134.

[2] *Ibid.* p. 111.

[3] Engels, *Streitschrift gegen Dühring*, 1877-78, pp. 10, 162 ; 2nd ed. (1886), pp. 10, 11, 12. See also below, § 9, p. 101, note 1.

[4] Cf. Rodbertus, *Vierter socialer Brief*, 1884, p. xv. (by Theophil Kozak) ; Engels's *Das Elend der Philosophie*, German edition, 1885, p. v. ;

owe their fundamental theories to the older socialists,—
Rodbertus to Proudhon and the Saint-Simonians,
Marx to William Thompson. The whole dispute as to
priority, which is not without a comic element, could
never have arisen if Rodbertus and Marx had not
refrained with equal care from confiding the sources of
their views to the public.

Rodbertus divides the income of every individual
into wages and rent, according as the owners "are
entitled to it by virtue of a direct participation in its
production or only by accidental possession. Rent is
therefore the income which an individual draws by
reason of his possessions without any resulting personal
obligation to work." [1] This distinction is to be found,
almost word for word, in the works of earlier economists
and socialists.[2]

Engels again in his preface to K. Marx's *Kapital*, vol. ii., 1885, p. viii.
The papers of K. Kautsky and Schramm in the *Neue Zeit* for the years
1884 and 1885 contain some information which is to the point. The *Neue
Zeit* for 1887 (pp. 49-62) contains, under the title *Juristen-Socialismus*,
a zealous criticism of the views I uphold here as to the origin of the main
principles of Socialism, but the anonymous author enters too little into
questions of literary history to make a scientific polemic possible.

[1] Rodbertus, *Zur Erkenntniss unserer staatswirthschaftlichen Zustände*,
1842, p. 64. *Zur Beleuchtung der socialen Frage*, 1875, p. 32. *Zweiter
socialer Brief an Kirchmann*, 1850, p. 59.

[2] Sismondi, *Nouveaux principes d'économie politique*, vol. i., 1st ed.
1819, p. 104 (above, § 5, p. 55, note 2). T. R. Edmonds,'*Practical, Moral,
and Political Economy*, 1828, p. 114. "The income of every individual
consists either of revenue or wages, or of both. *Revenue is what costs the
receiver no labour, it is generally derived from property in lands, houses,
money, machinery*, etc. Wages may be defined to be the commodities
which a man of ordinary talents, and possessing no property or credit,
receives in exchange for his labour." *Économie politique et Politique*

But how does unearned income—the *Rente* of the
Saint-Simonians and Rodbertus, the profit, *Mehrwert*, of
Thompson and Marx—arise? The cause of this institution lies, according to Rodbertus, in the existing legal
system, especially in private ownership of land and
capital. " For positive law," he says, " declares land and
capital to be as much the property of individual persons,
as the power to work is the property of the labourer.
By this the workers, in order to produce at all, are
forced to combine with the owners of land and capital,
and to share with them the produce of labour. . . .
This combination adds nothing to the natural productive
elements of all commodities, *but only removes a social
hindrance to production, the arbitrary 'quod non' of
landowner and capitalist, and does so by a division of the
product.*"[1]   Just so, and almost in the same words do

(Enfantin), 2nd ed., 1832, pp. 68, 69 ; cf. also above, § 6, p. 71, note 1 :
"Tous sentiront alors que les efforts qui auraient pour but de réduire
*l'intérêt, les loyers et les fermages, c'est-à-dire de diminuer la rente faite
par le travailleur au propriétaire oisif,* auraient, ainsi que ceux qui
favorisaient la hausse des salaires, l'immense avantage d'accroître l'importance sociale du travail et de déconsidérer progressivement l'oisiveté." H.
Feugueray (a pupil of Buchez the Saint-Simonian), *L'association ouvrière
industrielle et agricole,* 1851, p. 53 : " Ce prélèvement (by landowners
and capitalists) c'est ce qu'on appelle tantôt rente de la terre, tantôt loyers,
tantôt intérêts, tantôt dividendes, et que je comprends sous ce seul mot :
Rente." Cf. also the *Exposition de la doctrine Saint-Simonienne,* vol. xli.
p. 247 (below, p. 86, note 3) ; Ott, a pupil of Buchez, *Traité d'économie
sociale,* 1851, p. 201 ; and Ludwig Gall, *Was könnte helfen?* (above, § 2,
p. 35, note 5), pp. 84, 85, 93-97. We may probably assume from an
essay published by Rodbertus in 1837 (*Zur Beleuchtung der socialen
Frage,* ii. p. 210) that he borrowed his theory of rent from the Saint-
Simonians.

[1] *Ibid.* pp. 45, 46 (*Zweiter sociale Brief,* 1850, pp. 82, 83).

Proudhon,[1] Louis Blanc,[2] and even earlier the Saint-Simonians[3] explain the origin of rent or surplus value.

The decisive point is, that rent and interest accrue to individual landowners and capitalists not by reason of the productive qualities of land and capital, but as a result of the political ascendency which the possession of them confers. The application of this theory to particular forms of unearned income, especially to rent and interest, lies on the surface, and on both heads Rodbertus is in general agreement with Proudhon.[4]

The views, as to the nature and origin of unearned income, held by Rodbertus had thus been already expressed before him, not only by the older English socialists (§§ 3-5), but also by Proudhon and the Saint-

---

[1] Cf. the passage quoted, § 7, p. 76, note 3, from Proudhon's *Résumé de la question sociale* (1849), which Rodbertus has practically merely translated, and *Qu'est-ce que la propriété?* 1841, p. 162, *Œuvres*, i. p. 122.

[2] Louis Blanc, *Organisation du travail*, 9th ed. 1850, p. 156 ; 5th ed. 1848, same page.

[3] *Exposition de la doctrine Saint-Simonienne* (see above, p. 69), in the collected works of Saint-Simon and Enfantin, vol. xli., 1877, p. 247 : "La propriété, dans l'acceptation la plus habituelle du mot, se compose de richesses qui ne sont pas destinées à être immédiatement consommées, et qui donnent droit à un *revenu*. En ce sens elle embrasse les fonds de terre et les capitaux, c'est-à-dire, selon le langage des économistes, le fonds de production." "Revenu" here means unearned income, as is shown by the note to the passage.

[4] Cf. Proudhon, *Résumé de la question sociale* (§ 7, p. 77, note 4), p. 12 in the *Œuvres complètes*, vi. p. 158, with Rodbertus, *Zur Beleuchtung der socialen Frage*, i., 1875, p. 141 (*Dritter socialer Brief an Kirchmann*, 1851, p. 147). The first edition of Proudhon's work, 1849, directly preceded the first edition of Rodbertus's *Sociale Briefe*, 1850-51.

Simonians. There is no doubt that Rodbertus was directly indebted to the French socialists, whom he often mentions in his writings, the early English writers having been but little known in Germany.

If we inquire into the position assumed by Rodbertus with regard to property and the right to the whole produce of labour, we are obliged to recognise it as very vacillating and undecided,—qualities, indeed, characteristic of all conservative socialists. He declares, in his third economic letter,[1] his conviction that the right of inheritance is as well founded a right as that of property, and that he holds the right of property to have as firm a basis as any right can have. On the other hand, in the fourth economic letter, which was only published after his death,[2] he expresses himself in the following terms as to Proudhon's well-known formula (La propriété c'est le vol): "If the possession of land and capital be theft, because it robs the producers of a portion of the value they produce, and slavery be murder, because it deprives man of his free power of development, then even in democratic institutions which retain 'freedom of contract' for wages by the side of private property in land and capital, you have not only theft but murder. For so long as the labourers are cut off from the fruits of increasing production, even in their share of the product, they are as certainly

---

[1] Cf. Rodbertus, *Zur Beleuchtung*, i. p. 145.

[2] Rodbertus, *Das Kapital, Vierter Socialer Brief an Kirchmann*, 1884, p. 204 ; cf. also pp. 214, 215.

deprived of their full powers of development." In spite
of all the reservations made by Rodbertus, the contradictions of these two views, as to the justification of
property in land and capital, cannot be denied.

There are many indications, even in Rodbertus's earlier
works, that he had some scruples as to the legitimacy
of private ownership of land and capital, as when he
declares the injustice of rent and interest according to
natural rights to be indisputable;[1] that unearned income (rent and interest) is abstracted from the labourer
by the positive action of law and appropriated to others;
that the law, which has always allied itself with force,
only effects this abstraction by permanent compulsion;[2]
that the conception of property has always gone
hand in hand with false weights and measures, and
so on.[3]

The practical proposals made by Rodbertus for the
diminution of the most injurious effects of unearned
income in its present form share the obscurity of his
theoretical position. Already, in the *Fünf Theoremen*,
following older economists and socialists, Rodbertus had
given it as his conviction that, in consequence of the
private ownership of land and capital, the labourers
receive no more of the whole national income than is
necessary to their bare subsistence (Lassalle's iron law),
while the whole of the remainder goes to landowners

---

[1] Rodbertus, *Zur Beleuchtung*, i. p. 115.   [2] *Ibid.* p. 37.
[3] *Ibid.* p. 145; also see *Zur Beleuchtung der socialen Frage*, ii.,
1885, p. 44.

and capitalists as rent and interest.[1]   So that wages
being relatively constant while the product of labour
constantly increases, owing to inventions and other
improvements, it follows that "the wage of the working-
classes tends to become a smaller and smaller proportion
of the national production."[2]

Now Rodbertus, unlike all previously-mentioned
socialists, does not contemplate the total abolition of
unearned income.   On the contrary, he would retain
rent and interest, and even increase both in proportion
to the growing production of labour; but what he aims
at is, at the same time, to rouse wages from the immo-
bility in which they are held by the iron law, so that
they may increase at the same rate as unearned income.

Provisionally, then, Rodbertus looks to a compromise
between the existing economic system and Socialism.[3]
Eventually, however, he believed that private ownership
of land and capital would die out,[4] and he therefore
gave in his posthumous work on capital a sketch of his
proposals in the event of a communistic establishment.[5]
I will only take into account here the schemes published

---

[1] Rodbertus, *Zur Erkenntniss unserer staatswirthschaftlichen Zustände*,
1842, p. 72 ; cf. with this Thompson, *Distribution of Wealth*, 1824, pp.
163-173, from which the passage given above (§ 5, p. 54, note 4) is taken,
and the proofs given by Lassalle in his *Arbeiterlesebuch*.

[2] Rodbertus, *Zur Beleuchtung der socialen Frage*, i. p. 24 ; ii. p. 20.
Also *Zur Erklärung u. Abhilfe der heutigen Kreditnot des Grundbesitzes*,
2nd ed. 1876, vol. ii. p. 314.   The same law is given by Fourier,
Nouveau Monde Industriel, 1829, pp. 41, 42.

[3] *Das Kapital*, p. 228.   [4] *Ibid.* pp. 219, 221.

[5] *Ibid.* pp. 136-160.

by Rodbertus in his essay *Ueber den Normalarbeitstag*, in 1871, as he intended them to include those social reforms the accomplishment of which should be immediately attempted.[1]

The main contents of this scheme of reform are as follows. The State should no longer leave to free competition the regulation of prices of wage-labour and commodities, but should itself take this in hand by means of a comprehensive system of valuation; prices being fixed not as now in terms of metallic money, but in a labour currency. To this end the normal working day—six, eight, ten, or twelve hours respectively—must be settled for each trade, and over and above this the average production of such a day estimated, namely, that quantity of labour or production in each trade which can be effected in such a working day by an average workman, with average skill and average industry. This average measure of production per day, or per hour, would serve as a unit of value, and the labourer would be credited with no more than this proportion, whether he had spent more or less time over his work.

Private property in land and capital being maintained, as we noticed before, the labourer naturally cannot be allowed the full measure of normal production; far from this, deductions must be made for State expenditure and in favour of unearned income; and Rodbertus

---

[1] The essay appeared first in the *Berliner Revue*, 1871, and has been several times reprinted since. Cf. Kozak, *Rodbertus social-ökonomische Ansichten*, 1882, p. 8. I quote here the reprint in Moritz Wirth's *Kleinen Schriften von D. Carl Rodbertus-Jagetzow*, 1890, pp. 337-359.

estimates that out of ten million normal labour-hours, only something like three millions would be assigned to wages, one to State expenditure, and three each, that is six together, to rent and interest. So that, taking this estimate, the workman who delivered ten normal labour-hours, would only actually be credited with three to apply to the satisfaction of his wants. Of course, this fundamental proportion between the different branches of the national income (wages, State revenue, and un-earned income) would be determined by State authority.

In terms of such normal labour-hours or days, then, the prices of all goods and services are to be fixed. In the case of goods, allowance must be made not only for labour directly expended, but for the wear and tear of tools. As the production of labour is liable to variations, so that at different periods the same proportion of normal labour results in more or less product, the State must from time to time revise its price lists.

The labour-money is, however, not intended to com-pletely replace the metallic currency, but both are to circulate side by side. In order to bring the labour-money into circulation the State would reserve to itself the right of issue, granting cheap credit in this currency to employers of labour, and establishing State magazines to store the goods delivered by them in repayment of their loans, as well as exchanges for the conversion of labour-money into metallic coin; for Rodbertus does not contemplate a forced circulation of the labour currency.

The main advantage which Rodbertus aims at securing to the working-classes by these measures is that a fixed quota of the national income would be assured to them (for instance, $\frac{3}{10}$); so that whereas now, even with increasing production, the income of the labouring classes is kept down by the iron law of wages to the level of bare subsistence, it would then increase in the same proportion as unearned income.

These proposals of Rodbertus are not new. The settlement of prices and wages by the State and the creation of a labour currency have been tried again and again. The first comprehensive attempt to regulate the price of the chief necessaries and wages by law [1] was the edict issued by Diocletian in the year 301 (*Edictum Diocletiani de pretiis rerum venalium*),[2] that is shortly before the fall of the heathen state. This edict enacts that the chief provisions, articles of clothing and materials, wage-labour, and a number of tools and other commodities [3] shall for the future bear a fixed price throughout the whole Roman Empire.[4] Vendor [5]

---

[1] In special cases, assessments of wages and goods have, as is well known, existed always, and still exist, in most countries.

[2] I quote this famous law in Mommsen's edition in the *Proceedings of the Königl. sächsischen Gesellschaft* in Leipzig, philosophical and historical division, 1851.

[3] Cf. Mommsen's survey of the tariff laws, as above, pp. 63-80.

[4] *Edict. cit.:* " Placet igitur ea pretia, quae subditi brevis scriptura (the comprehensive tariff contained in the law) designat, ita totius orbis nostri observantia contineri, ut omnes intelligant egrediendi eadem licentiam sibi esse praecisam."

[5] *Edict. Diocl.:* " Placet, ut, siquis contra formam statuti huius conixus fuerit audentia, capitali periculo subigetur."

and purchaser alike,[1] concluding a transaction in
defiance of these regulations, as well as any one causing
a scarcity of provisions by withholding them from sale [2]
(the *accapareur* of the French Revolution), were amen-
able to a capital penalty, that is death, labour in the
mines, or banishment to an island.[3] The law became
ineffective after a very short period of operation,
certainly after Diocletian's abdication (1st May 305),
after much blood had been shed in enforcing it, and
having caused a great rise in prices, instead of the
desired cheapness of the necessaries of life.[4]

The *maximum* of the French Revolution was a
second attempt to fix the prices of the most important
necessaries by the State.[5] By the Decree of 29th September 1793, the Convention enacted that prices of
the chief commodities and services (provisions, clothing,
metals and ordinary wage-labour [6]) were to be fixed by

[1] *Edict. Diocl. cit.:* "Idem autem periculo etiam ille subdetur, qui
conparandi cupiditate auaritiae distrahentis contra statuta consenserit."

[2] *Edict. Diocl.:* "Ab eius modi noxa inmunis nec ille praestauitur qui
habens species victui atque usui necessarias post hoc siui temperamentum
existumaverit subtrahendas ; cum poena vel grauior esse debeat inferentis
paenuriam quam contra statuta quatientis."

[3] L. 27, § 2, L. 28. D. *de poenis* (48, 40).

[4] Lactantius, *de mort. pers.*, c. 7: "Tunc, ob exigua et vilia multus sanguis
effusus, nec venale quidquam metu apparebat et caritas multo deterius
exarsit, donec lex necessitate ipsa post multorum exitium solveretur."

[5] As to the gradual development of the *maximum*, cf. especially Louis
Blanc, *Histoire de la Révolution française*, vol. ii., 1861, pp. 382-421 ;
Joseph Garnier, in Guillaumin's *Dictionnaire d'économie politique*, sub
voce "Maximum."

[6] Art. 1 of the Decree of 29th September 1793 in the *Moniteur universel*,
1st October 1793, gives an exact list of the "objets de première nécessité."

the Republican authorities, and were to be in each department, for goods $1\frac{1}{3}$ times the market price of 1790, and for services $1\frac{1}{2}$ times that price.[1] Persons who accepted more than the *maximum* were not only threatened with a considerable material punishment, but were to be placed on the list of suspects and treated accordingly ;[2] which by the law, as to the treatment of suspected persons, of 17th September 1793 implied imprisonment until the completion of the peace ;[3] while in other ways the lives of such persons were seriously endangered in that time of revolutionary excitement. As a necessary consequence of these laws of a *maximum*, those persons had to be punished as *accapareurs* who withdrew the goods mentioned (marchandises ou denrées de première nécessité) from sale by buying them up or storing them, or who allowed them to go to waste.[4] Death was in all cases the punishment for this passive resistance to the law, which was, of course, far more dangerous and effective than active transgression.[5]

The price list (*tableau du maximum*) was actually drawn up in a comparatively short time, and came into operation on 21st March 1794.[6] After Robespierre's fall the *maximum* laws could not be enforced,

---

[1] Arts. 3, 8 of the Decree.   [2] Art. 7 of the Decree.

[3] Arts. 1, 7 of the Decree (17th September) in the *Moniteur* of 19th September 1773.

[4] *Décret sur les accaparements* (26th July 1793) in the *Moniteur* of 29th July 1793, arts. 2, 3.

[5] Decree of 26th July, Arts. 1, 8, 9.

[6] Cf. Barère's Report of the Sitting of the Convention of 30 Ventôse an II. (20th March 1794) in the *Moniteur* of the 21st, No. 181.

and they were repealed in entirety by a decree of the Convention of 23rd and 24th December 1794.[1]

Finally Proudhon, in his pamphlet on the organisation of credit and currency,[2] proposed that the State, in order to remove the stagnation of business caused by the Revolution of '48, should fix the prices of labour and commodities. Proudhon's suggestions are very like the *maximum* of the first Revolution, only he aims at a general reduction of prices in industry and commerce, from which he would exempt agricultural prices.

All these schemes, ancient and modern, agree in retaining the actual measure of value (money). Robert Owen, on the other hand, in his Equitable Labour Exchange, founded, long before Rodbertus, an institution which has all the characteristic features of the latter's proposals. In September 1832 Robert Owen opened his Labour Exchange, which was based on the following principles.[3] Every member of the society might deposit goods in the Exchange warehouses, and had the right to

---

[1] See the Decree in the *Moniteur*, 24th and 26th December. Cf. also Buchez, *Histoire Parlementaire*, xxxvi. p. 207.

[2] Proudhon, *Organisation du crédit et de la circulation et solution du problème social*, 1848, pp. 17-23, *Œuvres*, vol. vi. p. 105. See also Fichte's proposals, § 2, p. 35, note 2.

[3] Cf. Holyoake, *History of Co-operation in England*, vol. i., 1875, p. 160, for contemporary plans of like tendency. According to Noyes, *History of American Socialisms*, 1870, p. 95, the American socialist Josiah Warren communicated the plan of a Labour Exchange to Owen during the latter's visit to America, 1826. In his work *Practical Details of Equitable Commerce*, vol. i., 1852, p. 14, Warren gives an interesting description of a Time Store opened in Cincinnati on 18th May 1827, which, however, differs materially from Owen's Labour Exchange in many points.

draw for them labour-notes to the amount of their estimated value.[1] The unit of value was one hour's work, and was to equal 6d. in metallic money.

In the case of every commodity the value of the raw material, as well as the work expended on it by the labourer, was taken into account. Each depositor received not the number of labour-hours he had actually expended, but the amount of hours which the valuers considered an ordinary workman would employ on the articles in question.[2] At the same time a bank was to be founded for the exchange of labour-notes into metallic currency,[3] but so far as I can see this never came into existence.[4] As Owen wished to bring

[1] The original of one of these notes lies before me, and runs: "National Equitable Labour Exchange.—To the storekeeper of the Exchange.—22nd July 1833—Deliver to the bearer exchange stores to the value of One Hour by the order of—— " (here follow the signatures of the superintendent and the secretary).

[2] Booth, *Robert Owen, the Founder of Socialism in England*, 1869, p. 146 : ". . . In the exchange, valuators would fix the amount of hours which in their judgment an ordinary workman would employ on each article." This is clearly Rodbertus's "normal" working time, and does not differ materially from the "average or socially necessary" working time of Marx (cf. *Zur Kritik der polit. Oekonomie*, 1859, p. 9, and *Das Kapital*, 3rd ed. 1833, p. 6). Booth, p. 147, and Sargant, *Robert Owen*, 1860, p. 309, criticise this method of valuation. I have not got the first volume of the *Crisis*, the official organ of the labour bank, with its statutes and programme, from which Booth quotes the above passage. [The sentence quoted from Booth is a paraphrase of various statements by Owen, the earliest of which appeared in his *Report to the County of Lanark* in 1821. Cf. also his *Third Dublin Address*, 1823 ; and the *Crisis*, 1832, vol. i. pp. 50, 59-63, 77-81, 105, 106.—H. S. F.]   [3] Sargant, as above, pp. 306, 307.

[4] As early as 21st December 1833 (*Crisis*, vol. iii. p. 131) a member complains that the labour-notes are generally accepted not at 6d. the labour-hour, but only at 4½d. This, of course, would not have occurred had there been an exchange.

the Labour Exchange into being at once, it could of course only start as a private undertaking; but he was quite aware that comprehensive results could not be looked for without the intervention of the State, and he therefore, at a meeting held at the bank on 22nd January 1834, proposed a petition to the king and both Houses of Parliament, demanding as a provisional measure the establishment by the State of Labour Exchanges in every village.[1]

The objections to Owen's schemes raised by Rodbertus in his work on the normal working day are therefore completely unfounded. Rodbertus says of Owen's plan: "If one hour's shoemaker's work, reckoned by solar time, be accounted equivalent to one hour's weaver's work, reckoned in the same way, then certainly such a system will not advance matters, for it is nothing more than a general premium on idleness, quite apart from the really childish attempt to found such a system on a voluntary basis like a private speculation."[2] But we have already seen that Owen, long before Rodbertus, very clearly recognised the nature of normal labour and the necessity of State intervention.

Altogether the position which Rodbertus assumes with regard to Owen's project is characteristic of the dilettantism with which this writer, so much admired in Germany, treated the social question. Rodbertus confesses openly that in 1842, when he wrote his essay *Zur Erkenntniss unserer staatswirthschaftlichen Zustände,*

---

[1] *Crisis*, 1st February 1834, vol. iii. p. 184.

[2] Rodbertus in his essay "Der Normalarbeitstag," in the *Kleine Schriften*, 1890, p. 350.

he had no knowledge of Owen's experiments (1832), although they anticipated by a considerable interval his proposed creation of a labour currency.[1] Thirty years later, when Rodbertus was writing his paper on the normal working day, he had informed himself as to Owen's Labour Exchange, but only from Reybaud's *Études sur les Réformateurs ou Socialistes modernes*,[2] that is to say from a work, in which, as every one who has studied the subject can see at a glance, the crassest errors may be counted by hundreds.   Reybaud's inaccurate and incomplete account naturally led Rodbertus to false conclusions, as he had, to quote his own words, "obtained no further information" (in spite of the copious literature on the subject) as to the projects of Owen or others.[3]   Mazel's writings, too, whose pro-

---

[1] Rodbertus, *Zur Erkenntniss unserer staatswirthschaftlichen Zustände*, i., 1842, pp. 164-175.

[2] The passages cited by Rodbertus in the *Kleine Schriften* are to be found in the *Études*, vol. i., 7th ed. 1864, p. 245.

[3] Marx and Engels are no better informed than Rodbertus as to labour exchanges—decisive as these experiments are for the development of the socialist theory of value.   Marx, for instance, declares, in his *Misère de la Philosophie*, 1847, p. 62, in all seriousness that the equitable labour exchange bazaars originated in a treatise published in 1839 by J. F. Bray, *Labour's Wrongs and Labour's Remedy;* and Engels reprints the statement in the German translation of the *Misère de la Philosophie*, 1885, p. 62, adding one or two remarks about Proudhon's people's bank, which he fails to understand.   As a matter of fact, the labour exchanges were founded during and after 1832, and had failed (for instance, the London Exchange in 1834) some considerable time before 1839 (cf. the *Crisis* of 31st May and 7th June 1834, pp. 64, 71, and Owen's account in the *New Moral World* of 17th October 1835, vol. i. p. 400).   If Bray's proposals (as above, pp. 157-161, and *passim*), with regard to the labour currency, have a certain resemblance to Owen's, Bray of course was indebted to Owen and not Owen to him,

posals coincide on most points with those of Rodbertus
(§ 7, p. 74, note 2), seem quite unknown to him.

If we ask, in conclusion, What is the practical value
of Rodbertus's proposals? we are obliged to answer that
we are dealing here with a manifest Utopia. It appears
from the lately-published *Fourth Economic Letter*, that
Rodbertus originally intended his plans to apply to a
communist social organisation without private property
in land or capital ; so that a detailed criticism of his
schemes belongs to section 13, in which I propose to discuss the relations of the communistic system to the right
to the whole produce of labour. I will only consider here
the misgivings which arise when one imagines these proposals realised in a society based on private property.

Under such social conditions the State regulation of
prices of all goods and services, whether in terms of
metallic money or of a labour currency, would be in
constant conflict with the economic interests of large
and small employers in agriculture, industry, and
commerce. Now it is just these innumerable independent *entrepreneurs* who, in a State recognising individual ownership of land and capital, are the real
masters of the situation, whose will may indeed be bent
for a time by the extreme terrorism of the State, but can
never be broken so long as private property exists.
This was shown clearly enough during the enforcement
of Diocletian's edict and the *maximum* of the French
Revolution, although a legal determination of prices in
metallic money, such as they effected, is far easier to

carry out than a more or less arbitrary settlement in average working time. And both these attempts failed, although both Diocletian and the Terrorists of the French Revolution did not flinch from a resort to penalties of imprisonment and death for the enforcement of their decrees.

It must not be forgotten that a general State assessment of the price of goods and services involves the necessity of compelling the sale of such products as are not actually required by the dealers for their own consumption, as they could otherwise, by mere passivity, reduce the legal price-list to an absurdity. And the laws of Diocletian and of the French Revolution did actually apply as severe, nay severer, penalties to those who kept back from sale such goods (accapareurs), as to those who actively transgressed the legal price-list. But it stands to reason that a state of things in which the legal authorities prescribe to the dealers what they are to sell, is subversive of all the freedom and independence of an individualistic organisation, and combines all the evils of private and collective property. For this reason it is probable that the Roman Empire and France would have passed rapidly to pure communism, had the existing political conditions allowed the continued enforcement of these measures.[1]

[1] As to the question of the utility and feasibility of a State regulation of prices while an individualistic organisation is maintained, the debate of the French Convention on the repeal of the *maximum* of 23rd and 24th December 1794 (*Moniteur*, 26th and 27th December) may still be read with profit. It is true that the value of these debates is greatly lessened by the reactionary fanaticism which characterises nearly all the speeches.

§ 9. MARX

WHILE Rodbertus repeats in the main the thoughts of the French socialists, of the Saint-Simonians and Proudhon, Marx is completely under the influence of the earlier English socialists, and more particularly of William Thompson. Leaving out of account the mathematical formulæ by which Marx rather obscures than elucidates his argument, the whole theory of surplus value, its conception, its name, and the estimates of its amount are borrowed in all essentials from Thompson's writings.[1] Only Marx, in accordance with the aim of

[1] Cf. Marx, *Das Kapital*, English trans. 1887, pp. 156, 194, 289, with Thompson, *Distribution of Wealth*, p. 163 ; 2nd ed. p. 125. Engels, who, in his *Polemic against Dühring*, 1877, pp. 10, 162, and in his pamphlet, *The Development of Socialism from a Utopia to a Science* (cf. p. 103, note 2), hailed Marx as the discoverer of the theory of surplus value, from which epoch-making discovery he dates the rise of scientific Socialism, appears, however, in his preface to the 2nd vol. of *Kapital*, 1885, p. xiv., to admit that Marx had predecessors in the theory of surplus value amongst the older English socialists. But I doubt whether Marx drew his views on this question from the pamphlet quoted by Engels, *The Source and Remedy of the National Difficulties*, London, 1821, which contains only faint hints of the theory. The real discoverers of the theory of surplus value are Godwin, Hall, and especially W. Thompson (see above, §§ 3-5). Marx himself, like Rodbertus, is silent as to the sources of his views, although, as a rule, he is far from sparing of quotations. Cf.

his work, pays special attention to the one form of unearned income (interest on capital), and fails to give either that jural criticism of private property in instruments of production and useful commodities which is the necessary supplement of the theory of surplus value, or a rigorous exposition of the right to the whole produce of labour. In all these respects Marx is far inferior to Thompson, so that the work of the latter may be regarded as the foundation-stone of Socialism.

With regard, on the other hand, to practical measures for the abolition of surplus value, Marx and his friend Engels occupy a peculiar position. In the *Communistic Manifesto*, which belongs to the period preceding the revolution of '48, they both make a series of proposals borrowed, almost without exception, from older socialist literature.[1] Several of these measures manifestly aim at the abolition of unearned income, at any rate on a

---

Böhm-Bawerk, *Kapital und Kapitalzins*, 1884, vol. i. p. 361 ; Gustav Gross, *Karl Marx*, 1885, pp. 57, 59 ; Schramm in the *Zukunft*, 1878, p. 129 ; and Diehl's recent work on *Proudhon*, 2nd section, 1890, p. 269.

[1] Cf. the *Kommunistische Manifest*, 3rd ed. 1883, p. 17, authorised English translation, 1888, p. 22. "For the most advanced countries the following measures might come into very general application : (1) Expropriation of landed property, and application of rent to State expenditure ; (2) heavy progressive taxation ; (3) abolition of inheritance ; (4) confiscation of the property of all emigrants and rebels ; (5) centralisation of credit in the hands of the State by means of a national bank with State capital and exclusive monopoly ; (6) centralisation of means of transport in the hands of the State ; (7) increase of national factories, instruments of production, reclamation and improvement of land according to a common plan ; (8) compulsory obligation of labour upon all, establishment of industrial armies, especially for agriculture ; (9) joint prosecution of agriculture and manufacture aiming at the gradual removal of the distinction of town and

large scale, as for instance, the expropriation of landed
property, the abolition of inheritance, the concentration
in the hands of the State of credit and means of transport and of a part of industry. Marx and Engels
repeated some of these suggestions later on, as when,
for instance, Marx[1] prophesied that as soon as the
concentration of the means of production in the hands
of the rich becomes excessive, they will be expropriated
by a popular revolutionary crusade; while Engels expressed the same opinion when he characterised as
indispensable, given the preliminary economic conditions, the seizure of political power by the proletariate,
and the conversion into State property of the means of
production.[2] Both writers therefore maintain, on
the most important point, their position of 1848,
except that in the interval the expropriation of landed
property has transformed itself into a confiscation of
all instruments of production.

Essentially the same views are advocated by those
writers and societies who may be counted as belonging
to the party of the two socialists. Thus at Brussels in
1868 the Congress of the International decided in favour
of a communistic system of conducting the chief branches
of elementary production, namely, agriculture and

country; (10) public and gratuitous education for all children, abolition
of children's labour in factories in its present form, union of education
with material production," etc.

[1] Marx, *Das Kapital*, English trans. 1887, pp. 788, 789; 3rd ed.
p. 790.

[2] Engels, *Die Entwicklung des Socialismus*, Zurich, 1882, p. 42.

mining; that is to say, mines and arable land were to be the property of the State, and were to be worked by labour associations (common property and common usance). At the same time the Congress decided—and, as we shall see later on (§ 13), this decision is not in perfect agreement with the first—that labour must retain its full rights and its whole reward, and that accordingly all deductions made in the name of capital must be repudiated, whether as rent, interest, profits, or in any other form.[1]

At the Bâle Congress of the International in 1869 the question was again raised, and the right of society to annul private property in land and delegate it to the community was again asserted, while, moreover, this appropriation of land by the community was declared to be a necessity.[2]

The Congress could not agree on the further question whether the common property was to be used in common, or whether the community should allot portions of the common land to private persons and individual

---

[1] Cf. *Troisième Congrès de l'Association Internationale des Travailleurs, Compte Rendu officiel*, Brussels, 1868, pp. 40, 45. The decisions of the Congress are, moreover, somewhat obscure and contradictory in consequence of the disagreement of the respective followers of Proudhon and Marx.

[2] The two decisions run in the *Compte Rendu du iv*ᵉ *Congrès International, tenu à Bâle en Septembre 1869*, Brussels, 1869, pp. 84, 90: "iⁱᵒ Le congrès déclare que la société a le droit d'abolir la propriété individuelle du sol et de faire entrer le sol à la communauté ; iiⁱᵒ Il déclare encore qu'il y a aujourd'hui nécessité de faire entrer le sol à la propriété collective." Against these proposals, cf. Adolf Wagner, *Die Abschaffung des privaten Grundeigenthums*, 1870.

labour associations for temporary separate cultivation.[1]
This question was postponed to the next Congress, but
was never decided, owing to the notorious split in the
International which took place at the Congress of 1872
at the Hague.

The decisions of the International were authoritative
for the various national labour congresses. The general
German Social Democrat Labour Congress, which was
held at Eisenach from the 7th to the 9th of August 1869
(so before the Bâle meeting of the International), confined itself to declaring that the "economic dependence
of the labourer on the capitalist is the foundation of
every form of enslavement, and that therefore the social
democrat party aimed at obtaining for every labourer
the whole produce of his labour by the substitution of
associated for the present system of wage labour."[2] So
that, although the Brussels Congress had been held more
than a year before, the so-called Eisenach programme
only pronounced in favour of the right to the whole
produce of labour, and for associated labour in general,
without entering into the means by which this end was
to be obtained. Not until the Congress at Stuttgart (4th
to the 7th of June 1870) did the Social Democrat Labour
Party declare, in connection with the decisions of the
International in Brussels and Bâle, "That the economic
development of modern society made it a social necessity

[1] *Compte Rendu*, p. 72.
[2] *Protokoll über die Verhandlungen des allgemeinen Deutschen social-
demokratischen Arbeitercongresses in Eisenach am 7. 8. und 9. August
1869*, Leipzig, 1869, pp. 29-32.

to convert arable land into common property ; the State letting it to agricultural associations pledged to cultivate the land by scientific methods, and to divide the produce of their labour according to a fixed scale of partition amongst the members. . . . As a transition step between private and co-operative agriculture, the Congress demanded that a beginning be made with Government land, royal demesnes, trust lands, church and common lands, mines, railways, etc., and with this in view protested against all conversions of the said State and common property into private property." [1]

It can hardly be claimed that by these manifestos the socialist party explain clearly and definitely the social organisation at which they aim. They do not so much as answer the fundamental question of Socialism, whether the future social order is to be based on the right to the whole produce of labour, or on the right to subsistence ? The Gotha programme alone, which was adopted by the Congress held from the 23rd to the 26th of May 1875, and which still forms the basis of the socialist movement in Germany, is drawn up with an approach to scientific precision. The essential points of this programme justify us in concluding that the German socialist party regards the right to subsistence, distribution according to wants, as the basis of the future social order.

The Gotha programme lays down as a fundamental

[1] *Protokoll über den ersten Kongress der socialdemokratischen Arbeiterpartei in Stuttgart, vom 4. bis 7. Juni 1870*, Leipzig, 1870, pp. 16-18.

principle that labour is the source of all wealth and all civilisation, and that generally beneficial labour being only possible through society, *the whole produce of labour belongs to society : that is to say, that, work being universally compulsory, every member of society has an equal right to a share of the product according to his reasonable requirements.* The product of labour, then, belongs not to the labourer, as follows necessarily from the right to the produce of labour, but to society, and is by society allotted to every individual according to the measure of his reasonable wants (see above, § 1).

In order to pave the way for the solution of the social problem, the German socialist labour party demands in the Gotha programme the establishment of socialist productive associations for agriculture and industry by State aid under the democratic control of the working-classes, and that on such a scale as shall lead to the socialistic organisation of labour generally. So that the realisation of the schemes of Louis Blanc and Ferdinand Lassalle is recommended as a transitionary measure to a thoroughly socialistic organisation of society.[1]

At the first Congress of the German social democrat party held, after the repeal of the socialist law, at Halle from the 12th to the 18th of October 1890, the need for

---

[1] Cf. as to the Gotha programme and questions connected with it, Liebknecht, *Die Grund- und Bodenfrage*, 2nd ed. 1876, pp. 183, 184. Bebel, *Unsere Ziele*, 9th ed. 1886, pp. 23, 29, 30 ; *Die Frau in der Vergangenheit, Gegenwart und in der Zukunft*, 1883, pp. 148, 149. Schäffle, *Die Quintessenz des Socialismus*, 7th ed. 1879, pp. 2, 3, 44, 45. Hermann Bahr, *Die Einsichtslosigkeit des Herrn Schäffle*, 1886, pp. 78, 79.

a reform of these schemes, as of the whole programme, was recognised on all sides, though the discussion of the necessary alterations was postponed to the next Congress.[1]

The French labour movement took up the thread just where the Germans let it fall. The third French Labour Congress at Marseilles (1879) demanded the confiscation of land, machinery, means of transport, buildings, and accumulated capital, in favour of the human race, and declared further that this appropriation of instruments of labour and forces of production should be forwarded by all possible means.[2]

Having regard to the essential portions of these various utterances, the following appears to represent the views common to modern socialists. The socialist parties of the present day oppose not only unearned income (*Rente, Mehrwert*), but also private ownership

---

[1] Cf. the *Protokoll über die Verhandlungen des Parteitages der social-demokratischen Partei Deutschlands*, 1890, pp. 157, 158. Liebknecht's speech is especially deserving of notice as giving a clear insight into the intellectual currents of the German socialist labour party.

[2] Cf. *Rapports et Résolutions des Congrès Ouvriers de 1876 à 1883*, Paris, 1883, pp. 7, 8 : " Le Congrès . . . conclut à l'expropriation collective des sol, sous-sol, machines, voies de transport, bâtiments, capitaux, accumulés, au bénéfice de la collectivité humaine ; Le Congrès déclare que l'appropriation collective de tous les instruments de travail et forces de production doit être poursuivie par tous les moyens possibles." Until the Marseilles Congress, the labour congresses had maintained a conservative position with regard to private property ; even the Lyons Congress (1878) rejected by a large majority a resolution recognising the right to the whole produce of labour, and in favour of collective possession of the instruments of production. Cf. Mermeix, *La France socialiste*, 1886, pp. 80-86, and as to the English labour movement see below, § 12, p. 155, note 1.

of the means of production and of consumable commodities ; and they recognise quite generally the right
to the whole produce of labour in its negative sense
(see below, § 13), that is, in as far as it denies the justice
of rent and interest. It is as a direct consequence
of these tenets that modern Socialism demands the conversion of private property in instruments of production
and consumable commodities into collective property.

On the other hand, the present socialist parties have
not attained to any decided, unanimous conviction as to
the fundamental principle of Socialism, whether the
basis of the future social organisation is to be the right
to the whole produce of labour, or the right to subsistence.
Just as little are they agreed as to the future subject of
this common property. Shall, in the socialistic state, the
labour associations have possession of the instruments
of production and consumable commodities, using them
in common (Group Socialism)? Or is this task to fall to
the municipality, the State, or even as desired by the Marseilles Congress (p. 108, note 2) to mankind in general
(Municipal, State, Universal Socialism)? Or is there to
be a combination of these different positions in such a
way that, while the State or the municipality possesses
the means of production, it assigns them to individuals
or associations for separate use and management? To
all these questions the latest socialist writings, and the
decisions of socialist congresses, give only vague and
often contradictory answers.

This lack of decision is certainly caused in part by

the difficulty of these questions, dealing as they do with mainly juridical problems; while the examination from the juridical point of view of the socialist ideas has not yet even been attempted. But it is in a far greater measure due to the opinions held by Marx and Engels as to the scope of modern Socialism. According to these writers, a critical analysis of existing economic conditions in their historical connection, and of the theoretic principles which lie behind them, is the true method of scientific, as distinguished from Utopian Socialism (as of Saint-Simon,[1] Fourier, and others), and they expressly exclude, as purely visionary, every attempt at a detailed forecast of the social order by which existing conditions will be replaced in the future. The task of scientific Socialism, says Engels, is no longer to devise as complete a social system as possible, but to inquire into the historical course of economic events which inevitably produced the bourgeoisie and the proletariate, and the mutual antagonism of the two; and to discover in the resultant economic conditions the means to end the conflict. . . . Socialists hitherto (*i.e.* before Marx) did indeed

---

[1] Engels is quite wrong when he calls Saint-Simon (who must be distinguished from his school) Utopian ; cf. the *Polemic against Dühring*, pp. 219, 223 ; *Die Entwicklung des Socialismus von der Utopie zur Wissenschaft*, p. 3 of Introduction to *Dühring* (see p. 103, note 2).   It is true that Saint-Simon's writings, just as do those of Marx and Engels, contain occasional plans for the reform of society, but we look in vain for a Utopia, that is a detailed account of the future social organisation.   The school of Saint-Simon was the first to draw such a picture of the future order of society in the *Exposition de la doctrine Saint-Simonienne* (see above, § 6). Owen, also, can hardly be termed Utopian.

criticise the existing capitalistic mode of production and its results, but, having never arrived at a clear comprehension of its origin and nature, they could not reform it. All this Marx was the first to accomplish by his "discovery" of surplus value.[1]

Now I take such a synthetic forecast of a complete social organisation to be not only strictly scientific, but absolutely indispensable, if the socialist movement is even partially to realise its aims. That only is an unscientific Utopia which, under the new order, expects men to be moved by essentially different springs of action, or contemplates another sequence of cause and effect than that of our actual conditions. Many socialists, old and new—Engels[2] himself not excepted—have, it is true, constantly violated both these essential conditions. I need only recall Cabet[3] who declared a

---

[1] Engels, *Die Entwicklung des Socialismus*, p. 11. Engels follows here the "petit bourgeois" Proudhon who also, in his *Système des contradictions économiques*, vol. ii. p. 330, rejects all previous communistic systems as Utopias.

[2] Thus Engels, in the *Polemic against Dühring*, 1886, p. 270, expresses himself as follows on the probable consequences of the establishment of a socialistic system : "To ensure by social production to every member of society an existence that is not only materially sufficient and improves from day to day, but which also guarantees the completely free development and exercise of his bodily and intellectual capabilities. The possibility of this exists for the first time, but it does exist." I consider these assurances, which represent as actually attainable the ultimate goal of human effort, to be more Utopian than all the promises of peculiar gastronomic, sexual, and intellectual pleasures with which Fourier fills his bulky volumes.

[3] Cabet had been reproached with the fact that his *Journey to Icaria* contained no connected scientific theory of Socialism. To which Cabet gave, in the monthly magazine, *Le Populaire*, 4th November 1844, p. 3, of

sense of brotherhood to be the sole motive of action, as it was the only object of his social system, although he could not possibly hide from himself that experience of human nature up to the present time gives no cause to expect such an unconditional sway of brotherly affection, even in a communist state.   Or, again, remember Fourier and Pierre Leroux,[1] who so greatly misunderstand the historical relations of cause and effect that they predict as the immediate result of the realisation of their schemes a fourfold or fivefold increase in the quantity of social production.   Needless to say that when some of these socialist systems (for instance those of Fourier and Cabet) were put to the test of practical experiment these fantastic promises were in no case fulfilled.[2]

Marx and Engels, it is true, believe that the concentration of the instruments of production on the one hand, and the socialisation of labour on the other, will gradually reach a point at which there must inevitably follow the collapse of private property.   But a glance at the fall of

which he was editor, the fine but fantastic answer, " If we are asked what is your *science*, we answer : *Fraternity !*   What is your *principle ?* *Fraternity !*   What is your *doctrine ?*   *Fraternity !*   What is your *theory ?* *Fraternity !*   What is your *system ?*   *Fraternity !* "

[1] In the *Nouveau Monde Industriel*, p. ii., 1829, Fourier gives as the result of his invention : " The means of quadrupling suddenly the gross product, and of multiplying by twenty the relative product, the sum of enjoyment."   The title of a paper published in 1853, and addressed by Pierre Leroux to the Parliament of New Jersey, runs *On a Method of increasing by five Times, not to say more, the Agricultural Produce of the Country.*

[2] Cf. for the practical trials of Fourierism made in North America, Noyes, *History of American Socialisms*, p. 200.

the Roman Empire will show how little power the
greatest social evils have to effect a recasting of
society, unless a nation has before its eyes a clear,
unexaggerated picture of the organisation which is to
replace them. Never were the means of production
so centralised as at the time when half the African province was the property of twenty-four individuals;[2] never
were the sufferings of the working-classes greater than
when almost every productive labourer was a slave.
Nor was there any lack of violent criticism of the existing social conditions—for instance, in the writings of
the Fathers—such as need not fear comparison with the
best socialist writings of the present day.[1] In spite of
all this, the fall of the Western Empire was followed not
by Socialism, but by the legal order of the Middle
Ages.

The course of the French Revolution of 1848,
distinctly social in character as it was, shows the
necessity of a thorough investigation of socialist policy
from a legal point of view, as much in the interests of
the propertied as of the working-classes. Bearing in
mind how unfavourable to the labouring class were the
political relations at the time, and that these rendered
any radical measure of reform impossible, I must still
point out that the few measures which were carried did
not, as Marx and Engels would have had them, obey a
historical necessity inherent in the economic relations,

[1] Cf. Villegardelle, *Histoire des Idées sociales*, 1846, p. 50.
[2] Plin. *Hist. Nat.* xviii. 35 ed. Sillig.

but had been discussed long beforehand in books and newspapers. A reference to the account given in Chapter I. of the historical development of the right to labour, will show that the way was prepared for its recognition by a, very Utopian discussion of many years' duration.

Take another measure of undoubtedly socialist tendency, the appointment of a Government Labour Commission by a Decree of the Provisional Government of 28th February 1848.[1] On that date the Parisians demanded the establishment of a labour progress department (Ministère du Travail et du Progrès) endowed with adequate executive powers for the protection of labour interests.[2] But Louis Blanc was persuaded by his colleagues in the Provisional Government to accept, instead of this labour and progress department, the Government Commission, which was purely theoretical in character, and was a kind of academy for the discussion of labour interests. Now the progress department, like the right to labour, was an old scheme of the Fourierist school.[3]

To take a final illustration, the Constituent Assembly, by a Decree of 5th July 1848, voted a grant of

---

[1] Carrey, vol. i. Nos. 42, 58. The Proceedings of this Commission were published by Louis Blanc in a pamphlet, *La Révolution de Février au Luxembourg*, Paris, 1849.

[2] Louis Blanc, *Histoire de la Révolution de 1848*, 5th ed. 1880, vol. i. p. 133.

[3] Cf. *Bases de la politique positive, Manifeste de l'école Sociétaire fondée par Fourier*, 2nd ed. 1842, p. 207.

three millions for the support of labour associations,
which was applied in the form of loans, sums under
25,000 francs at an interest of 3 per cent, larger
amounts at 5 per cent. The three million francs were
accordingly almost entirely taken up by labour associations in Paris and the provinces ; and many of them
flourished exceedingly until their dissolution after the
Coup d'État of 2nd December 1851, owing to the
republican opinions of their members.[1]   It is easy to
recognise in these measures the proposals already made
by Louis Blanc in his work on the organisation of
labour, and again during the revolution of February
on the Luxembourg Commission.[2]

But if we ask what decides the leaders of the socialist
movement in the face of these sufficiently well-known
historic facts to refrain from a detailed exposition of the
social organisation at which they aim, or, in other words,
from a statement of the socialist ideals, two considerations
may perhaps give an explanation of a circumstance in
itself so surprising.   In the first place, remember that the
most distinguished socialist theorists are generally also

---

[1] *Enquête de la commission extraparlementaire des associations ouvrières*,
vol. i., 1883, p. 10 ; vol. ii. p. 329.

[2] Louis Blanc, *Organisation du Travail*, 1st ed. 1841, pp. 76, 107, 113,
114 ; English trans. 1848, pp. 78, 122.   *La Révolution de Février au
Luxembourg* (1849), p. 100.   Again in his monthly review, *Le Nouveau
Monde*, 15th September 1849, p. 129 (*Le socialisme en projet de loi*).
Again in the *Organisation du Travail*, 9th ed. 1850, p. 119 ; 5th ed.
1848, p. 102, and in the 10th edition in the *Questions d'aujourd'hui
et de demain*, vol. iv., 1882, p. 152.   The proposals mentioned here
do not agree perfectly.

the most influential leaders of the socialist parties. Now experience shows that it is far easier to keep political and economic parties united on a negation of existing conditions than on the formulation of a definite scheme.

Moreover, a misapprehension of the distinction between theoretical and applied science may be partly responsible for this position assumed by an important group of socialist theorists. In theoretical science the mere proof of error is of importance, even when the investigator is not in a position to replace the abolished misconception by the right view; so that Copernicus would have earned undying fame by the mere refutation of the Ptolemaic system, even if he had not established his own in its place.

But it is otherwise in the province of applied science. Here the aptest criticism of existing conditions is not permissible without sufficient proof of the possibility of a better state of things. However heavily unearned income (rent, surplus value) may press upon the working classes, the people will never decide upon a comprehensive social experiment until they are possessed of a socialist scheme on lines laid down by experience.

Even the political efforts at reform of the eighteenth and nineteenth centuries would have had no permanent success had not the world possessed, in the writings of Montesquieu and Rousseau, a sketch of the political conditions at which to aim.

§ 10. LOUIS BLANC AND FERDINAND LASSALLE

LOUIS BLANC and Ferdinand Lassalle are the two most distinguished adherents of that form of Socialism which I called in the last chapter (p. 109) Group Socialism, of which the main principle is the common ownership and employment of instruments of production by larger or smaller associations of workmen in each trade. A central organisation of all the groups of each trade, or indeed of all trades, is, of course, merely a further development of this idea, and in no way invalidates the definition. The essential distinction between this and other forms of socialist opinion (Municipal, State, and Universal Socialism) is, that Group Socialism makes a group or society of workmen the unit of ownership and production.

The relative positions of Louis Blanc and Lassalle may be thus characterised : in Louis Blanc's work the historical and philosophical foundations of group Socialism are of the scantiest; whereas Lassalle is master not only of the historical and philosophical sides of the question, but also of a portion of its earlier literature, so far as it concerns the main problem of Socialism, unearned income. On the other hand, in all his practical schemes Lassalle is absolutely dependent on Louis Blanc.

Louis Blanc belonged to a group of young men who, after the July revolution (1830), gathered round Philippe Buonarroti, the companion of Babeuf and the historian of the Babeuf conspiracy; [1] and Blanc's relations with the old communist Jacobin were not without influence on his socialistic writings. His system lacks that economic garb in which, since Thompson and Ricardo, socialists were wont to disguise social problems which in reality are questions of law and politics. A reference to eternal justice, which they took to require economic as well as political equality (égalité de fait, égalité réelle), sufficed for the determined revolutionaries who joined with Babeuf to inaugurate a new social order by force of arms.

Louis Blanc's system, therefore, does not start from any special definition of value. He neglects the disparity between the wages and the product of labour, which is so emphasised by most socialists; nor does he assert the right of the labourer to the entire produce of his industry, though it is true that in the ninth edition of his chief work [2] he examines the justification of unearned

[1] Advielle, *Histoire de Gracchus Babeuf et du Babouvisme*, vol. i., 1884, p. 360.

[2] Louis Blanc, *Organisation du Travail*, 9th ed. 1850, p. 156; English trans. 1848, p. 8. Cf. also his paper, *Le Socialisme. Droit au Travail*, 1848, pp. 20-24.

income, a question which the writings of Proudhon and
Bastiat had brought to the fore during the revolution of
February. Louis Blanc takes the view that unearned
income, especially interest on loans, is in itself unjust
(differing from Bastiat), but that it must be regarded as
an absolute necessity under our present legal system,
which distributes land and the other instruments of
production to private persons (differing from Proudhon).
But he does not carry these ideas sufficiently far to
claim for the labourer the right to the whole produce of
labour; he rather asserts the right of every human being
to subsistence (*droit à la vie*),[1] and lays down as the
organising principle of the social order the rule that
every one should produce according to his ability and
consume according to his wants.[2]   It is clear from this
that the centre of Louis Blanc's socialistic system is
not the right to the whole produce of labour, but the
right to subsistence, and that it is based, not on an
economic principle, but on the philanthropic conception
of brotherhood.

In order, then, to the realisation of this aim Louis Blanc
makes a series of proposals, to the following of which I call
attention.   He advocates the foundation of a Department

---

[1] Louis Blanc, *Organisation du Travail*, in the *Questions d'aujour-
d'hui et de demain*, vol. iv. p. 202.

[2] *Ibid.* p. 91 : "L'égalité n'est donc que la proportionnalité, et elle
n'existera d'une manière véritable que lorsque chacun, d'après la loi écrite
en quelque sorte dans son organisation par Dieu lui-même, *produira selon
ses facultés et consommera selon ses besoins.* Cf. also Louis Blanc, *La
Révolution de Févrie rau Luxembourg*, 1849, pp. 71, 75. See also above,
§ 1, p. 8, note 2, and p. 9, note 1.

of Progress, as Fourier's school had proposed before him (see above, § 9, p. 114, note 3), whose chief task would be to inaugurate by reforms the gradual abolition of the proletariate. This department would undertake the control of railways, mines, the note issue, and insurance, would found bazaars for retail, and warehouses for wholesale trade, this last with the right to issue a sort of commodity-money against the deposited goods. The profits which would accrue to the State from all these institutions would defray, in the first place, the capital and interest of the compensation fund required by these operations, the remainder being the workmen's budget.

This workmen's budget would be applied to found agricultural and industrial labour associations, by means of an allowance of State credit made to them for the purchase of instruments of production. But the labour associations who claim State credit must incorporate the following rules in their statutes. Out of the earnings of the association must be paid, firstly, all the expenses of production, including wages ; and, secondly, the interest on the capital advanced by the State. Of the remainder one-fourth is to go to form a sinking fund for the repayment of the capital, another fourth is to found a pension fund for persons unable to work, while a third quarter is to be divided amongst the associates. The last quarter is to go to a general reserve fund destined to support the associations in times of crisis.

The workshops of all the trade associations (ateliers

sociaux)[1] are to be united in one organisation, all those of the same trade depending on one central agency.[2] This would allow prices to be fixed for the different factories, thus preventing competition between them. At the head of all the associations, industrial and agricultural, there would be a supreme council, which would also administer the reserve fund mentioned above.[3]

If, now, we examine the relation in which Ferdinand Lassalle, the second of the above-named advocates of Group Socialism, stands to Louis Blanc, the first thing to

---

[1] The social workshops proposed by Louis Blanc must be clearly distinguished from the national workshops founded by the Provisional Government after the Revolution of February, Louis Blanc himself protesting emphatically against their identification. As a matter of fact, the difference between the two establishments is sufficiently marked. The social workshops are, according to Louis Blanc's intention, associations of workmen of the same trade, who work on their own account and are therefore bound together by a certain community of interest. The national workshops, on the other hand, were turbulent assemblies of unoccupied proletarians of all trades, who were organised in military fashion and were only occupied with earthworks to remove the idea of alms. Cf. Louis Blanc, *Pages de l'histoire de la Révolution de Février*, 1848, p. 55 ; *Le Socialisme. Droit au Travail : Réponse à M. Thiers*, 1848, p. 16 ; *Nouveau Monde* of 15th July 1850, p. 31 ; *Histoire de la Révolution de 1848*, vol. i., 5th edition, 1880, p. 221. The director of the national workshops declared, moreover, repeatedly that they did not owe their origin to Louis Blanc's schemes, but were secretly intended to reduce them to absurdity by a pretence at experiment. Cf. *Rapport de la commission de l'enquête sur l'insurrection qui a éclaté dans la journée du 23 Juin et sur les évènements du 15 Mai*, vol. i., 1848, p. 352. Thomas, *Histoire des Ateliers nationaux*, 1848, p. 142. See also above, § 1, p. 21, note 4.

[2] *Organisation du Travail* in the *Questions*, vol. iv. p. 98.

[3] *Ibid.* p. 152 (cf. also the references, § 9, p. 115, note 2). Louis Blanc materially modified his proposals, especially with regard to the division of the profits of the labour associations, after the Revolution of February.

notice is that Lassalle reiterates as a basis for his schemes
a great part of the philosophical and economic theories
which had been elaborated by English, French, and
German socialists since Godwin; though he refers
directly to Proudhon, Marx, and Rodbertus, without apparently knowing the real sources of their theories. In
the *Open Letter to the Central Committee for the summon-
ing of a General German Labour Congress at Leipzig*,
1st May 1863, with which Lassalle began his socialist
agitation, he laid down already "the iron economic
law which kept down the average wage for labour
to the level of bare subsistence, which the custom of a
nation renders indispensable to the continuance of existence and reproduction."[1]   From the entire product of
labour so much is, in the first place, deducted and divided
amongst the labourers as will suffice for their bare existence (wages), the entire surplus falling to the share of
the *entrepreneur*.   So that the workmen are deprived of
any share in the increased productivity of their own
labour due to the advance of civilisation.[2]   All Lassalle's
later socialist writings, particularly the *Arbeiterlesebuch*[3]

[1] Ferd. Lassalle, *Collected Speeches and Writings*, edited by George
Hotschick, New York, vol. i. pp. 36, 37.   Cf. v. Plener, *Ferd. Lassalle*,
1884, p. 40 and *passim*.   At the Congress of the Social Democrat party
at Halle (1890), in the debate on the Gotha programme, which ranks the
"breaking down of the iron law of wages" as one of the chief aims, Liebknecht spoke against the assumption of such a law, and demanded its
erasure from the party programme.   Cf. the *Report of the Proceedings of
the Congress*, 1890, p. 167.

[2] Lassalle, *Works*, vol. i. p. 38.   Cf. above, § 8, p. 89, notes 1, 2.

[3] *Arbeiterlesebuch*, Lassalle's speech at Frankfurt a/M., 17th and 19th
May 1863.

and the *Polemic against Schulze-Delitzsch*,[1] have in the main no other object than the historical, philosophical, and economic proof and elucidation of these few propositions.

Lassalle's practical proposals follow in all respects those of Louis Blanc, only they lack that detailed elaboration which Louis Blanc's owe solely to his position at the head of the Luxembourg Commission. Lassalle's proposals, which he never defined more closely, are much on a level with those of Louis Blanc in the earlier editions of his book on the *Organisation of Labour*,[2] and in the Decree of the French National Assembly of 5th July 1848.[3] In his *Open Letter* he sums up his proposals as follows : " Once more, then, free individual association of workmen—free association, remember, rendered possible by the supporting and promoting hand of the State—this is the only road out of the desert open to the working-class." [4] He designates the proposed associations shortly, in his attack on Schulze, as State-supported productive associations of workmen.[5] As a rule, there would be only one association of a trade in each place, all associations of the same kind being united by an organisation of credit and

---

[1] *Herr Bastiat-Schulze von Delitzsch, Der ökonomische Julian*, Berlin, 1864.

[2] Louis Blanc, *Organisation du Travail*, 1st ed. 1841, p. 76.

[3] A good summary of the history leading to this Decree is given in the *Enquête de la commission extraparlementaire des associations ouvrières*, vol. ii., 1883, p. 329.

[4] Lassalle, *Werke*, vol. i. p. 55.

[5] *Ibid.* vol. ii. pp. 391, 392.

insurance.[1] As regards the loans to the labour associations, which, of course, would only be founded gradually, Lassalle estimates that they would be covered, in the first instance, for the whole of Germany, by a sum of one hundred million thalers.[2]

Lassalle regarded his proposals as merely transitional measures which were to prepare for the solution of the social question,[3] and had never thought out so much as their immediate consequences. But even the plans of Louis Blanc, which are immeasurably better worked out, do not seem adapted to attain the object at which they aim, namely, to abolish competition and secure a satisfactory existence to the mass of labourers. It might be possible for the authority of the central factory to prevent competition between the workshops belonging to the same branch of production ; but the conflict of interests between the separately-organised branches would only flame the more fiercely. For it must not be forgotten that a socialist system would reign only within the individual associations ; for the entire field of consumption, as well as for the relations between the different branches, the individualistic system was to remain intact with its unavoidable consequences, freedom of contract and competition.

Still less would Group Socialism succeed in abolishing

---

[1] Lassalle, *Offenes Antwortschreiben, Werke,* vol. i. pp. 47, 48. *Bastiat-Schulze,* Berlin, 1864, p. 217. *Briefe an Rodbertus,* 1878, pp. 43, 80.

[2] Lassalle, *Arbeiterlesebuch,* Frankfurt, 1863, p. 43.

[3] *Ibid.* note, p. 41. *Bastiat-Schulze,* p. 211. *Briefe an Rodbertus,* pp. 44, 46, 81. Rodbertus, *Briefe an Meyer,* vol. i. p. 226.

unearned income. Lassalle, it is true, in his *Open
Letter* [1] held that when the working-class (by means of
labour associations) became their own employers, wages
as the reward of work must of necessity be replaced by
the product of labour. But who can fail to see that the
proposals of Louis Blanc and Lassalle only replace
private by corporate property, which latter exists to a
very large extent under our present system ; that it
follows that private property in land and capital, with
the ascendency conferred upon them by the law, remain ;
and that rent and interest would not be abolished.
Indeed without the Utopian supposition that the labour
associations would be guided solely by brotherly love,
it must, on the contrary, be assumed that the separately
organised trade societies (especially those producing,
like agriculture, the absolute necessaries of life) would,
thanks to their position of ascendency, wring more
unearned income out of the community than private
individuals are able to do to-day in open market.[2]

[1] Lassalle, *Werke*, vol. i. p. 43 ; cf. *Briefe an Rodbertus*, p. 77.

[2] Cf. the criticism of Louis Blanc's proposals (entirely from the
" Manchester " point of view) which Thiers gave in his speech before the
French National Assembly on the 13th September 1848 (Girardin, *Le
droit au travail au Luxembourg et à l'Assemblée Nationale*, vol. ii., 1849,
p. 221. Also Louis Blanc's answer in his work, *Le Socialisme. Droit au
Travail. Réponse à M. Thiers*, 1848, p. 56.

§ 11. MODERN AIMS

(1.) Conservative Socialism in Germany

During the last decade, socialist principles, having become an element in imperial politics, have been made the plaything of political and religious parties. I take it that Marx and Engels[1] are wrong in their so-called materialistic view of history, which regards the ideal categories of human life—the State, the Church, art, and science—as merely the product of temporary economic conditions. The great diffusion of religious convictions, tempering the sorrows of life and the terrors of death, is itself enough to contradict this assumption; seeing that the striving for a blissful life beyond the grave must necessarily counteract in innumerable cases the influence of purely economic motives. We cannot concede to economic conditions so sovereign an influence on the course of human development. They do not suffice of themselves to explain any great historic event, though it is

[1] Marx, *Misère de la Philosophie*, 1847, pp. 99, 113 ; also *Zur Kritik der politischen Oekonomie*, book i., 1859, p. v. ; Engels, *Streitschrift gegen Dühring*, 1886, p. 9 ; and *Die Entwicklung des Socialismus von der Utopie zur Wissenschaft*, p. 253 of *Dühring*.

equally true that none can altogether escape their influence. Thus in actual life we see political and religious parties pursuing economic aims side by side with ideal interests, and in particular striving to take from their opponents and appropriate to themselves the largest possible share of unearned income, of which no more than a fixed amount is available at any given time. From this results a circumstance, astounding at first sight, that many modern social writers in the service of political or religious parties emphatically defend those forms of unearned income which are in the hands of their own partisans, while they violently attack all others as a revolting injustice.

But there is another cause for this discrimination between the various forms of unearned income. The owner's title to unearned income is founded, not in economic conditions, but in a positive legal enactment, and it is peculiarly important in the case of such property that his title should be supported by corresponding effectual power. Although, as De Tocqueville has shown, feudal burdens were far less oppressive in France just before the Revolution than in England or Germany, yet the French people were especially embittered against this form of unearned income, because the Crown had gradually deprived the nobles of all those powers of jurisdiction, which might have, at any rate apparently, legitimatised the enforcement of the feudal exactions.[1]

[1] Tocqueville, *L'ancien régime et la révolution*, book ii. chap. i.

It becomes manifest on inquiry, that of all existing forms of unearned income, the possessions of the middle and poorer classes most nearly reconcile might and right. A step further on, in the case of larger landed and industrial properties, the situation is less favourable, because the authority of the owner has to be exerted by independent agents whose interests are anything but identical with the proprietor's. But the disproportion is most glaring in the case of those persons who draw unearned income by virtue of a legal claim, particularly in the case of the holders of public and private securities, which form of property has so immeasurably increased of late. For here the holder has no authority whatever, and the legislature can at any moment annul his rights by simply withdrawing its recognition of them.

Now the greater the disproportion between legal and effectual power, the more small and moderate properties become merged into large proprietorship, and these again into money investments on paper securities, so much the weaker does the inner structure of the whole system of private property become. The continually increasing dislocation of might and right, which is without doubt peculiarly characteristic of our epoch, is to my mind the most important impetus which is driving our system of private property towards Socialism. This political factor is of far greater moment than the economic concentration of the means of production in a few hands, on which Marx and other socialists lay most stress; for under certain conditions, if industry, for instance, were carried on as in ancient times by slave labour, such a concentration might conceivably strengthen the foundations of private property.

It is natural that those forms of private property in which the political power of the claimant is weak, and which depend practically on the sanction of the Legislature, should be attacked with special vehemence by modern socialist writers; and accordingly in Germany, where owing to the large number of small estates the position of landed property is very strong, the attack of one-sided socialists is mainly directed against so-called mobile capital; while in England, where the existence of *latifundia*, by concentrating private property in comparatively few hands, has greatly weakened the political power of landowners as a class, it is round landed property that the battle rages.

The violent attack led by the conservative social writers in Germany and Austria against interest on loans and similar forms of unearned income (particularly interest on outstanding debts and settlements) is one form of this partial and one-sided Socialism. Interest on credit of every kind (which I will term shortly interest on loans) is, from the socialist point of view, just as much unearned income accruing to the owner by virtue of positive legal enactment, as the rent of land or those forms of rent which landlords and capitalists draw from their personal undertakings. The only difference between interest on loans and other forms of unearned income is that in the former case capital and interest are of the same denomination, the interest being generally expressed as a percentage of the capital. So that the debtor is in a position, without the aid of any economic or juridical reasoning, to recognise clearly the amount of his exploitation, which in the other forms of unearned income is obscured to the unpractised eye by the want of homogeneity between the service and what is paid for it, *e.g.* work and wage, tenancy and rent, etc.

The circumstance that oppression by interest on loans (loan-usury) is so patent to every one has two important consequences. The first is, that loan-usury is only practised by persons of low social standing, and has therefore from the earliest times been the object of violent abhorrence, public opinion being always coincident with social ascendency. On the other hand, oppression by means of rent and wages bargains (rent-usury and wage-usury),.emanating as a rule from the upper classes, has met with a less unfavourable judgment even at the hands of the masses of the people. And yet the oppression of loan-usury is confined to a comparatively narrow sphere; while it is notorious that wage - usury has caused the degeneration of whole populations (especially in manufactures), and that rent-usury has been the scourge of rising towns,[1] and reduced the agricultural population of whole countries (Great Britain, Italy,

---

[1] Cf. D. Engel, *Die moderne Wohnungsnot,* 1873, p. 24 and *passim.*

South of France, and Spain [1]) to a condition resembling slavery.

The easily recognisable injustice of loan - usury, secondly, caused the Church and the State to discountenance it at a time when the other aspects of the social question were absolutely ignored. In Rome, originally, no limits were imposed on usury; but the law of the Twelve Tables and a long series of laws down to the reign of Justinian [2] fixed a legal maximum of interest, and it would even appear that during the republican period loans at interest were for a time absolutely forbidden.[3] The Christian Church likewise promulgated strict prohibitions against the taking of interest, on the authority of Christ's words in St. Luke's Gospel (vi. 34, 35), which, however, do not relate to the taking of interest, but exhort to "lend, hoping for nothing again," that is, without hope of return of the sum lent.[4] But about

---

[1] For the cruelties of which the English landed aristocracy have been guilty towards their tenants, cf. Wallace, *Land Nationalisation*, 2nd ed. 1882, chaps. iii.-v. Sugenheim's *Geschichte der Aufhebung der Leibeigenschaft*, 1861, contains important information on this point.

[2] L. 26, § 1, Cod. de usuris (4. 32). Cf. Glück, *Ausführliche Erläuterung der Pandekten*, vol. xxi., 1820, p. 1.

[3] Tac. *Ann.* vi. 16 ; cf. Liv. 1. vii. c. 16. 42.

[4] The passage in St. Luke runs literally : καὶ ἐὰν δανείζητε παρ' ὧν ἐλπίζετε ἀπολαβεῖν, ποία ὑμῖν χάρις ἐστί; καὶ γὰρ οἱ ἁμαρτωλοὶ ἁμαρτωλοῖς δανείζουσι, ἵνα ἀπολάβωσι τὰ ἴσα. πλὴν ἀγαπᾶτε τοὺς ἐχθροὺς ὑμῶν, καὶ ἀγαθοποιεῖτε καὶ δανείζετε μηδὲν ἀπελπίζοντες· καὶ ἔσται ὁ μισθὸς ὑμῶν πολύς, καὶ ἔσεσθε υἱοὶ τοῦ ὑψίστου (Luke vi. 34, 35). These words, as is clearly shown by the connection of *doing good* and *lending*, are meant as a moral, not a legal, precept. But even if the passage, in contradiction to its whole sense, be interpreted as a legal precept, it must be taken to forbid the demand for the return of the sum lent, or, the

the thirteenth century the doctrine of the so-called titles to interest (Zinstitel) arose, the substance of which was that loans, as such, should never bear interest, but that the creditor might accept compensation when justified by particular circumstances ; for instance, if the creditor was in any way harmed by the loan (*damnum emergens*), or if it caused him a loss of profit (*lucrum cessans*), or if the capital lent suffered any risk in the hands of the debtor (*periculum sortis*), and so on.[1] It stands to reason that such extremely comprehensive titles to interest practically abolished the canonical prohibition. In fact, very few Catholic social writers still uphold the prohibition,[2] the far greater number countenancing the demands for a moderate rate of interest, and only attacking usury ;[3] a position which is shared by modern legislation.

Thus the abandonment of the war waged by the Catholic Church for thousands of years upon loans at interest is the inevitable result of the one-sided estimate of economic and social relations from which the controversy started ; for there is not the remotest reason,

promise of repayment being an essential part of the contract of a loan, to forbid not only lending at interest but lending at all. Cf. Funk, *Zins u. Wucher*, 1868, p. 220 ; and for the opposite view Vogelsang, *Zins u. Wucher*, 1884, p. 7.

[1] See Funk, *Zins und Wucher*, 1868, p. 78. Endemann, *Studien in der romanisch-kanonistischen Wirtschafts- u. Rechtslehre*, 2nd vol., 1883, divs. viii., ix.

[2] Vogelsang, *Zins u. Wucher*, pp. 49, 73 and *passim*.

[3] Funk, p. 215. Ratzinger, *Die Volkswirtschaft in ihren sittlichen Grundlagen*, 1881, p. 231. Jäger, *Die Agrarfrage der Gegenwart*, 2nd div. 1884, pp. 275, 276.

from a moral and religious standpoint, for opposing interest and usury any more than the other forms of unearned income and their abuses. To dispute the justification of interest, implies logically, the rejection, as inadmissible, of all kinds of returns on capital, particularly of medieval feudal charges and rent for land, as these forms of income involve no personal work on the part of the proprietors. Hence it could always be maintained against the canonical prohibition of interest, that the creditor instead of lending his money might have applied it to the purchase of the means of production, thus obtaining, by virtue of his legally recognised possession of wealth, an unearned income sanctioned by the Church. The ecclesiastical position would only have been logical had the Church opposed unearned income in general; for which a Scriptural foundation might have been found in St. Paul's declaration, "If any would not work neither should he eat" (2nd Thess. iii. 10).

The more modern ecclesiastical views have determined the present constitutional practice as to unearned income. The civil and criminal codes of almost all states contain more or less severe articles against usury, but lack any effectual provisions against abuses in wage, house - rent, farm - rent, and trade contracts. It is only during the last few decades that most European states have even attempted the protection of the industrial labourer against the extreme rigour of the wages contract, by restricting

the hours of labour for women and young persons, by
fixing a normal working day for all workmen, and by
similar measures. Besides this, England has been
in advance of the other European states in the repression of rack-renting (as in the protection of the wage-
earners), by the Irish Land Acts of 1881 (44 and 45
Vict. ch. 49 [1]), though her example has not yet been
followed elsewhere. With regard to all other forms of
usury, the system of unrestricted freedom of contract
still reigns everywhere.

The ecclesiastical disapproval of money-lending has
also exerted a marked influence on the schemes of social
reform proposed by conservative and catholic writers.
While these writers take up a strongly conservative
position in relation to those private rights which ensure
unearned income to the favoured classes, they look upon
money-lending as an institution which the Legislature
may at pleasure modify, or even partially or totally
abolish. The influence of political party interests is
here peculiarly operative, for interest on loans is drawn
almost entirely by the liberal urban population, while
the unearned income of the rural conservative electors
chiefly takes the form of rent. It is a perfectly
gratuitous assumption on the part of clerical-conservative writers that this position takes higher ethical
ground than that of the bourgeois political economy,
which recognises the same justification for all forms of

---

[1] Cf. Eduard Wiss, *Das Landgesetz für Irland vom Jahre 1881*,
Leipzig, 1882.

unearned income ; it is rather the old conflict of landed
interest and money interest, which is almost identical
with the strife between the liberal and clerical-conservative parties in Germany and Austria.

The proposals of the clerical-conservative socialists
for the reform of money-lending fall into two essentially
distinct categories. The proposals of the first class are
merely formal in character; they do not touch the distribution of unearned income between the different classes
of the population, nor diminish the creditor's share, but
only aim at altering the mode of prosecution of his
claim. The second set of proposals, on the other hand,
affect the material side of money-lending by diminishing,
in one way or another, the unearned income of the lender
for the benefit of the debtor, particularly of heavily-
burdened landowners ; actually contemplating, therefore,
an increase in the unearned income of a particular class.[1]

Amongst proposals of the first order I wish specially
to emphasise the principle of yearly returns (*Renten-
princip*), which Rodbertus suggested as the basis of a
reorganisation of agricultural credit.[2] This writer regards
land merely as a perpetual capital fund producing a
permanent yearly return, but incapable of producing a
capital sum of money representing its value. Accordingly, such a piece of land cannot be mortgaged for a
capital sum, but only for an annual interest ; in other

[1] Jäger (vol. ii. p. 304) gives an account of the newest proposals for the
relief of burdens on land.

[2] Rodbertus, *Zur Erklärung und Abhilfe der heutigen Kreditnot des
Grundbesitzes*, vol. ii., 2nd ed. 1876, p. 72.

words, he would abolish the present capital mortgage and replace it by the purchase of an annuity. In the same way all valuations of land must be made in terms of annual return or rent value, not in a capital sum; for instance, the value of an estate would be not £5000, but only £250 net annual return. All transactions affecting land are to be made in terms of rent. Thus the purchaser of the land, whether the sale be by private contract or by judicial order, undertakes to pay to the vendor a certain annuity, having the option of taking over all existing charges on the estate, on account of the price, or rather the rent. Again, in the case of the division of an inheritance amongst the heirs, the shares must be paid not in capital, but in the form of an annuity payable by the holder of the land. Loans, too, could be made only in the shape of the purchase of an annuity; that is to say, the owner of the land undertakes to pay a yearly rent for the sum received in loan. Of course the parties interested might agree upon a capital sum which should be accepted by the creditors as redeeming the debt, but without such a mutual arrangement the obligation of the landowner would extend only to interest, never to capital. The land, not the owner, would be answerable for the annual debt; and in the documents the name of the estate only, not that of a personally responsible debtor, would appear.

With the object of promoting agricultural credit, the landowners of a whole state, or of a county, would be formed into a union analogous to the Prussian *Land-schaft*.[1] These unions would estimate the maximum return which might be safely expected from an estate, and would for this amount issue to the owner of an unencumbered estate land-bills (*Landrentenbriefe*) payable to bearer for fixed amounts (for instance, for a yearly rent of £5), secured on the total property of the union. These land-bills would form also a kind of land currency, being the legal tender for payment of interest. The landowner may at any time redeem all encumbrances by these land-bills, which would be negotiable, though the creditor cannot enforce such a redemption; in other words, these debts of interest would be at any time redeemable by the debtor alone.[2] For that part of the value of the estate which does not fall within the limit of certain return, estate-bills (*Guts-rentenbriefe*) may be issued, for which, however, the encumbered estate only would be security, and which therefore would not be in the nature of a land currency.

All existing capital mortgages are to be compulsorily converted into annuities,[3] excepting only such

[1] [The Prussian *Landschaften* are associations, under State license, of the landowners in each district for the purpose of founding a sound and cheap agricultural credit, by the issue of mortgage bills up to a certain quota of the value of the estates as valued by the Landschaft. At the same time, they aim at facilitating and shortening the process of transfer of real property. They were first started under Frederick the Great in 1770 for the larger landowners (the *Ritter*), but were afterwards extended to the smaller properties. In some parts of Germany they are called "Ritterschaften." See Schoenberg, *Handbuch der Polit. Oek.*—Trans.]

[2] Rodbertus, vol. ii. pp. 196, 197, 270 and *passim*.

[3] *Ibid.* pp. 251, 246.

mortgage claims as do not represent arrears of purchase-money, or inherited shares of an estate, but bona-fide loans; these may retain their original form. Rodbertus did not explain the manner of this forced conversion, but it could hardly be effected in any other way than by the issue to the mortgagee of rent-bills (*Landrentenbriefe*) to such an amount of his claim as lay within the limit of certain return, the remainder being paid to him in the estate bills (*Gutsrentenbriefe*).

Eugen Jäger[1] adopted the main principles of Rodbertus, but gives the State authorities wider powers of interference. At the request of a landlord they can reduce excessive rates of interest,[2] and fix from time to time the rate at which landowners may redeem annuity debts by a capital payment (p. 136).[3]

In a book which deals only with the theory of the right to the whole produce of labour, it is no part of my task to enter into the numerous economic and legal objections to Rodbertus's plans. Such merely formal changes could not in any case be of effectual assistance to landowners, because they do not touch the distribution of unearned income. Moreover, once ignore, in the same measure as he does, the rights of mortgagees, and his objects may be attained without any such complicated apparatus, simply by depriving actual and future creditors of the power of foreclosing.

But I would note how entirely the schemes of this

---

[1] Eugen Jäger, *Die Agrarfrage der Gegenwart*, Part 2, 1884, p. 320.
[2] *Ibid.* p. 831.   [3] *Ibid.* p. 322.

conservative radical writer are determined by the class interests of the landowners. For not agricultural lands only, but houses let at a rental, and workshops of every kind, are merely a permanent rent-fund ; again, the economic activity of persons who live on a wage or salary or a fixed income produces an annuity no more and no less than agricultural land. And unless we acquiesce in pure class legislation, all enforcible capital-indebtedness must be forbidden in these cases too, and only interest claims redeemable by the debtor be allowed. Indeed the logical conclusion of this annuity principle applied to the other classes of the people, who are certainly not less important to the State than the rural population, would be that all debts would be declared invalid which the debtor from his economic position had no prospect of being able to meet. But every competent judge will allow the impossibility of constructing a practically enforcible law on this principle.

While Rodbertus's proposals and those of his followers are restricted mainly to the mode of distribution of unearned income, the very existence of unearned income is threatened by the second group of projects (p. 135). The one-sided position of the social writers who advocate these reforms is shown by the circumstance that they strive to prejudice only that form of unearned income which is levied by monied capitalists on the rural population. The material portions of their schemes may be summarised in a State redemption of all existing mortgage claims on landed property, similar to that of the feudal charges formerly, and the prohibition, or at any rate restriction, of such encumbrance for the future.

The oldest advocate of such a disencumbrance known to me is François Vidal, who, in a paper published in 1848,[1] proposes to reconstruct the whole mortgage system by means of land banks (*banques agricoles*), to be established in every department.[2]   He makes three separate proposals for the redemption of mortgage claims. The first suggests that all mortgagees should be forced by law to accept land bank stock at 3·65 per cent in settlement of their claims, against which the debtor would pay the bank 4 per cent and a fraction for a sinking fund.[3]   According to the second, the State itself is to redeem mortgages, issuing 4 per cent stock to the creditors to the amount of their claims.[4] By his third and last proposal, Vidal suggests that the State should authorise the land banks to issue a kind of land currency, convertible only after the lapse of a given period, and bearing a low rate of interest (1 per cent), but which could be used for payment to the State and the land banks.   In this way the land banks would redeem all mortgage claims, even apparently against

----

[1] François Vidal, *Vivre en travaillant*, 1848.   The scheme was to have been included in the *Exposé de la Commission de Gouvernement pour les travailleurs* (§ 9, p. 114, note 1), to which Vidal was secretary, but this was prevented owing to the premature dissolution of the Commission.

[2] *Ibid.* p. 117.   [3] *Ibid.* pp. 147, 148.

[4] *Ibid.* pp. 148, 149.

the will of the creditors.[1] A criticism of these proposals,
which evidently greatly overestimate the economic
efficiency of the modern State, seems hardly necessary.
But we should notice that Vidal was quite innocent of
any intention to prejudice unfairly the urban population
in favour of the landowners, for his book contains well-
meant plans of benefit for all classes in the philanthropic spirit of his day.

During the last few years the idea of a disencumbrance of land, and especially of peasant properties, has
been revived in Austria, and amongst the authors who
advocate it we should mention v. Vogelsang.[2] According to his proposals, which, however, go but little into
details, the redemption would be effected at the cost of
the encumbered estates, but under Government control,
and would deal particularly with the peasant properties.
The autonomous associations which would be formed
for the purpose would first revise all claims, excluding too heavily-burdened landowners from the
benefit of the redemption; they would collect the sums
due as interest, and those due to the liquidation fund
from the debtors, and pay them over to the creditors. The
process would be lightened for the peasant proprietors
by a legal moratorium of ten years, and if necessary of
a longer duration. At the same time the mortgage
accounts would be definitely closed, and the encum-

[1] Vidal, *Vivre en travaillant*, pp. 149-158.

[2] Baron v. Vogelsang, *Die Notwendigkeit einer neuen Grundentlastung*,
1880, p. 30. Cf. also Hitze, *Kapital u. Arbeit*, 1881, p. 465 ; Stœpel,
Die freie Gesellschaft, 1881, pp. 25-47.

brance of agricultural land (except for purposes of cultivation) prohibited for the future.[1]

A detailed criticism of this scheme is hardly possible, because, according to the author's intention, it deals only with the principle of the question. But this we may say, that if the disencumbrance of peasant properties is really to be carried out solely at the cost of the encumbered owners, it can be of no material advantage to them ; for the mischief lies just in the fact that the peasant owner has to give up too large a proportion of his income to his creditors. But if his obligations are to be effectually reduced by the redemption, it can only be carried out in two ways—either by a restriction of the capital and interest claims of the creditors, or by a State contribution levied mainly from other classes of citizens.[2] Should the Legislature ever decide on a revolutionary measure of such far-reaching effect as this new land disencumbrance, it will certainly have to sanction a considerable reduction of the obligations of the peasant proprietors in one or other of these two ways.

The result of such a measure would be to increase by legal compulsion the unearned income of moderate and small landed proprietors, proportionately diminishing that of many needy persons who, by savings bank accounts, mortgages, or other investments, were interested in the rent of the peasant properties. Even a mere

[1] Cf. for a similar scheme the earlier writer, Albert Tebeldi (pseudonym for Beidtel), *Die Geldangelegenheiten Oesterreichs*, 1847, p. 257.

[2] [They may also be reduced, as under the Ashbourne Act in Ireland, by the substitution of State for individual security.—H. S. F.]

moratorium without any loss of capital or interest would bring economic ruin on a great part of the poorer urban population, and yet confer no benefit on agricultural labourers; and, on the other hand, only an insignificant fraction of the great sum of mobile capital, which is very rarely lent on the security of peasant owner-ships, would be touched. I therefore fail to see in these schemes anything but the expression of a crass egoism on the part of the peasant class, and certainly not the outcome of a Christian view of life.

Of more importance than such a redemption would be the cancelling or restriction of the power of mortgag-ing agricultural land. But such a measure, if introduced without abolishing free sale of peasant properties and equal inheritance by the children, could only lead to the establishment of *latifundia*. For on the occasion of a sale, or the division of an inheritance, the land could only pass under such circumstances to purchasers who were in a position to pay down the whole value at once ; and this is exactly the condition to lead to *latifundia*, because it would regularly exclude the children of the dead owner, and the less wealthy peasants, from acquiring landed property.

Generally, however, the conservative socialists assume free sale of allotments and equal inheritance by the children to be abolished with the closing of the mortgage accounts ; and there can be no doubt that if the Legislature were to extend to peasant proprietor-ships of a certain size the institution of entail, now confined mainly to the large properties of families of rank, the abolition or restriction (to about a third of the value) of mortgages could be practically realised. Such a measure, it is true, would ensure to the eldest son the possession of a practically unencumbered property, and with it a considerable unearned income, but all the younger children would be relegated to the ranks of the unpropertied proletariate, and that by the positive action of the State. I do not ignore the technical advantages of such close peasant proprietorships from the point of view of rational agriculture; and the great landlords may cherish the hope of finding in the holders of these peasant entails a defence of their own privileges, and in the disinherited children a cheap and willing labour supply. But all these advantages are more than compensated by the social and political drawbacks. In old times, when the unpropertied labourers bore their lot in silence, it was possible in all lightness of heart to originate or retain measures which condemn the preponderating majority of the coming generation of the rural population to an artificial indigence; to-day such a measure would be a pernicious folly. For it must not be forgotten that the unpropertied classes of all civilised countries are more and more possessed by a common *esprit de corps,* and that the time is perhaps not far distant when every labourer, whether of the hammer or the plough, will find himself in a certain antagonism to the existing legal order of things.

The annuity principle, the new disencumbrance of

agricultural land, and the abolition or restriction of the power to mortgage, are the three main principles on which are based all schemes for the relief of agriculture, in so far as they do not touch the right of inheritance. These very numerous projects, amongst which I would call special attention to those of Ratzinger,[1] Schaeffle,[2] and Preser,[3] need not therefore be discussed and described here.

---

[1] Ratzinger, *Die Volkswirtschaft in ihren sittlichen Grundlagen*, 1881, p. 345.

[2] Schaeffle, *Die Inkorporation des Hypothekarkredits*, 1883, pp. 6-9.

[3] Preser, *Die Erhaltung des Bauernstandes*, 1884, p. 324.

§ 12. MODERN AIMS

(2.) Land Nationalisation in England

In no country in the world is the whole economic life so completely dominated by that system of production, which since Louis Blanc has been called capitalism, as in England. We should therefore expect to find the socialist campaign directed mainly against so-called *mobile capital* (*mobiles Kapital*). In point of fact, the exact opposite is the case. Those socialist systems which have as yet attained any great degree of popularity in England direct their attack against landed property and rent, and concern themselves but little with profits and property in capital. As in Germany so here, the reason of this striking circumstance lies in existing political conditions. The gradual concentration of landed property in comparatively few hands has reduced the actual authority of the landlords to a negligible quantity, while repeated parliamentary reforms have materially diminished their political power. It is true, however, that in the last few years, since the first appearance of this work, these conditions have undergone considerable modifications.

Thomas Spence [1] is the oldest advocate of land nationalisation, or more properly land municipalisation, who, after the manner of modern socialists, appealed directly to the masses. He was born in 1750, at Newcastle-on-Tyne, of parents in straitened circumstances, and became a schoolmaster in his native town. On 8th November 1775 he read a paper before the Philosophical Society of Newcastle, which contained already the main principles of his system, beyond which during a forty years' agitation he never advanced.[2] As a result of this address he was forced to remove to London, where he devoted himself to the diffusion of his opinions, thereby repeatedly drawing upon himself, especially during the revolutionary wars, the persecutions of the Government. He died in September 1814, leaving an appreciable number of followers, who, if the official parliamentary papers may be credited, attempted a riot in London in 1817 for the realisation of their master's views.[3] But their plans were frustrated by the Government, and the societies of the followers of Thomas Spence were dissolved. As about this time Robert Owen began his successful agita-

---

[1] For the life and teachings of Spence, cf. Allen Davenport, *The Life, Writings, and Principles of the Spencean System: or Agrarian Equality*, London, 1836.

[2] I use here the edition of this paper published by Spence himself under the somewhat high-flown title, *The Meridian Sun of Liberty : or the whole Rights of Man displayed and most accurately defined*, London, 1796. Hyndman published a reprint of this important work (London, 1882).

[3] Cf. Report from the Committee of Secrecy, 19th February 1817 ; Second Report from the Committee of Secrecy, 20th June 1817.

tion which was supported by large means, the social
system of Spence very soon lost the foremost place in
the public attention.

The fundamental ideas of this system are as follows.
Spence assumes that the inhabitants of a country by
virtue of their right to subsistence have an equal claim
to the land and all appertaining to it.[1] The unjust
appropriation of the land by the landlords is the source
of all the misery of the working-classes, forcing them
to work and sacrifice themselves for the benefit of idle
landowners.   For this reason the ownership of land is
to be transferred to the municipality or the parish in
such a manner that all inhabitants have an equal right,
and that the municipality may not alienate their landed
property.   They need not, however, cultivate it themselves ; on the contrary, it is assumed that they will let
it at a rental to the highest bidders on a seven years'
lease, employing the rents to defray taxes and other
public expenditure, the surplus being divided in equal
shares amongst the inhabitants.   This agrarian Socialism,
on the border-line between individualistic and communal
economy, is not to extend to movable property.[2]

---

[1] *Meridian Sun*, p. 6 : "Hence it is plain that the land or the earth,
in any country or neighbourhood, with everything in or on the same, or
pertaining thereto, belongs at all times to the living inhabitants of the said
country or neighbourhood in equal manner.   For, as I said before, there
is no living but on land and its productions, consequently what we cannot
live without, we have the same property in, as in our lives."

[2] *Ibid.* pp. 8-11.   Thomas Evans, Librarian to the Society of Spencean
Philanthropists, *Christian Policy, the Salvation of the Empire*, 2nd ed.
1816, p. 25 ff.   Davenport, *Life of Thomas Spence*, p. 11.   For Charles

Spence's ideas, which were relegated for a considerable time to the background by the measures taken for their suppression by the English Government and by Robert Owen's agitation, revived again soon after the July revolution. Land nationalisation became a favourite cry with radical political reformers, who without exactly subscribing to Robert Owen's communism, were still of opinion that Catholic emancipation, parliamentary reform bills, and similar political measures were far from sufficient to cure the fearful diseases of our social organisation. Amongst these radical democrats I must mention William Carpenter [1] and James Bronterre O'Brien.[2] William Cobbett, too, preached a violent crusade against English landlordism, in a widely-read work published shortly before his death (1835) ; but far from demanding the abolition of private property in land, he only reaches the modest result that landowners have no right to arbitrarily clear their estates of the labouring population, and that in cases of necessity the poor have a claim to adequate relief, not as a matter of charity, but of right.[3]

Hall, whose proposals often coincide with those of Spence, see above p. 49.

[1] William Carpenter, *Monthly Political Magazine*, vol. i., 1831, pp. 23, 24.

[2] Cf. the work first published in a complete form after O'Brien's death, *The Rise, Progress, and Phases of Human Slavery*, 1885, p. 126.

[3] William Cobbett, *Legacy to Labourers : or what is the Right which the Lords, Baronets, and Squires have to the Lands of England*? 1835, p. 99 : "Can the landlords rightfully use their land so as to cause the natives to perish of hunger or of cold ?"

While most of the writers we have mentioned are almost completely forgotten, the idea of land nationalisation lived on in a series of theorists by whom the intellectual life of the present day has been directly influenced. John Stuart Mill is the most distinguished English writer who, from an economic and jurisprudential point of view, holds ownership of land to be less justifiable than ownership of capital. In his *Principles of Political Economy* he founds private property—curiously enough —on the right to the whole produce of labour. " The institution of property, when limited to its essential elements, consists in the recognition, in each person, of a right to the exclusive disposal of what he or she have produced by their own exertions, or received either by gift, or by fair agreement, without force or fraud, from those who produced it." [1]   Now as land, apart from improvements, is not a product of human labour, this principle of property cannot be applied to the ownership of land; [2] there is a far-reaching contrast between it and property in the actual produce of labour. So that, while the State may freely dispose of landed property and even entirely dispossess the owners, provided that they receive its whole pecuniary value in capital or annual income, Mill holds that property

[1] Mill, *Principles of Political Economy*, book ii. chap. ii. § 1.

[2] *Ibid.* book ii. chap. ii. § 5.   Similar views, as to the different equitable position of land and the improvements brought about by labour, were already upheld by Thomas Paine in a work written in 1795-96, *Agrarian Justice opposed to Agrarian Law*, Paris and London, 1797, pp. 6, 7 ; ed. 1842, pp. 5-7.

in the products of human industry can and should be
absolute.[1]

These views, which manifestly belong to the border-
land between economics and Socialism, had a very
powerful influence on later English socialists, amongst
whom I need only mention Herbert Spencer,[2] Alfred
Russel Wallace, and Henry George, who in England
promoted the movement for the nationalisation of land.
For the sake of shortness, I will confine myself more
particularly to Henry George's[3] doctrines, which would
seem to have attained the greatest influence amongst
the advocates of land nationalisation.

Henry George recognises the inborn right of every man
to a joint enjoyment of natural resources, but he limits
this right to the land, while according to him the work
of men's hands may without injustice be appropriated

---

[1] *Principles of Political Economy*, book ii. chap. ii. § 6.

[2] Herbert Spencer, *Social Statics : or the Conditions essential to Human
Happiness specified, and the first of them developed*, London, 1851, pp.
129-144. [In the later edition of the *Social Statics* (1892) the passage is
omitted. In the preface to this edition Spencer states that he has "re-
linquished some conclusions" drawn in the earlier editions. In *Principles
of Ethics*, 1893, vol. ii. Appendix B, p. 446, he develops the *practical
impossibility* of land nationalisation, with the remark that he formerly
"overlooked the foregoing considerations."—Trans.]

[3] Henry George, *Progress and Poverty : an Inquiry into the Cause of
Industrial Depressions and of Increase of Want with Increase of Wealth*,
1879 ; *Social Problems*, 1884 ; *The Land Question : What it is, and how
only it can be settled.* Among German writers the following have pronounced in favour of land nationalisation : Stamm, *Die Erlösung der
darbenden Menschheit*, 3rd ed. 1884, p. 142 ; Samter, *Das Eigentum in
seiner socialen Bedeutung*, 1879, p. 462 ; Flürscheim, *Auf friedlichem
Wege*, 1884, p. 179 ; Hertzka, *Die Gesetze der socialen Entwicklung*, 1886,
p. 156, and many others.

by the producers. " The equal right of all men to the
use of land was clear as their equal right to breathe the
air—it is a right proclaimed by the fact of their existence. For we cannot suppose that some men have a
right to be in this world and others no right." [1] But
George deduces from this right of participation not, as
did Considérant (§ 1), the right to labour, but the
competency of the State to appropriate rents. On the
other hand, he asserts, in agreement with John Stuart
Mill, the absolute right of the producer to the product
of his industry. [2]

As a consequence of this position George necessarily
regards all unearned income drawn from landed property
or rent as an injustice. Just as conservative German
socialists see in movable capital and interest the root
of all economic evil, so Henry George, on the contrary,
attributes pauperism, [3] commercial crises, [4] and the iron
law of wages, [5] to landed property and rent. He justifies
the right of the State to appropriate rents without compensating the owners, and suggests as the best means
of doing this a tax which would as far as possible absorb
all rent and would allow the abolition of all other
taxation. [6]

Seeing that George concedes the legitimacy of

---

[1] Henry George, *Progress and Poverty*, book vii. chap. i.

[2] *Ibid.* book vii. chap. i.   [3] *Ibid.* book v. chap. ii.

[4] *Ibid.* book v. chap. i. ; *Social Problems*, ed. 1884, pp. 168, 169.

[5] *Progress and Poverty*, book iii. chap. vi.; *Social Problems*, pp. 191-194.

[6] *Progress and Poverty*, book viii. chap. ii. ; *Social Problems*, pp. 274-
276 ; *The Land Question*, 3rd ed., p. 32.

property in capital he is bound to justify also the resulting unearned income, interest.[1] In contradiction to Bastiat, George does not explain interest on the ground that human labour is rendered more productive by the use of tools and the application of capital, but from the circumstance that many articles of capital, such as wine, herds, etc., increase in quantity or value through the action of natural forces, by mere effluxion of time.[2] This reacts on other forms of capital which, like tools, are not capable of any intrinsic increase of quantity or value, and which if they ceased to produce interest would never be made at all for purposes of exchange. " Thus interest springs from the power of increase which the reproductive forces of nature, and the in effect analogous capacity for exchange, give to capital. It is not an arbitrary, but a natural thing; it is not the result of a particular social organisation, but of laws of the universe which underlie society. It is therefore just." [3] And consequently the State, which may without scruple appropriate rents, has no right to touch capital and interest.

Alfred Russel Wallace, in his book on *Land Nationalisation*,[4] takes up the same one-sided position as George, and, like him, sees in rent the cause of all economic evils; [5] but his deductions from this position

[1] As to the difference between profit and interest, see *Progress and Poverty*, book iii.   [2] *Ibid.* book iii. chap. iii.

[3] *Ibid.* ; and somewhat differently, *The Land Question*, pp. 29, 30.

[4] Alfred Russel Wallace, *Land Nationalisation : its Necessity and its Aims*, 1882.   [5] *Ibid.* chap vii.

differ materially from those drawn by George. Wallace proposes a general appropriation of the land by the State, which, however, shall not include actual applications of capital (buildings, fences, drains, gates, private roads, plantations, etc.). With respect to the land itself, the State will take the place of the former owner, compensating him by a fixed sum of purchase money, or better, by granting him an annuity equal to the income he hitherto derived from the land. The improvements will remain in the hands of the former owner, constituting a tenant-right which may be sold, but not let. I cannot enter here into the details of these schemes, which are closely connected with English agrarian conditions ; but this much may be said, that the ideal to which Wallace looks makes the State the universal landlord, under whose supervision independent tenants cultivate the land on their own account.[1]

If we inquire into the intrinsic justification of these views, we must characterise them as just as one-sided and partial as those of the German conservative socialists ; for the English repudiate unearned income drawn from landed property, while the Germans direct their attack against unearned income drawn from capital, especially interest on loans and other credit contracts. Now it is quite certain that no sufficient grounds exist for submitting land and capital to perfectly different principles of equity, excluding private property in land and allowing private property in

---

[1] *Land Nationalisation*, chap. viii.

capital ; nor can I recognise as accurate the assumption
on which English socialists base their dualism, namely,
that land is a free gift of nature, while capital is the
work of men's hands. For objects of capital (machines,
tools, provisions, etc.) consist just as much as the
land of materials provided by nature, which labour only
shapes and adapts to human needs. Nor is the circumstance decisive that land is available only in a
limited quantity, because there are numerous articles
of capital which are also incapable of indefinite
increase. In no case are these differences of sufficient moment to develop perfectly separate economic
relations.

It is quite comprehensible that those English
socialists, who follow the traditions of German socialism,
should have repudiated the one-sided tendency of Mill,
Spencer, George, and Wallace. From the appearance
of H. M. Hyndman, whose first work of importance was
published in 1881,[1] may be dated the penetration of
German Socialism into England, or more truly the
revival of socialist ideas originated by earlier English
theorists. In this work Hyndman already declares
land nationalisation to be necessarily the ultimate aim
of all organic reform, but maintains that it will be of little
practical benefit to the mass of labourers unless railways
and capital are nationalised at the same time. Provisionally, however, he restricts himself to making one
or two proposals which belong rather to the radical than

---

[1] *The Text-book of Democracy : England for All*, London, 1881.

to the socialist programme, such as the abolition of primogeniture, the simplification of the transfer of real property by the introduction of registration of title, and so on.[1]

The manifesto of the Social-Democratic Federation (June 1883), of which Hyndman was the leader, contains, however, land nationalisation as the most important item of its programme;[2] the English Trades Union Congress of 1882 having in the meanwhile declared in favour of the same measure.[3] The latest manifestations of the social democratic party in England, take up unanimously the position that land and capital ownership must be treated alike, and that therefore both land and capital should be nationalised.[4] In the programme article of the Social-Democratic monthly review, *To-day*, January 1884,[4] Hyndman says that the land nationalisation demanded by George and Wallace " is the only means, combined with the simultaneous or prior nationalisation of capital, machinery, and communications, to meet our own future wants in a greater degree at home, and to avert great dangers." We may therefore say that, in spite of George's agitation, English social democracy takes the same position as French and

[1] *Text-Book of Democracy*, as above, p. 26.

[2] *Socialism made plain. Being the Social and Political Manifesto of the Social-Democratic Federation*, p. 6.

[3] Hyndman, *The Historical Basis of Socialism in England*, 1883, p. 449.

[4] *Ibid.* p. 449.   Hyndman, in *To-day*, No. 1, January 1884, p. 14. See *The Meaning of Socialism* (a new manifesto of the Social-Democratic Federation) in *To-day*, No. 13, January 1885, p. 7.

German socialists with regard to the most important question.

The socialist agitation in England has continued on the same lines during the last few years without, however, anything like as important political results as the German social democrat party has attained. The reason of this lies, doubtless, in the fact that English political parties are not as nervously apprehensive of Socialism as the German, and that the radical party, in particular, includes more and more distinctly socialist elements in its programmes. It is therefore probable that English socialists will remain in the future a comparatively small group, with the historical task of providing the existing political parties with ideas and schemes for the progressive reform of the established order; ideas and schemes, which, in the natural course of things, are at first abhorred by the other classes of the population as revolutionary and impracticable, then gradually attain toleration, approval, and practical realisation, until, finally, what was a criminal delusion comes to be treasured as one of the sacred foundations of human society.[1]

We can hardly overestimate the practical importance of the opinions we have discussed in this and the preceding chapters (§§ 11, 12). For the very reason that the attacks of many English, and of the German conservative socialists are directed only at particular forms of unearned income, they are in a high degree fitted to be

[1] Cf. Sidney Webb, *Socialism in England*, 1890, p. 19.

the object of a political agitation, which can only take account of such aims as are relatively practicable. For all that, this agitation lacks all intrinsic justification. Our present system of private property and freedom of contract, which recognises unearned income without any qualification, as well as Socialism which gives it as unqualified a repudiation, both rest on a logical philosophy ; but the social political systems which would retain our actual social conditions, reducing or abolishing the unearned income of particular classes of the population only, are fighting against reason and justice. We may, therefore, rest assured that such a social organisation could never be permanently maintained, but must lead to the ultimate extinction of private property, and all other institutions which ensure unearned income to the propertied classes.

§ 13. THE RIGHT TO THE WHOLE PRODUCE OF LABOUR, IN RELATION TO THE VARIOUS FORMS OF PROPERTY

In the preceding exposition (§§ 3-12) I have endeavoured to show how the conception of a new right—the right to the whole produce of labour—gradually developed within the socialist parties, and further what practical suggestions for its realisation have been made within the last century. My account would, however, be incomplete without a more detailed dogmatic discussion of the right to the whole produce of labour, now that the study of the historical evolution of the right has placed us on firm ground.

The right to the whole produce of labour, in the sense in which it figures in socialist theories, leads on the one hand to a criticism of existing conditions, and on the other hand to constructive proposals for their modification. In its negative critical function it repudiates as an intolerable injustice all unearned means of existence, whether in the form of rent or interest. Its positive constructive function is to allot to every labourer such a share of the value of the total production as he by his labour has produced.

Consciously or unconsciously, all socialists accept the right to the whole produce of labour in its negative function; indeed, this recognition may be taken as the distinguishing mark between the true socialist parties and the parties of mere reform, who aim at improving the actual social organisation whilst holding fast by its first principles. This repudiation of unearned income is the fundamental revolutionary conception of our time, playing the same dominant part as the idea of political equality in the French Revolution and its offshoots. Both conceptions are of a purely negative character, and contain no positive principle for the reconstruction of an economic order; but, seeing that the masses are most easily united on negations, an immense revolutionary force must be ascribed to them both.

There is no such unanimity on the positive aspect of the right to the whole produce of labour. The idea that every labourer ought to receive the entire value that he produces without any deduction in favour of land or capital,[1]—this is, in fact, a new principle of distributive justice, one of the two positive programmes (§ 1) for a new organisation of society which Socialism places at our disposal. The realisation of this principle must in the nature of things affect every legal institution, and first and foremost, the accepted forms of property.

---

[1] It stands to reason that a deduction must be made from this value for State expenses, the State being the necessary foundation of production.

We may distinguish three fundamentally different forms of property, each of which stands in a distinct relation to the right to the whole produce of labour; they are:—

(1) Private property, always united with separate usance of the objects possessed.

(2) Community of property with separate usance.

(3) Community of property with community of usance.

Under the sway of private property with separate usance (1), that is under the conditions actually dominant in almost the whole of Europe, the right to the whole produce of labour can never be realised. For under such an organisation, the means of production and consumable commodities being legally assigned to separate individuals, the owners are enabled, by virtue of their legal monopoly, to draw unearned income in the form of rent or interest.   All proposals to combine separate usance and private property with the right to the whole produce of labour, whether by a reorganisation of credit (Proudhon), or of purchase, exchange, and wage contracts (Rodbertus), are inevitably wrecked upon this legalised ascendency of landowners and capitalists.

The second of the above-mentioned forms of property, namely, common ownership with private usance, can at any rate approximately realise the right to the whole produce of labour.   We possess an example of this applied to agriculture in the Russian village com-

munity (the *Mir*). In Russia the land of the village is
the property of the community, but the separate fields
and meadows are allotted to individuals to cultivate on
their own account. "The field and meadow land of
the community is divided amongst the existing families,
but only for a time and for cultivation, not as a
possession. Originally, perhaps annually, but now to
avoid expense and inconvenience after a term of years,
the land, due allowance made for its quality, is allotted
equally amongst the different married couples of the
village."[1] Only arable and grass land, however, is
thus distributed, pasture and forest remaining for common use. Similar proposals were made, as we have
seen (§ 4), by the English socialist Hall.

It is clear that such organisations are applicable to
agriculture only, because, unlike land which is divisible
at pleasure, factories and workshops cannot be divided,
and their component parts allotted to the private use
of individuals, because their several parts, buildings,
machinery, and raw materials can only be worked in
conjunction. But a similar result may be at any rate
approximately reached in the field of industry, if the
community (State or municipal authorities) let the
workshops to labour associations who work them on
their own account. It is immaterial whether the State
makes over the workshops to the associations direct, or

---

[1] Haxthausen, *Studien über Russland*, vol. iii. (1852) p. 125. Cf. also
Keussler, *Geschichte und Kritik des bäuerlichen Gemeindebesitzes in
Russland*, vol. i. (1876) pp. 4, 5.

whether, as proposed by Louis Blanc and Lassalle, it enables them to procure workshops by the aid of State credit.

Under the domination of a system such as we have just sketched in outline, every one would be provided with the necessary instruments of production, and therefore within the community (municipality or labour association) unearned income would disappear. But the socialisation of society, if I may use such an expression, would be confined to industrial production within the community or the association, the individualist economies of the members would still exist, and exchange between them would retain the form of the present system. The economic success of every individual, or of each association, would be solely dependent on the amount of labour applied to production; but the produce of this labour must, as under our actual conditions, be made available by exchange in open market. The Russian peasant, who receives from the *Mir* as good a piece of land as his fellows, can never draw an unearned income so far as they are concerned; but he must part with such a portion of the produce as he cannot himself consume according to the forms of an individualistic system, that is by open contract and free competition.

Thus the right to the whole produce of labour is only approximately realised, even by community of property combined with separate usance. For we have already seen, in our criticism of the proposals of Louis Blanc and Lassalle (§ 10), that unearned income would disappear only as regards the internal intercourse of the associations and communities, and not in the mutual relations of these bodies; nay, that in such a state of society powerful associations or communities would probably extort just as large an unearned income as the individual owners of land and capital do now.

The third possible form of property is community of possession and community of use, and is represented in the communistic societies, of which a considerable number have for a long time existed in North America. In all these communities production is established on a thoroughly communistic basis; which, however, extends to consumption only in a minority of the communities (common residence and common meals!), the majority retaining individual family households.[1] It cannot be ignored that production, in these days of the factory system, encourages the combination of workmen; while consumption has always a certain tendency towards the isolation of individuals and families, even in a socialist organisation, so long as family life is maintained intact.

But what is the relation of this form of property (community of possession and community of use) to the right to the whole produce of labour? There can be no question that this right can be realised under such a

---

[1] According to Hinds, in his work on American communistic associations (see p. 165, note 2), common living is to be found amongst the Shakers (Hinds, p. 109) and in Oneida Community (pp. 121, 134); family life, on the other hand, in Zoar (p. 131) and Amana (p. 51) and Icaria (Constitution of Icaria, art. 78). The Oneida community, however, has been dissolved within the last few years.

communistic social organisation ; that is to say, that the
State or the municipality, as the owner of all useful commodities and instruments of production, can minutely
control the work done by every labourer, and allot him
articles of consumption in proportion to his performance.   Indeed Rodbertus, in his fourth economic letter,[1]
has actually sketched an economic society in which land
and capital belong to the State, but where, nevertheless,
each individual can only claim that which he produces
(the return of his labour).   But, at the same time, so
great are the difficulties which surround the realisation of
the right to the whole produce of labour in an absolutely
communistic order of society, that the second fundamental right, the right to subsistence, will be generally
preferred as the basis of distribution.

There is no trace of the right to the whole produce
of labour in the statutes of the North American communities, which are for the present the most important
examples of practical communism.   William Alfred
Hinds, who until quite lately was secretary of the
Oneida community in the State of New York, has given,
in his interesting work on the American communities,[2]
some of the covenants which every new member is
required to sign on joining.[3]   In them the community

---

[1] *Das Kapital*, 1884, p. 109.

[2] Hinds, *American Communities : Brief Sketches of Economy, Zoar,
Bethel, Aurora, Amana, Icaria, the Shakers, Oneida, Wallingford, and the
Brotherhood of the New Life*, Oneida, 1878.

[3] Hinds (p. 165) gives the covenants of the communities of Economy,
Zoar, and Oneida, and of the Shakers ; their contents are in essentials
identical, so I quote from that of Economy.

undertakes to supply the newcomer and his family with the necessaries of life,[1] to educate the children,[2] and support those who are incapable of working.[3]   In return the new member promises for himself and his family to further by their work, according to their ability, the good of the community.[4]

Thus the American communities lay down exactly that balance of rights and duties which I have characterised (§ 1) as the right to subsistence. There is no mention here of an understanding that each member shall receive only such an amount of necessaries as is covered by the value of the work he does; on the contrary, it is distinctly asserted that no member on leaving the community has any

---

[1] The Covenant of Economy, a community inhabited by followers of George Rapp's communistic religious sect, runs : "Art. 5. The said George Rapp and his associates agree to supply the undersigned severally with all necessaries of life, as clothing, meat, drink, lodging for themselves and for their families."

[2] Article 4 of the Covenant of Economy promises the members, not only for themselves, but also for their children and families, such instructions in church and school as may be reasonably required both for their temporal good and for their eternal felicity.   Orphans would retain their rights according to art. 5.

[3] Article 5 of the Covenant : "And this provision (that mentioned in note 1) is not limited for their days of strength ; but when any of them shall become sick, infirm, or otherwise unfit for labour, the same support and maintenance shall be allowed as before, together with such medicine, care, attendance, and consolation as their situation may reasonably demand."

[4] Article 2 of the Covenant, the new member promises "to promote the interest and welfare of the said community, not only by the labour of our hands, but also by that of our children, our families, and all others who now are, or hereafter may be, under our control."

claim to a special remuneration for the work he has done.[1]

This at the same time does away with a popular objection to Socialism, which is evidently at the root of Rodbertus's plans also,[2] namely, that in a socialist society no one would work for others, and that they must therefore fall a prey to general indolence and carelessness. As a matter of fact, the working-classes now in all larger undertakings have no interest at all in the produce of their labour, while in a socialist state they are always concerned to a certain extent. Moreover, our legal system, though it does allow employers to enforce the wages-contract, lacks any effectual protection against indolence or carelessness on the part of the workman; the dismissal of the workman being in effect the only means at the employer's disposal. But this is also ready to the hand of the socialist community (in the expulsion of the idle member), and that with far greater effect. And, in point of fact, the history of the numerous socialist experiments shows that though they generally did not make the satisfaction of wants

[1] Article 3, the members promise, "We never will claim or demand, either for ourselves, or our children, or for any belonging to us, directly or indirectly, any compensation, wages, or reward whatever for our or their labour or services rendered to the said Community, or to any member thereof, but whatever we or our families, jointly or severally, shall or may do, all shall be held and considered as a voluntary service for our brethren."

[2] Cf. *Das Kapital* (1884), pp. 115, 135, 136, and the essay, *Der Normalarbeitstag*, in Moritz Wirth's edition of the *Kleine Schriften von Rodbertus*, 1890, pp. 338, 350.

dependent on the work done, they yet hardly ever failed from the indolence of their members. The regular causes of their failure were rather unfavourable situations, want of the necessary capital, and lack of discipline.

The methods which make the workman's reward, even in a communistic society, dependent on his activity, are of two kinds. It is possible, in the first place, to take as the measure of remuneration the working time put in by the worker, without regard to the results achieved (system of time work). Or, on the other hand, the amount produced by average work in a given time (day or hour) may be taken as the unit of valuation of the work delivered by the workman, the time actually employed being of no account (system of average work). In the first case, therefore, the community, if I may use terms applying to a very different social organisation, pays its members time wages, in the second case piece wages.

I know of no socialist experiment by which the right to the whole produce of labour has been combined with a system of pure time work; though, up to a certain point, we may reckon as such a number of Fourierist communities in North America, who, in a Congress at Bloomfield (New York) on 15th May 1844, laid down the following rules for the distribution of the produce of labour. All labour is divided into necessary, useful, and pleasant, and in each group the foreman enters exactly the weekly working hours of each member,

which are then multiplied by a coefficient depending
on the individual worker and the kind of work. As a
maximum for this coefficient, the figures 30, 25, and 18
were fixed for the three groups respectively, but these
amounts applied only to the best workmen, and were
reduced in proportion to age, sex, and capability; so
that an average worker in the tailor group, which was
reckoned as a useful trade (maximum coefficient, 25),
would have, for instance, the coefficient 15 or 20, and
working sixty hours a week, would be credited with
the figures 900 or 1200. For a thousand (?) units a
workman in the Clarkson Phalanx, from which these
figures are taken, could obtain provisions to the amount
of $\frac{3}{4}$ dollar.[1]

We are clearly dealing here as little with a pure
piece-wage system as with a system of pure time-wage,
for, as we have seen, the co-efficient expresses the
difference between classes of work and efficiency of
workmen. In other words, the co-efficient is not
an expression for the work actually done, but for the
work which may be expected from the personal qualifications of a particular workman.

The second of the systems distinguished above (p.
168) takes as the measure of the workman's reward
not the time during which he really worked, but the
time in which on an average the work could be done
(system of average work). Rodbertus is a logical
advocate of this method, while Weitling upholds a

---

[1] Noyes, *History of American Socialisms* (1870), p. 276.

combination of the right to subsistence with the right
to the whole produce of labour, the nature of which we
have already explained.

Rodbertus [1] assumes a condition of things in which
the State, by means of a process of redemption, has
already possessed itself of land and capital. In these
circumstances unearned income cannot exist, but every
workman has a right to the whole value produced by
his labour,[2] subject only to a deduction for government
expenses.[3] The workman is paid for his work in labour
hours according to the system of average work, and
with the labour money he can buy goods or services in
the Government stores to the given amount ; [4] but as
the whole State is a working community, "the value of
a given quantity of produce must be estimated not
only in the normal (or average) work of the locally-
distributed workers, but also in proportion to the
average work which the total social produce in the
particular category has cost." [5] That is to say, the
average production is calculated, not from the amounts
produced by the various localities, but from the amounts
produced in the different trades all over the country.
According as the productive power of labour increases
or diminishes, the tariffs of prices of wares and

---

[1] *Das Kapital*, p. 117. Cf. the criticism of Rodbertus's proposals
in George Adler's *Rodbertus, der Begründer des wissenschaftlichen
Socialismus*, 1884, pp. 68-73 ; Böhm-Bawerk, *Kapital u. Kapitalzins*
vol. i., 1884, p. 376.

[2] Rodbertus, pp. 115-117.   [3] *Ibid.* p. 158.

[4] *Ibid.* pp. 149, 150.   [5] *Ibid.* p. 146.

services in terms of labour hours are to be periodically revised.[1]

The objections to these schemes lie on the surface. If every workman is entitled only to what he produces, what is to happen if work which is intended to be productive remains without result ; for instance, if a hailstorm destroy the harvest in a district ? Again, if the average time applied to their production be the sole measure of the value of goods, are we to pay the same number of labour hours for a poor wine as we pay for a fine one, which, by reason of the favourable aspect of the vineyard, costs no more labour to produce ? And if these questions be answered in the affirmative, as would logically follow from Rodbertus's plans, to whom are these naturally favoured products to be assigned ? Similar questions in great numbers might be opposed to these schemes, which have obviously been very insufficiently thought out by their author.

But even leaving these rather economic objections out of the question, very material scruples arise on the legal aspect. The quantity of work required on an average for the creation of a given product is in many cases extremely difficult to determine, and as a matter of fact, at Owen's Labour Bank, which was established on this system, the declaration of the workman who delivered the goods at the store was generally accepted.[2]

---

[1] Rodbertus, *Das Kapital*, p. 148.

[2] Cf. the official organ of the labour exchanges in London and Birmingham, *The Crisis*, 25th January 1834, p. 171. [But it appears from this

Moreover, the productiveness of labour not only varies greatly in the course of time by reason of discoveries and other improvements, but it is also liable to great fluctuations at a given time (especially agricultural produce, the quantity and quality of which depend so much on weather and other natural causes). To settle continuously the just prices of innumerable necessaries on such a daily shifting basis is a task which far transcends the powers of the most absolutely perfect State. And yet the solution of such a problem is vital to the realisation of the right to the whole produce of labour.

Far better thought out than the projects of Rodbertus are those put forward by William Weitling in his work, *Garantien der Harmonie und Freiheit*, published in 1842.[1] According to Weitling's proposals, society would be bound to provide every citizen with necessary and useful products and services, in return for which he is obliged to labour a certain time (six hours a day). So far Weitling recognises the right to subsistence. But beyond this every member is required to work extra time (commercial hours) to earn for himself merely agreeable products or services, the prices of these being valued in terms of labour hours which are to be exchanged for commercial hours. Like Robert Owen at an earlier date, Weitling advocates the valua-

and other passages, that the declarations of the depositors were checked by valuers.—H. S. F.]

[1] The second edition appeared in 1845, the third in 1849.

tion of all produce and services in average labour. "The time taken by a majority of capable workmen to produce any articles gives the most accurate measure of their value."[1] But the time taken to produce a ware is not to be, as with Robert Owen, the sole measure of value; on the contrary, the rarity and the demand are to be determining factors in the price, just as in our present economic system.[2]

It is clear that these proposals avoid the most glaring of the faults we found in Rodbertus. As Weitling recognises the right to subsistence with regard to necessary and useful commodities, his proposed society would not need a special State Poor Law for those incapable of work and for unsuccessful workers, an institution which would be absolutely indispensable—strangely enough—in Rodbertus's "communistic" State. Weitling also reconciles practical needs by giving an increase of price to rarer and more sought-after objects, which are produced at no greater cost of labour. But his remaining proposals, in so far as they regard the distribution of "agreeable" objects amongst the members, are open to the same criticisms as Rodbertus's schemes.

The results of this exposition may be summarised as follows. The right to the whole produce of labour is simply incompatible with our present society, which in the greater part of Europe recognises private property

---

[1] Cf. *Garantien*, 3rd edition, 1849, p. 190.

[2] *Ibid.* p. 187 ; 1st edition, p. 154. Cf. also Weitling's *Die Menschheit, wie sie ist und wie sie sein sollte*, 2nd edition, 1845, pp. 36, 37 ; the first edition appeared anonymously in 1838.

in land and capital. Under a legal system which unites common property with separate usance, the right to the whole produce of labour is the natural principle of distribution. In a communistic organisation of society, which combines common property and common usance, the realisation of this right seems at first sight not impossible; but a nearer consideration of the circumstances reveals so many impracticable difficulties that in such a community the natural basis of the distribution of wealth must be sought in the right to subsistence.

§ 14. CONCLUDING REMARKS

OF what importance for the practical aspirations of our day are these two conceptions of natural rights—the right to the whole produce of labour and the right to subsistence, which in the course of a century have gradually evolved themselves in the consciousness of the mass of the working-classes ? It can hardly be a matter of doubt that the development of a legal system completely dominated by these fundamental rights belongs to a far distant future. Many supporters of revolutionary Socialism are indeed of opinion that the working-classes need only possess themselves of political power in order to institute a socialist order of society in a relatively short time, just as a change of constitution has so often been achieved by a fortunate *coup de main.* But we must not overlook the fact that political upheavals only slightly affect the intrinsic life of nations, while the failure of a social experiment may bring a people face to face with the question of bare existence. So that the social question will not be solved like the political in one night (from the 4th to the 5th of August 1789). It is true that our existing economic system no

longer completely coincides with the actual political relations between landlords and capitalists and the working-
classes, whose influence on society has greatly increased
with their advance in education and class feeling.   But
the necessary changes will come about by a long process
of historical evolution, just as in the course of centuries
our present system undermined and decomposed the
feudal organisation, until at last only an impulse was
needed to consummate its overthrow.

But is the tendency of our social development
towards the realisation of the right to the whole produce
of labour, or of the right to subsistence?   Many signs
would seem to point to the latter.   An analogy, though
a very imperfect one, to the right to subsistence is
already recognised by many countries in the duty of
the community to provide for the poor; and, moreover,
many elements of the right to subsistence, as we
have explained it (§ 1), are in part already realised or
approaching realisation.

The right to subsistence, so far as it affects minors,
entitles them to support and education, and a part of
these claims is at present realised by compulsory education, which may be more correctly specified as the right
of children to a certain amount of intellectual culture.
Again, in the case of persons who are incapable of work,
whether from age, illness, or other infirmity, the right to
subsistence extends to periodical or permanent support—
claims which are satisfied (to a very limited degree, it is
true) by the German Imperial laws as to insurance

against illness,[1] accident,[2] infirmity, and old age.[3] Similar efforts are being made in Austria, France, and other countries.

The most difficult question remains, the realisation of the right to subsistence in the case of the labourers themselves, of the able-bodied; for one reason most difficult, because it affects enormous masses of people, and for another because in this case the recognition, in however limited a degree, of the right to subsistence implies an organic modification of traditional forms of property. So that, as far as the labourers themselves are concerned, modern legislation generally restricts itself to limiting the working time of women and children after the manner of the English Factory Acts, to supervising sanitary conditions, and in some cases to fixing a maximum of hours for factory work (normal working day). But these protecting measures extend only to industrial operatives, and not to agricultural labourers, whose position is far less favourable than that of the factory hands, partly because their interests clash with those of the larger landed proprietors, who in most parts of Europe monopolise political power, and also because agricultural labourers, owing to their local isolation, have but little social influence. But even with the factory operatives it is a matter purely of trade and sanitary police regulations, and in modern factory legisla-

[1] German Imperial law of labourers' insurance against illness, 15th June 1883.

[2] German accident insurance law, 6th July 1884.

[3] Imperial law of invalid and old-age pensions, 22nd June 1889.

tion particularly there is no trace of an approach to the right to subsistence.

This tendency does, however, lie at the root of the hitherto unsuccessful efforts to obtain recognition in our modern legislation for the *right to labour*. The essential features and the historical development of this new legal conception have been treated above (§ 1). We need only remark here that just because it connects itself with, and, in a certain sense, like our poor law, completes the existing system, the right to labour is peculiarly adapted to be a transitional measure ; while, once recognised and realised, it is just as certain to be only the starting-point of a new process of human development.

Whether the development of the social question takes the direction of the right to the whole produce of labour, or of the right to subsistence, it is in both cases imperative that the weaknesses of our present system should not be artificially increased, and the gradual transformation of our economic organisation rendered impossible by a revolutionary outbreak.

According to my view, two points must be emphasised which modern legislation has too little regarded.

In the first place, it should be recognised as a guiding principle of legislation that all measures are to be avoided which create or increase unearned income. It may, without exaggeration, be asserted that every increase on a large scale of the unearned income of the propertied classes is an impulse hurrying our present

organisation over the precipice. The cases in which
the State creates artificial unearned income are very
numerous. I need mention only the contracting of
State and municipal debts, especially for unproductive
objects, the imposition of duties on industrial and agricultural products in so far as they aim at increasing
rent and interest, the founding of sinecures and disproportionately remunerated offices, etc. Generally the
parties who propose such measures look only at their
political and economic objects, ignoring the social consequences, because the working-classes—the ultimate
producers of unearned income—are but sparely represented in parliaments.

Even more injurious than the creation of new
sources of unearned income is every transfer of rent
and interest from one class to another, so far as it is
effected by legislation or State compulsion. To this
category we must refer, as we saw before, every
redemption of mortgage burdens on landed property at
the cost of the State ; for such a process practically
amounts to depriving the urban populations of that part
of the rent which they draw as interest on mortgages,
and presenting it to the owners of agricultural estates.
It cannot be doubted that such a breach of equity,
aiming, as it does, not at the protection of honest
labour, but at assigning unearned income to one class at
the cost of another, must greatly shake the foundations
of the whole social system.

It cannot be argued that just such a breach of equity

was committed in the matter of the feudal charges, and that without materially damaging the respect for property; for mortgage burdens are not, like the feudal charges, an unearned income resting on obsolete titles, or on no title at all, and accruing to a comparatively small group of landowners. In their case rights come in question which are mostly founded on legal contracts of the last generation, and in which, in the form of mortgages, stocks, and savings bank accounts, large sections of the people are interested. It may therefore be prophesied with considerable certainty that private property would not outlive such a process of mortgage remission by a single generation.

APPENDIX I

PREFACE TO KARL MARX'S *ZUR KRITIK DER POLITISCHEN OEKONOMIE, 1859*

I HAVE arranged my critique of the system of bourgeois economics under the following heads :—

Capital, Landed Property, Wage Labour, The State, Foreign Trade, The International Market.

The three first sections contain an inquiry into the conditions of life in each of the three great classes into which modern society is divided ; the three remaining headings need no explanation. The first part of the first book deals with "capital," and contains the following chapters :—

(1) Commodities ; (2) Money, or elementary circulation ; (3) Capital in general.

The present.volume consists of the two first of these chapters. All the materials for the work lie before me in the shape of monographs written at long intervals, not for publication but for my own instruction ; and their elaboration into a connected whole, according to the above scheme, will depend on extraneous circumstances.

I have suppressed a general introduction which I had sketched, because, on reflection, any anticipation of results, the proofs of which can only be given in the sequel, seemed to me a disturbing element ; and, in any case, the reader who cares to follow me at all must reconcile himself to proceeding from particular cases to generalisations. A few remarks as to the course of my own economic studies may, perhaps, fitly replace it here.

My special study was jurisprudence, which, however, I always regarded as a subordinate branch of philosophy and history.   In the year 1842-43, as editor of the *Rhenish Gazette*, I had, for the first time, occasion to raise my voice in discussions on so-called material interests. The debates of the Rhenish *Landtag* on wood stealing and the allotment of landed property ; the official discussion into which Herr v. Schaper, then President of the Rhenish Province, entered with the *Gazette* as to the condition of the peasants of the Moselle ; and finally, debates on free trade and a protective tariff, first incited me to study economic questions.   Moreover, at that time, when willingness to "press forward" often turned the scale against scientific knowledge, an echo of French socialism and communism, slightly coloured by philosophy, began to make itself heard in the *Rhenish Gazette*.

This kind of patchwork I openly opposed, though confessing frankly, in a controversy with the *Augsburg Gazette*, that my studies did not enable me to form an independent estimate of the value of the French tendencies.   I therefore eagerly availed myself of the opportunity of retiring from the public platform to the library which was afforded me by the delusion of the managers of the *Gazette*, who hoped, by moderating the tone of their paper, to obtain the repeal of the sentence of suppression under which it lay.

The first task which I undertook for the solution of the doubts which assailed me was a critical revision of Hegel's *Jurisprudence*, of which the introduction appeared in the *Deutsch-Französische Jahrbücher*, published in Paris in 1844. My researches led to the result that economic conditions, like forms of government, cannot be explained as isolated facts, nor even as the outcome of what we call the general development of the human mind ; but that they are deeply rooted in the material conditions of life, which Hegel, following the example of French and English eighteenth-century writers, summed up in the term, *bourgeois society*. Of this *bourgeois society*, the anatomy must be sought in political economy.   Expelled from France by M. Guizot, I continued in Brussels the economic researches begun in Paris.   I will briefly formulate here the general results to which they led me, and which became the guiding thread of my studies.   Through the organised industry of their social life, men become involved in certain necessary, involuntary relations — industrial relations — which correspond to a given stage of development of their powers of material production.   The aggregate of these industrial relations forms the economic fabric of society, the concrete basis on which a political and legal superstructure is raised, and to which correspond given forms of social consciousness.   The system of industrial production determines the whole social, political, and intellectual process of life.   It is not men's consciousness which determines their being, but their social being which determines their consciousness.   At a given stage of their evolution the material powers of production of society begin to clash with existing industrial conditions, or, to use what is only the jurist's term for the same thing, with the actual laws of property, under which they had worked till then.   These laws, themselves the result of the development of the productive powers, are converted into fetters to hamper them.   A period of social revolution ensues.   With the modification of the economic foundation, the whole enormous superstructure oscillates more or less rapidly.

In observing such revolutions two things must be distinguished. The material revolution in economic industrial conditions must be determined with scientific accuracy, and must not be confused with the legal, political, religious, artistic, or philosophic—in short, the ideal—form in which the conflict presents itself to men's consciousness, and in which it is fought out. Such a revolutionary epoch can no more be judged by its own consciousness than an individual by what he thinks himself; rather must this consciousness itself be explained by the contradictions of material life, by the actual conflict between social powers of production and industrial conditions. A social formation is never submerged until all the powers of production for which it is sufficiently advanced are developed ; and a new and better industrial system never replaces the old until the material conditions necessary for its existence have been evolved by the old society itself. For this reason mankind only sets itself problems which it can solve, for closer observation will always show that the problem itself only arises when the material conditions for its solution are either actually in existence or in process of evolution. In rough outline, Asiatic, ancient, feudal, and modern systems of production may be characterised as progressive epochs of the economic evolution of society. The bourgeois industrial system is the last antagonistic phase of the social evolution ; antagonistic, not in the sense of an individual antagonism, but of an antagonism arising out of the social conditions of individual life. But the powers of production developing in the very midst of bourgeois society are, at the same time, producing the material conditions required to end the conflict. With this stage of social evolution, the bourgeois system, then, ends the preliminary period of the history of human society.

Friedrich Engels, with whom I have maintained a

constant interchange of ideas since the appearance of his
very able critical studies on the economic categories (in
the *Deutsch-Französische Jahrbücher*),[1] had arrived by other
paths at results identical with my own (cf. his *Condition of
the Working-Classes in England*) ; and when he settled in
Brussels, in the spring of 1845, we determined to work out
together the contradiction between our view and the
abstract results of German philosophy ; in fact, to close
accounts with our philosophical consciences. The plan was
carried out in the shape of a critique of philosophy after
Hegel. The manuscript, two thick octavo volumes, had been
some time at its publishèrs in Westphalia, when we were informed that altered circumstances would not allow of its being
printed. We were the more willing to abandon the manuscript to the gnawing criticism of the mice, inasmuch as we
had attained our chief object—a clear comprehension of our
own position. I will only mention two of the disconnected
works in which at that time we submitted our views
on one point or another to the public, namely, the *Manifesto of the Communist Party*, the joint work of Engels and
myself, and the *Discours sur le libre Échange* published by
me. The first scientific, though polemical, account of our
position was contained in my attack on Proudhon, *Misère
de la Philosophie*, in 1847. The revolution of February,
and my consequent forcible expulsion from Belgium,
interrupted the printing of a German essay on wage labour,
in which I had collected my addresses on this subject delivered to the German Workmen's Association of Brussels.

The editing of the *Neue Rheinische Zeitung* in '48 and
'49, and the events which ensued, interrupted my economic
studies, which could only be resumed in London in 1850.

[1] *Umrisse zu einer Kritik der National-oekonomie*, pp. 86-114, 1843-44.

The enormous mass of material for the history of political economy collected in the British Museum, the favourable position which London offers for the observation of bourgeois society, and lastly, the new period of development on which this latter appeared to enter with the discovery of the Californian and Australian gold-fields, induced me to begin again from the very beginning, and work my way critically through this new material. These studies led, partly spontaneously, to excursions into other subjects, apparently remote from my main path, and which detained me more or less. But the time at my disposal was especially curtailed by the imperative necessity, under which I laboured, of following some remunerative occupation. My collaboration in the first Anglo-American newspaper, the *New York Tribune*, which has now lasted eight years, consisting as it does but rarely in actual newspaper correspondence, forced me to spread my studies over a very wide field. At the same time, articles on noteworthy economic events in England and on the Continent formed so large a part of my contributions, that I was forced to familiarise myself with practical details which lie outside the actual field of economic science.

This sketch of the course of my studies in the province of political economy is only intended to show that my views, much as they may be criticised, and little as they may agree with the interested prejudices of the ruling classes, are at any rate the outcome of long years of conscientious research. At the gates of science, as at those of hell, the demand is made :

> Qui si convien lasciare ogni sospetto,
> Ogni viltà convien che qui sia morta.

KARL MARX.

London, *January* 1859.

APPENDIX II

BIBLIOGRAPHY OF THE ENGLISH SOCIALIST SCHOOL

I. SIX SELECTED WRITERS

II. THE SCHOOL GENERALLY: WRITINGS, SOURCES, CRITICISM

III. PERIODICAL PUBLICATIONS

IV. BIOGRAPHIES AND HISTORIES

1. SIX SELECTED WRITERS

William Godwin. 1756-1836.

1793. An Inquiry concerning Political Justice and its Influence on General Virtue and Happiness. *London.* 2 vols. 4to. Vol. I. pp. xiii. Contents (18 pp.), 378. Vol. II. Contents (21 pp.), 379-895.

[2nd edn. 2 vols. 8vo. 1796 ; 3rd edn. 1798. A reprint was issued by *James Watson*, the secularist, 1842, in two vols. 6s. 6d., or to be had in 11 parts at 6d. each. 4th edn. 1843.

Book VIII., *On Property*, was reprinted and edited by *H. S. Salt.* Cr. 8vo. 1890.]

1797. The Enquirer. Reflections on Education, Manners, and Literature. In a Series of Essays. Pp. xii. 481. *London.* 8vo.

[There was a *Dublin* edn. in the same year.]

1801. Thoughts occasioned by the perusal of *Dr. Parr's* Spital Sermon, preached at Christ Church, 15th April 1800 : being a reply to the attacks of *Dr. Parr, Mr. Mackintosh*, the author of an Essay on Population, and others. 82 pp. *London.* 8vo.

1820. Of Population. An Inquiry concerning the power of Increase in the numbers of Mankind, being an Answer to *Mr. Malthus's* Essay on that Subject. Pp. xvi. 626. *London.* 8vo.

1831. Thoughts on Man, his Nature, Productions, and Discoveries ; interspersed with some particulars respecting the Author. Pp. vi. 471. *London.* 8vo.

Charles Hall, M.D. 1745 (?)–1825 (?)

1805. The Effects of Civilisation on the People of the European States. Printed for the Author. Pp. viii. 328. *London.* 8vo. 7s.

[Reprinted by *J. M. Morgan* in the *Phœnix Library*, 1850. Pp. xvi. 252. *Charles Gilpin. London.* 12mo.]

Hall's argument in this work was controverted in *The Economist*, 1821. Vol. I. pp. 49, etc. (the first Owenite journal).

1805. Observations on the principal Conclusion in *Mr. Malthus's* Essay on Population. Printed for the Author. *London.* 8vo.

[With title-page, but paged continuously with the larger work. Pp. 325-350. Sheet Z.]

William Thompson.   1783 (?)–1833.

1824. An Inquiry into the Principles of the Distribution of Wealth most conducive to Human Happiness; applied to the newly-proposed System of Voluntary Equality of Wealth. Pp. xxiv. 600. *London.* 8vo.

[Written about 1822, acc. to *Wm. Pare.*]
A New Edition by *Wm. Pare. London,* 1850.
[Editor's Preface, few biographical details.]
A New Edition by *Wm. Pare.* Ward and Lock, 1869. 10s. 6d.

1825. Appeal of One-Half the Human Race, Women, against the Pretensions of the other Half, Men, to retain them in Political, and thence in Civil and Domestic Slavery; in reply to a Paragraph of *Mr. Mill's* celebrated "Article on Government." Pp. xvi. 222. *London.* 8vo.

1827. Labour Rewarded. The Claims of Labour and Capital conciliated: or How to secure to Labour the Whole Products of its Exertions. By one of the Idle Classes. Pp. viii. 127. *London.* 8vo.

[Dated at end, 25th December 1825. Advertisement, 1st March 1826.]

1830. Practical Directions for the Speedy and Economical Establishment of Communities, on the Principles of Mutual Co-operation, United Possessions, and Equality of Exertions, and of the means of Enjoyments. Title, Contents, pp. iv. 266, xvi. Plan. *London.* 8vo.

[Very badly printed.]

John Gray.

1825. A Lecture on Human Happiness; being the first of a Series of Lectures on the Causes of the Existing Evils of Society. To which are added the Articles of Agreement recommended by the *London Co-operative Society.* Pp. 72, 16. *London.* 8vo.

["A few hundred copies were sold immediately, and the rest were put into the hands of a London publisher, who failed shortly afterwards. The pamphlet was afterwards reprinted in *Philadelphia*, where an edition of 1000 copies was rapidly sold off."—Preface, ix. *The Social System*, 1831.]

1826. A Word of Advice to the *Orbistonians* on the principles which ought to regulate their present proceedings. 29th June 1826.

[A few hundred copies printed for distribution at *Orbiston*.]

1831. The Social System : a Treatise on the Principle of Exchange. Pp. xvi. 374. *Edin.* 8vo.

1842. An Efficient Remedy for the Distress of Nations. Pp. xvi. 224. *Edin.* and *Lond.* 8vo.

1847. The Currency Question. A Rejected Letter to *The Times*. Challenge to *The Times* to discuss the subject for the sum of 500 guineas. Pp. 24. *Edin.* and *Lond.* 12mo.

1848. Lectures on the Nature and Use of Money. Delivered before the Members of the *Edin. Phil. Inst.* during the months of February and March 1488. Pp. xvi. 344. *Edin.*

Thomas Hodgskin.

1825. Labour defended against the Claims of Capital : or the Unproductiveness of Capital proved with reference to the Present Combinations amongst Journeymen. By a Labourer. *Knight and Lacy.* 34 pp. 18mo.

1827. Popular Political Economy. Four Lectures delivered at the *London Mechanics Inst.* By *Thomas Hodgskin*, formerly Honorary Secretary to the Institution. *Charles Tait.* Pp. xxxii. 268. 24mo.

1831. Labour Defended against the Claims of Capital : or the Unproductiveness of Capital proved. By a Labourer.

2nd Ed. [with a Notice to 2nd ed. added]. *Steil.* Pp. iv. 34, 2 blank. 18mo.

[This 2nd Ed. was an acknowledgment of *Brougham's* attack in the Rights of Industry. Published 15th November 1831.]

1832. The Natural and Artificial Right of Property contrasted. A Series of Letters addressed, without permission, to *H. Brougham*, Esq., M.P., F.R.S., etc. (now the Lord Chancellor). By the Author of " Labour defended against the Claims of Capital." *B. Steil.* Pp. vi. 188. 16mo.

J. F. Bray.

1839. Labour's Wrongs and Labour's Remedy : or the Age
of Might and the Age of Right.   Pp. 216.   *Leeds.*   12mo.
[The book was also published by Heywood in 9 Nos. at 2d.
each ; and Chap. II. was afterwards published (*Leeds,* 1842) as
No. 4 of the *Labourers' Library.*]

2. THE SCHOOL GENERALLY : WRITINGS, SOURCES, CRITICISM

1756. Edmund Burke. A Vindication of Natural Society : or, a View of the Miseries and Evils arising to Mankind from every Species of Artificial Society. In a Letter to Lord ——. By a late Noble Writer. 8vo.

[2nd edn., with a new Preface, 1757. 8vo. 3rd edn. 1780. New edn. *Oxford.* 1796. Sm. 8vo.]

1858. —— The Inherent Evils of all State Government demonstrated. Being a Reprint of Edmund Burke's Celebrated Essay, entitled *A Vindication of Natural Society*, with Notes and an Appendix briefly enunciating the principles through which " Natural Society " may be gradually realised. *Holyoake and Co.* VI. 66 pp. 8vo.

[Edition by B. R. Tucker. *Boston.* 1885. 8vo.]

1768. Richard Woodward, LL.D. An Argument in support of the Right of the Poor in . . . Ireland to a National Provision . . . on the footing of Justice. *Dublin.* 8vo.

[Another edn. in 1772. *Dublin.* 8vo.
Also reprinted in 1775 as an appendix to An Address to the Public on the Expediency of a Regular Plan for the Maintenance and Government of the Poor. . . . *Dublin* printed ; *London* reprinted. 8vo.]

1775. Thomas Spence. On the Mode of Administering the Landed Estate of the Nation as a Joint-Stock Property, in Parochial Partnerships, by dividing the Rent. A Lecture read at the Philosophical Society in Newcastle, on the 8th November 1775.

[In a reprint of this Lecture in 1796, Spence says he has been publishing it in various editions for more than twenty years. The 4th edn. appeared in 1793.]

For a modern reprint see

The Nationalisation of the Land in 1775 and 1882. Being a

Lecture . . . by *Thomas Spence*, 1775. Reprinted and edited
with Notes and Introduction by *H. M. Hyndman*, 1882. 16mo.

1776. [John Cartwright.] Take Your Choice ! Representation
and Respect : Imposition and Contempt. Annual Parliaments and Liberty : Long Parliaments and Slavery. 8vo.
A 2nd enlarged edn. was published in 1777, with the title,
The Legislative Rights of the Commonalty Vindicated. 8vo.

1782. William Ogilvie, A.M. An Essay on the Right of
Property in Land, with respect to its Foundation in the
Law of Nature ; its present Establishment by the
Municipal Laws of Europe. 8vo.
[Reprinted in 1839 ; also in 1891, under the title *Birthright in
Land ;* with Biographical Notes by D. C. Macdonald.]

1789. Jeremy Bentham. An Introduction to the Principles of
Morals and Legislation. 4to.

1791. Thomas Paine. Rights of Man : being an Answer to
Mr. Burke's Attack on the French Revolution. [Part I.]
8vo.

1792. —— Rights of Man. Part II. Combining Principle and
Practice.

1792. Mary Wollstonecraft. A Vindication of the Rights of
Woman : with Strictures on Political and Moral Subjects.
Vol. I. (all published). 8vo.

[1792 (?).] The *London Corresponding Society's* Addresses and
Regulations. 8vo.

1795. The Correspondence of the *London Corresponding Society*
revised and corrected, with Explanatory Notes and a
Prefatory Letter, by the Committee of Arrangement [viz.
John Moody, John Maxwell, James Lapworth]. 8vo.

1793. Proceedings of the *Society of Friends of the People ;*
associated for the purpose of obtaining a Parliamentary
Reform, in the year 1792. 8vo.

1793. A. D. R. S. An Essay on Civil Government or Society
Restored. Translated from the Italian MS. 8vo.

1793 (?). [George Dyer.] The Complaints of the Poor People
of *England.* 12mo.
[2nd edn., corrected, altered, and much enlarged, 1793. 8vo.]

1793–94. **T. Ruggles.** The History of the Poor, their Rights, Duties, and the Laws Respecting them. 2 vols. 8vo. [New edn. 1797. 4to.]

1793. **Thomas Spence.** The Rights of Man, as exhibited in a Lecture, read at the Philosophical Society, in Newcastle, to which is now first added an interesting Conversation. 4th edn. 8vo.
[This Lecture was originally read on 8th November 1775.]

1793–95. —— Pigs' Meat : or Lessons for the Swinish Multitude. 3 vols. 12mo.
[2nd edn. 1793-95. 3 vols. 12mo. 3rd edn. 1796 (?). 3 vols. 12mo.]

1795 (?). —— The End of Oppression ; being a Dialogue between an old Mechanic and a young one, concerning the Establishment of the Rights of Man. 2nd edn. 12mo.

1795 (?). [——] A Letter from *Ralph Hodge* to his cousin *Thomas Bull*. 12mo.

1795. **Rev. David Davies.** The Case of the Labourers in Husbandry stated and considered. *Bath*, printed. *London*. 4to.

1795. **William Hodgson.** The Commonwealth of Reason. 1st and 2nd edns. 8vo.

1796. **Thomas Spence.** The Meridian Sun of Liberty. . . . A Lecture read at the Philosophical Society in Newcastle 8th November 1775. 12mo.

1796. —— A Fragment of an Ancient Prophecy. Relating, as some think, to the Present Revolutions. [Includes Resignation: an Ode to the Journeymen Shoemakers, who refused to work except their Wages were raised.] 12mo.

1796. —— The Reign of Felicity, being a Plan for civilising the Indians of North America . . . In a Coffee-house Dialogue, between a Courtier, an Esquire, a Clergyman, and a Farmer. 12mo.

1797. **Thomas Paine.** Agrarian Justice opposed to Agrarian Law, and to Agrarian Monopoly, being a Plan for meliorating the Condition of Man, by creating in every Nation a National Fund. [Three different edns. in London.] Printed *Paris*. Reprinted *London*. 8vo.
[Other edns. *Dublin*. 12mo. *Philadelphia*. 8vo. Same date.]

1797. **Thomas Spence.** The Rights of Infants: or, The Imprescriptable Right of Mothers to such a Share of the Elements as is sufficient to enable them to suckle and bring up their Young. In a Dialogue between the Aristocracy and a Mother of Children. To which are added . . . Strictures on *Paine's Agrarian Justice.* 8vo.

1798. —— The Constitution of a Perfect Commonwealth : being the French Constitution of 1793, amended, and rendered entirely conformable to the Whole Rights of Man. 2nd edn., with a Preface, showing how to study Politics. 12mo.

1798. **T. R. Malthus.** An Essay on the Principle of Population, as it affects the Future Improvement of Society : with Remarks on the Speculations of Mr. Godwin, M. Condorcet, and other writers. 8vo.
[Other edns. in 1803, 1806, 1807, 1817, 1826, etc.]

[1798.] **W. C. Proby.** Modern Philosophy and Barbarism : or, a Comparison between the Theory of *Godwin,* and the Practice of *Lycurgus.* 8vo.

1799. **Thomas Green.** An Examination of the Leading Principle of the New System of Morals, as that Principle is stated and applied in *Mr. Godwin's* Enquiry concerning Political Justice, in a Letter. . . . 2nd edn. 4to.

1803. **Thomas Spence.** Dhé 'Import'ant Tri'al ŏv *T'om'is Sp'ens.* . . . Ma 27ᵗʰ 1801 . . . 16mo.

1803. —— Dh'e K'onst'ituti'on 'ov Sp'ensoné'a, a Kŭntre ĭn Fare Lănd . . . 16mo.

1807. **Thomas Spence.** The Important Trial of *Thomas Spence,* for a Political Pamphlet, intitled, *The Restorer of Society to its Natural State,* on 27th May 1801, at Westminster Hall, before *Lord Kenyon* and a special Jury. [Includes (1) The Restorer of Society to its Natural State ; in a Series of Letters. (2) The Constitution of Spensonia, a Country in Fairy-land, situated between Utopia and Oceana. 4th edn.] 2nd edn. 12mo.

1807 (?). —— *Spence's* Songs. 12mo.

1807. —— —— Part Second. 12mo.

1809. Whole Proceedings on the Trial of an Indictment against *Joseph Hanson*, for a Conspiracy to aid the Weavers of Manchester in raising their Wages. 8vo.

1812. [**Robert Owen.**] A Statement regarding the New Lanark Establishment. 8vo.
Privately printed, *Edinburgh*.

1812. **John Melish.** Account of a Society at Harmony (twenty-five miles from Pittsburg), Pennsylvania, United States of America. Taken from "Travels . . . in 1806, 1807, 1809, 1810, and 1811. By *John Melish.*" From *The Philanthropist*, No. xx. 8vo.
[Another edn. 1820. 8vo.]

1812. [**Beaumont.**] The Beggar's Complaint against Rack-Rent Landlords, Corn Factors, Great Farmers, Monopolizers, Paper-Money Makers, and War . . . Also some Observations on the Conduct of the Luddites in reference to the Destruction of Machinery, etc. etc. By one who pities the Oppressed. 2nd edn. *Sheffield.* 12mo.
[The real date must be 1813. See p. 100 of the work.]

1813. [**Robert Owen.**] A New View of Society: or, Essays on the Principle of the Formation of the Human Character, and the Application of the Principle to Practice. By one of His Majesty's Justices of Peace for the County of Lanark. 8vo.

1813–14. —— A New View of Society: or, Essays on the Principle of the Formation of the Human Character, etc. Privately printed. 8vo.
[2nd edn. 1816. Royal 8vo. 3rd edn. 1817. Royal 8vo. 4th edn. 1818-19. Royal 8vo. Another edn. 1826. *Edinburgh.* Post 8vo. Another edn. 1837. *Manchester.* 16mo.]

1814. **P. Colquhoun.** A Treatise on the Wealth, Power, and Resources of the British Empire. 4to.
[2nd edn. 1815. 4to.]

1815. The Address and Regulations of the *Society of Spencean Philanthropists;* with an Abstract of *Spence's* Plan. 12mo.

1815. **Robert Owen.** Observations on the Effect of the Manufacturing System: with Hints for the Improvement of

those Parts of it which are most injurious to Health and
Morals. Royal 8vo.
[Another edn., privately printed, without author's name and
date. 3rd edn. 1818.]

1816. **Robert Owen.** An Address delivered to the Inhabitants
of New Lanark, on the 1st of January 1816, at the opening
of the Institution established for the Formation of Character. 1st and 2nd edns. Royal 8vo.
[3rd edn. 1817. Royal 8vo. 4th edn. 1819. Royal 8vo.]

1816. **Thomas Evans,** *Librarian to the Society of Spencean
Philanthropists.* Christian Policy, the Salvation of the
Empire. 1st and 2nd edns. 8vo.

1817. **D. Ricardo.** On the Principles of Political Economy
and Taxation. 8vo.
2nd edn. 1819. 8vo. 3rd edn. [modified by *Barton's* criticism]
1821. 8vo.

1817. **Robert Owen.** Peace on Earth . . . Development of the
Plan for the Relief of the Poor, and the Emancipation
of Mankind. 8vo.

1817. —— No. 1. New View of Society. Extracted from the
London Daily Newspapers of the 30th of July, and the
9th and 11th of August 1817. With reference to a Public
Meeting held at the City of London Tavern, on Thursday,
14th August 1817, for the consideration of a Plan to
relieve the Country from its present Distress. Broadside folio.

1817. **Robert Owen.** No. 2. New View of Society. *Mr. Owen's*
Report to the Committee of the Association for the Relief of
the manufacturing and labouring Poor . . . accompanied
by his Address delivered at the City of London Tavern,
on Thursday, 14th August 1817, at a Public Meeting expressly convened to consider a Plan to relieve the Country
from its present Distress. . . . With a Letter from *Mr.
Owen.* . . . Broadside folio.

1817. —— Article from the *The Times* of 29th May, with
Plans; published in the *Evening Mail* of 28th and 30th
May. Large folio.

1817. **Rev. John Brown.** Remarks on the Plans and Publications of *Robert Owen* of New Lanark. *Edinburgh.* 8vo.

1817. Exposition of One Principal Cause of the National Distress, particularly in Manufacturing Districts; with some Suggestions for its Removal.   8vo.

1817. **Thomas Evans.**   The Petition of *Thomas Evans*, Librarian to the *Spencean Philanthropist Society* . . . to the . . . House of Commons, 28th February 1817. 8vo.

1817 (?). —— Address of the *Society of Spencean Philanthropists* to all Mankind, on the means of promoting Liberty and Happiness.   12mo.

1817. Report from the Committee of Secrecy on Papers, which were presented (sealed up) to the House by *Lord Viscount Castlereagh*, on the 4th day· of February, by Command of His Royal Highness the Prince Regent. 19th February 1817.   34.   Folio.

1817. Second Report.   20th June 1817.   387.   Folio.

1817. Report of the Secret Committee of the *House of Lords*, appointed to take into consideration the several Papers sealed up in a Bag, and delivered by command of His Royal Highness the Prince Regent.   23rd June 1817. 399.   Folio.

> [These Reports deal with the Spencean movement and the disaffection in the manufacturing districts.   Cf. the Act 57 Geo. III. c. 3, "to empower H.M. to secure and detain such persons as H.M. shall suspect are conspiring against His Person and Government"; also the continuing Act, 57 Geo. III. c. 55.]

1817. The Present State of Public Affairs.   *Edin. Rev.*, August 1817.   [*Spencean Conspiracy*, etc.]   8vo.

1818. **Robert Owen.**   Observations on the Effect of the Manufacturing System.   3rd edn.   To which are added two Letters on the Employment of Children in Manufactories, and a Letter on the Union of Churches and Schools. Royal 8vo.

1818. **[William Allen.]**   Reply on behalf of the London Proprietors to the Address of the Inhabitants of New Lanark.   8vo.

1818. **Robert Owen.**   New View of Society.   Tracts Relative to this Subject, viz. :——

Proposals for Raising a Colledge of Industry of all
useful Trades and Husbandry.   By *John Bellers*.   (Re-
printed from the Original, published in the year 1696.)
Report to the Committee of the Association for the
Relief of the Manufacturing and Labouring Poor.
A Brief Sketch of the Society of People called Shakers.
With an Account of the Public Proceedings connected
with the subject which took place in London in July and
August 1817.   Royal 8vo.

1818. **Robert Owen.** Two Memorials on behalf of the Working Classes; the first presented to the Governments of
Europe and America, the second to the Allied Powers
assembled at . . . Aix-la-Chapelle.   8vo.

1818. Sketch of a proposed Plan for the Formation of a
National Agricultural Banking Company; with Remarks
on the Plans of *Mr. Owen*, etc.   By *Liberius Fortinbras*,
pseud.   8vo.

1818. **Morris Birkbeck.** Letters from Illinois . . . Map of the
United States . . . and . . . of English Prairie . . . By
John Melish.   Philadelphia.   12mo.
[2nd edn. *London*, 1818.   8vo.]

1818. Christian Policy in full Practice among the People
of Harmony . . . To which are subjoined, a Concise
View of the Spencean System of Agrarian Fellowship.
By a Spencean Philanthropist.   8vo.

1819. **H. G. Macnab.** The New Views of *Mr. Owen* of Lanark
impartially examined . . . Also Observations on the New
Lanark School, and on the Systems of Education of *Mr.
Owen*, of the *Rev. Dr. Bell*, and that of the New British
and Foreign System of Mutual Instruction.   8vo.

1819. [**J. Minter Morgan.**] Remarks on the Practicability of
Robert Owen's Plan to improve the Condition of the
Lower Classes.   By *Philanthropos*.   8vo.
[Reprinted in the *Phœnix Library*, 1849.]

1819. **Christianus.** *Mr. Owen's* proposed Villages for the Poor
shown to be highly favourable to Christianity; in a
Letter [signed C.] to *W. Wilberforce*.   8vo.

1819. *Mr. Owen's* Establishment at New Lanark a Failure ! !
Reprinted 1838, *q.v.*

1819. *Mr. Owen's* . . . Arrangements . . . Consistent with . . .
Political Economy . . . Three Letters . . . to *Ricardo*.
8vo.

1819. *Mr. Owen's* Plans for Relieving the National Distress.
Edin. Rev., October 1819.   8vo.

1819. Observations on the Critique, contained in the *Edinburgh Review* for October 1819, of *Mr. Owen's* Plans for
relieving the National Distress.   By a Lover of Truth.
Edinburgh.   8vo.

1820. A Vindication of *Mr. Owen's* Plan for the Relief of the
distressed Working-classes, in Reply to the misconceptions
of a Writer in No. 64 of the *Edinburgh Review*.   8vo.

1820. **John Barton.**   An Inquiry into the Causes of the Progressive Depreciation of Agricultural Labour in Modern
Times ; with Suggestions for its Remedy.   8vo.

1820. Why are we Poor ?   An Address to the Industrious
and Laborious Classes of the Community ; proving their
Distresses to arise from the Combination of the Rich and
Powerful.   By *Roger Radical*.   8vo.

1820. **Thomas Hodgskin.**   Travels in the North of Germany,
describing the present State of the Social and Political
Institutions, the Agriculture, Manufactures, etc., particularly in the Kingdom of Hanover.   *Edinburgh*.   2 vols.
8vo.

1820. **George Courtauld.**   Address to those who may be dis-
posed to remove to the United States of America, on the
Advantages of Equitable Associations of Capital and
Labour, in the Formation of Agricultural Establishments
in the Interior Country.   Including Remarks on *Mr.
Birkbeck's* Opinions upon this Subject.   *Sudbury*.   8vo.

1820. **Ellis.**   New Britain.   A Narrative of a Journey to a
Country so called by its Inhabitants, discovered in the
Vast Plain of the Missouri, in North America, and in-
habited by a People of British Origin, who live under an

Equitable System of Society, productive of peculiar Independence and Happiness. 8vo.

1821. **Robert Owen.** Report to the County of Lanark of a
Plan for relieving Public Distress. *Glasgow.* 4to.
[Reprinted in 1833.]

1821. **H. G. Macnab.** Examen impartial des nouvelles Vues
de . . . *R. Owen* et de ses Etablissemens à New Lanark
. . . Traduit de l'Anglais par *Laffon de Ladébat* . . . On
y a joint une Préface. . . . *Paris.* 8vo.

1821. **Van den Bosch.** De la Colonie de *Frederiks-Oord* et
des Moyens de subvenir aux Besoins de l'Indigence par le
Défrichement des Terres vagues et incultes. Traduction
. . . par le *Baron de Keverberg.* Avec une Préface du
Traducteur. *Gand.* 8vo.

1821. The Source and Remedy of the National Difficulties, deduced from Principles of Political Economy, in a Letter
to *Lord John Russell.* [(?) By *John Gray.*] 8vo.

1821. Report of the Committee appointed at a Meeting of
Journeymen, chiefly Printers, to take into consideration
certain Propositions submitted to them by *Mr. George
Mudie*, having for their object a System of Social Arrangement. 1st and 2nd edns. 8vo.

1822. Proceedings of the First General Meeting of the British
and Foreign Philanthropic Society for the permanent
Relief of the Labouring Classes . . . 1st June 1822.
[*Owenite.*] 8vo.

1822. Third Report of the Economical Committee of the
Practical Society. *Edinburgh.* 8vo.

1822. **Francis Place.** Illustrations and Proofs of the Principle
of Population : including an Examination of the proposed Remedies of *Mr. Malthus*, and a Reply to the
Objections of *Mr. Godwin* and others. 8vo.

1822. **Thomas Hopkins.** Economical Inquiries relative to
the Laws which regulate Rent, Profit, Wages, and the
Value of Money. 8vo.

1823. A New Theory of Moral and Social Reform ; founded
on the Principal and most general Facts of Human Nature :

or, Essays to establish a Universal Criterion of Moral Truth . . . and to found thereon a Plan of Voluntary Association and Order . . . By a Friend of the Utmost Reform. . . . 12mo.

[This work was issued with *A Prospectus of a Real Society* (1828), in paper covers, with outside title *A New Theory of Moral and Social Reform, to which is added A Prospectus of a Real Society.* Price 2s. 6d. 12mo.]

1823. **Robert Owen.** An Explanation of the Cause of the Distress which pervades the civilised Parts of the World, and of the Means whereby it may be removed.   12mo.

1823. —— Report of the Proceedings at the several Public Meetings, held in Dublin, by *R. Owen*, Esq., on the 18th March, 12th April, 19th April, and 3rd May.   Preceded by an Introductory Statement of his Opinions and Arrangements at New Lanark ; extracted from his Essays on the Formation of Human Character. *Dublin.*   8vo.

1823. A Letter containing some Observations on the delusive Nature of the System proposed by *R. Owen* . . . for the Amelioration of the Condition of the People of Ireland, as developed by him at the Public Meetings held . . . in Dublin 18th March. *Dublin.*   8vo.

1823. **Wm. M'Gavin.** Letters on *Mr. Owen's* New System. [7 Letters in 4 Parts.]   From the *Glasgow Chronicle.* 12mo.

1823. **Jasper Beatson.** An Examination of *Mr. Owen's* Plans for relieving Distress, removing Discontent, and "Re-creating the Character of Man." *Glasgow.*   8vo.

1823. A Report of the British and Foreign Philanthropic Society, with other Statements and Calculations explanatory of *Mr. Owen's* Plan for the Relief of Ireland, etc. *Dublin.*   8vo.

1823. **Robert Jackson,** M.D.   An Outline of Hints for the Political Organisation and Moral Training of the Human Race. *Stockton.*   8vo.

1823. **Abram Combe.** Observations on the Old and New Views, and their Effects on the Conduct of Individuals, as manifested in the Proceedings of the *Edinburgh Christian Instructor* and *Mr. Owen.*   *Edinburgh.*   8vo.

1823. **Abram Combe**. An Address to the Conductors of the Periodical Press upon the Causes of Religious and Political Disputes, with Remarks on the . . . Definition of certain Words and Terms which have been often the Subject of Controversy. *Edinburgh.* 8vo.

1823. —— Metaphorical Sketches of the Old and New Systems, with Opinions on interesting Subjects. *Edinburgh.* 24mo.

[1823.] **W. Longson**. The Impolicy, Injustice, Oppression. and Commercial Evils resulting from the Combination Law exposed, with a View of obtaining its Repeal ; s. sh. [*Manchester.*] Folio.

1824. **Abram Combe**. The Religious Creed of the New System, with an Explanatory Catechism . . . *Edinburgh.* 8vo.

1824. A Diagram illustrative of the Formation of the Human Character suggested by *Mr. Owen's* Development of a New View of Society. 4to.

1824. **Robert Dale Owen**. An Outline of the System of Education at New Lanark. *Glasgow.* 8vo.

1824. **W. M'Gavin**. The Fundamental Principles of the *New Lanark* System exposed. *Glasgow.* 12mo.

1824. **George White**. A Digest of the Minutes of Evidence taken before the Committee on Artizans and Machinery 8vo.

1824. —— A Digest of all the Laws at present in existence respecting Masters and Workpeople : with Observations thereon . . . 8vo.

1824. First, Second, Third, Fourth, Fifth, and Sixth Reports from Select Committee on Artizans and Machinery. 23rd Feb., 10th March, 23rd March, 5th April, 15th April, 21st May, 1824. [51.] Folio.

1824. Report from the Select Committee on Labourers' Wages 4*th June.* [392.] Folio.

1824. **Alex. B. Richmond**. Narrative of the Condition of the Manufacturing Population . . . State Trials in Scotland. 8vo.

1825. **Robert Owen.** Discourses on a New System of Society, as delivered in the Hall of Representatives of the United States, etc. *Louisville.* 8vo.
[Another edn. *London.* 8vo.]

1825. —— The First Discourse on a New System of Society; as delivered in the Hall of Representatives, at Washington . . . on the 25th of February 1825. *Manchester* and *London.* 16mo.

1825. A Letter to *R. Owen* (Author of Two Discourses on a New System of Society). By a Son of the Mist. *Philadelphia.* 8vo.

1825. **James Hamilton.** Owenism rendered consistent with our Civil and Religious Institutions : or, A Mode of forming Societies for Mutual Benefit on rational and practical Principles, without the Assistance of the Rich . . . 12mo.

1825. **Edward King.** An Essay on the Creation and Advantages of a Cultural and Commercial triform Stock, as a Counter-fund to the National Debt, and for the unlimited Investment of Capital at £5 per cent per annum, etc. 8vo.

1825. **Abram Combe.** The Sphere for Joint-Stock Companies : or, The way to increase the Value of Land, Capital, and Labour. With an Account of the Establishment at Orbiston, in Lanarkshire. Pp. iv. 70. *Edinburgh.* 8vo.

1825 (?). Prospectus of a Plan for establishing an Institution on *Mr. Owen's* System in the Middle Ward of the County of Lanark. 4to.

1825. Articles of Agreement for the Formation of a Community on Principles of Mutual Co-operation, within Fifty Miles of London. Drawn up and recommended by the *London Co-operative Society.* [See 1826.] 8vo.

1825. **William Hebert.** A Visit to the Colony of Harmony, in Indiana . . . recently purchased by *Mr. Owen* for the Establishment of a Society of Mutual Co-operation and Community of Property . . . Also a Sketch for the Formation of a Co-operative Society. 8vo.

1825 (?). A Bird's-eye View of one of the New Communities at Harmony, in the State of Indiana, North America. An Association of 2000 Persons, formed on the Principles advocated by *Robert Owen*. Folio.

1825. Report . . . *Select Committee* on Combination Laws . . . 5 Geo. IV. c. 95. 16*th June*. [437.] Folio.
Evidence . . . *Select Committee* on Combination Laws . . . 5 Geo. IV. c. 95. 8*th* and 24*th June*. [417.] Folio.
Report . . . *Select Committee* on Combination Laws . . . 5 Geo. IV. c. 95 [Lords]. 30*th June*. [209.] Folio.
Minutes of Evidence . . . *Select Committee* on Combination Laws . . . 5 Geo. IV. c. 95 [Lords]. 30*th June*. [210.] Folio.

1825. **F[rancis] P[lace]**. Observations on *Mr. Huskisson's* Speech on the Laws relating to Combinations of Workmen. 8vo.

1825. **Francis Jeffrey**. Combinations of Workmen. Substance of the Speech of *Francis Jeffrey*, Esq., upon introducing the Toast, "Freedom of Labour . . .," at the Public Dinner at Edinburgh to *Joseph Hume*, Esq., M.P., on 18th November 1825. *Edinburgh*. 8vo.

1826. **L. Byllesby**. Observations on the Sources and Effects of Unequal Wealth. *New York*.

1826. Articles of Agreement (drawn up and recommended by the *London Co-operative Society*) for the Formation of a Community within Fifty Miles of London, on Principles of Mutual Co-operation. 8vo.
[This is a 2nd edn. of the Articles published as an Appendix to *Gray's* Lecture in 1825. A very curious *Owenite* creed of 4 pp. is appended.]

1826. **[J. Minter Morgan.]** The Revolt of the Bees. 8vo.
[2nd edn., 1828. 3rd edn., 1839. 4th edn. (*Phœnix Library*), 1849.]

[1826.] **William Allen**. Colonies at Home : or, The Means for rendering the industrious Labourer independent of Parish Relief. *Lindfield*. 8vo.
[Another edn. *Lindfield*, 1828. 8vo. New edn., with Additions (Appendix to the 6th edn.). *Lindfield*, 1832. 8vo.]

1826. **William Hale.** An Address to the Manufacturers of the United Kingdom, stating the Causes which have led to the unparalleled Calamities of our Manufacturing Poor; and a Proposal of a Remedy. 8vo.

1826–27. **William Cobbett.** COBBETT'S POOR MAN'S FRIEND: or, Useful Information and Advice for the Working Classes; in a Series of Letters, addressed to the Working Classes of Preston. Nos. I.-V., 1st August 1826 to 18th October 1827. 12mo.

> In another edn. [1827 (?)] Nos. I. and V., which relate to election-eering and personal matters, are omitted, and the title becomes—
> COBBETT'S POOR MAN'S FRIEND: or, a Defence of the Rights of those who do the Work and fight the Battles. Nos. I., II., III., 26th August to 13th October 1826. 12mo.
> ["This is my *favourite* work. I bestowed more labour upon it than upon any large volume that I ever wrote" (*Cobbett*, in an advertisement).]
> A New Edition, all five numbers, in 1829, with the title—
> THE POOR MAN'S FRIEND: or, Essays on the Rights and Duties of the Poor. 12mo.

1827. **Robert Owen.** An Address to the Agriculturists, Mechanics, and Manufacturers, both Masters and Opera-tives, of Great Britain. Published in the *Sphynx* news-paper, September 1827. [Advocates labour notes.]

1827. Address delivered by *R. Owen*, at a Public Meeting . . . in . . . Philadelphia. . . . To which is added an Exposition of the pecuniary Transactions between that Gentleman and *W. M'Clure*. *Philadelphia.* 8vo.

1827. An Address to the Members of Trade Societies, and to the Working Classes generally; being an Exposition of the Relative Situation, Condition, and Future Prospects of Working People in the United States of America. Together with a Suggestion and Outlines of a Plan. . . . By a Fellow Labourer.

> Reprinted from the original edn. published in *Philadelphia*. *London.* 12mo. Another edn. in 1833.

1827. **Paul Brown.** Twelve Months in New Harmony; presenting a faithful Account of the principal Occurrences which have taken place there within that Period; inter-spersed with Remarks. *Cincinnati.* 8vo.

1827. Outlines of a Plan for an Agricultural Model School. *Cork.* 8vo.

1827. **J. C. Ross.** An Examination of Opinions maintained in the *Essay on the Principles of Population*, by Malthus ; and in the *Elements of Political Economy*, by Ricardo ; with some Remarks in Reply to Sir J. Graham's *Address to the Land-Owners.* 2 Vols. 8vo.

1827. Plain and Practical Observations on the Use and Application of Machinery, in a Series of Letters, drawn up at the Request of the Frome Committee ; addressed, by permission, to the Right Honourable *George Canning* . . . *Bath.* 8vo.

1828. Prospectus of a Real Society, regulated but by One Law : a System highly to be desired, and easily practicable, by all rationally and sincerely honest, independent, and religious Persons . . . 12mo.

1828. **Robert Owen.** Memorial . . . to the Mexican Republic and to the Government . . . of Coahuila and Texas. 4to.

1828. **Charles Fourier.** Political Economy made Easy. A Sketch . . . presented to the *London Co - operative Society* . . . 8vo.

1828. **Joseph Rey.** Lettres sur le systême de la co-opération mutuelle et de la communauté de tous les biens, d'après le plan de *M. Owen. Paris, Santelet,* 1828. 18mo.
  [The greater part of these letters had appeared in *Le Producteur.*]

1828. [**George Green Ward.**] London Co-operative Trading Fund Association. Address and Report. 8vo.

1828. The Nature and Reasons of Co-operation, addressed to the Working Classes. 8vo.

1828. An Account of the Poor-Colonies, and Agricultural Work-houses, of the Benevolent Society of Holland. By a Member of the Highland Society of Scotland. *Edinburgh.* 12mo.

1828. **T. R. Edmonds.** Practical, Moral, and Political Economy : or, The Government, Religion, and Institutions most conducive to Individual Happiness and to National Power. 8vo.

1828. **Thomas Hopkins.** On Rent of Land and its Influence on Subsistence and Population : with Observations on the Operating Causes of the Condition of the Labouring Classes in various Countries. 8vo.

1828. The Emigrants of the Nineteenth Century. *Knight and Lacey. London.*

1828 (?). The New Political Economy of the Honey-Bee. By the Author of *The Emigrants.*

1828 (?). A Letter to *Sir James Graham. Poole and Edwards, Ave-Maria-Lane.*

1829. **Samuel Read.** Political Economy : An Inquiry into the Natural Grounds of Right to Vendible Property, or Wealth. 8vo.

1829. **Robert Owen.** Opening Speech, and his Reply to the *Rev. Alex. Campbell* in the recent public Discussion in Cincinnati, to prove that the Principles of all Religions are erroneous . . . also, *Mr. Owen's* Memorial to the Republic of Mexico, and a Narrative of the Proceedings thereon, etc. *Cincinnati.* 8vo.

1829. Debate on the Evidences of Christianity ; containing an Examination of the " Social System " . . . held in the City of Cincinnati . . . 1829, between *R. Owen* . . . and *A. Campbell* . . . Reported by *C. H. Sims.* With An Appendix written by the Parties. [Edited by *A. Campbell.*] 2 Vols. *Bethany, Va.* 8vo.
[Another edn. *London,* 1839. 8vo. 5th edn. 1854.]

1829. **Frances Wright.** Course of Popular Lectures, as delivered . . . in . . . the United States. With Three Addresses, on various public occasions. And a Reply to the Charges against the French Reformers of 1789. *New York.* 12mo.
[Another edn. *Lond.* [1830 (?)]. 8vo. 4th edn. (Supplement : Course of Lectures, etc.). *New York,* 1831. 12mo. (The Supplement is in 4 parts separately paged.) Another edn. *New York,* 1853. 12mo.]

1829. **Frances Wright.** Introductory Address, delivered at the opening of the Hall of Science ; New York . . . 1829. *New York.* 8vo.

1829. —— A Lecture on existing Evils and their Remedy ; as delivered in the Arch Street Theatre, to the Citizens of Philadelphia, 2nd June 1829. *New York.* 8vo.

1829. **Robert Southey.** *Sir Thomas More :* or, Colloquies on the Progress and Prospects of Society. 2 Vols. 8vo.
[2nd edn. 1831. 2 Vols. 8vo.]

1829. A Letter to the *Rev. W. L. Pope*, Tunbridge Wells, in reply to Two Sermons preached by him on the Subject of Co-operation. *Tunbridge Wells.* 8vo.

1829 (?). A Diagram relating to the Formation of the Human Character. [*Circa* 1829.]

1830. **Thomas Cooper.** Lectures on the Elements of Political Economy. 2nd edn. *Columbia.* 8vo.
[This edn. contains a reference to the English Socialists. The 1st edn. appeared in 1826. The date on the title of this edn., 1829, appears to be a mistake. Cf. p. 349.]

1830. **Robert Owen.** The New Religion : or, Religion founded on the immutable Laws of the Universe, contrasted with all Religions founded on Human Testimony, as developed in a Public Lecture . . . at the *London Tavern*, 20th October 1830. 8vo.

1830. —— Second Lecture on the New Religion . . . at the *Freemasons' Hall*, 15th December 1830. 8vo.

1830. —— Lectures on an Entire New State of Society ; comprehending an Analysis of British Society, relative to the Production and Distribution of Wealth. 8vo.
[Appended is an Address delivered at *New Harmony*, 13th April 1828.]

1830. —— The Addresses of *Robert Owen* (as published in the London Journals), preparatory to the Developement of a Practical Plan for the Relief of all Classes, without Injury to any. 8vo.

1830. **Robert Dale Owen.** Moral Physiology : or, A Brief and Plain Treatise on the Population Question. [1st edn.] *New York.* 8vo.
3rd edn. *New York.* 1831. 12mo. 8th edn. *Lond.*, 1832.

8vo. 10th edn. *Lond.*, 1833. 8vo. [Another edn.] *Lond.*
1840. 8vo. Another edn. *Lond.*, 1852. 12mo. New edn.
Lond. [1870]. 8vo.

1830. **Frances Wright.** An Address to Young Mechanics, as
delivered in the Hall of Science, 13th June 1830. *New
York.* 8vo.

1830. —— Address to the Industrious Classes. (*Popular
Tracts*, No. 3.) 12mo.

1830. —— *Frances Wright* unmasked by her own Pen. Explanatory Notes, respecting the Nature and Objects of the
Institution of Nashoba. 3rd edn. *New York.* 8vo.

1830. **J. Minter Morgan.** Letter to the *Bishop of London.*
1st and 2nd edns. 8vo.
[Condition of the People.]

1830. [——] The Reproof of Brutus. 8vo.
[Metrical Critique of Economists.]

1830. —— Address . . . at the Theatre of the Mechanics'
Institution, on Thursday, 6th May 1830. 8vo.
[Paged 37-58 incl.]

1830. **John Evelyn.** Co-operation : an Address to the
Labouring Classes, on the Plans to be pursued and the
Errors to be avoided in conducting Trading Unions.
8vo.
[Against Community.]

[1830.] An Address to the Working Classes of Walsall on the
Objects and Advantages of Societies or Working Unions,
established on the Principles of Mutual Co-operation.
By a Member of the *Walsall Co-operative Society.*

1830. **Stedman Whitwell.** Description of an Architectural
Model from a Design by *Stedman Whitwell*, Esq., for a
Community upon a Principle of United Interests, as
advocated by *Robert Owen*, Esq. 8vo.

1830. **Henry Clissold.** Prospectus of a Central, National
Institution of Home Colonies ; designed to instruct and
employ distressed, unoccupied Poor, on waste Lands, in
Spade Husbandry. 8vo.

1830. Words of Wisdom, addressed to the Working Classes . . .
To which are subjoined the Laws of the *First Armagh
Co-operative Society. Armagh.* 8vo.

1830. Co-operation: Dialogue between a Shoemaker and a
Tailor. 2nd edn. 8vo.

[1830.] The Rise, Course, and Uses of Co-operation explained,
in an Essay addressed to the *First Norwich Co-operative
Society.*

1830. **Henry M'Cormac**, M.D.   An Appeal on Behalf of the
Poor . . . [advocates Co-operative Communities]. *Belfast.*
8vo.

1830. —— Plan for the Relief of the Unemployed Poor.
Belfast. 12mo.

1830. —— On the Best Means of Improving the Moral and
Physical Condition of the Working Classes. Being an
Address . . . *Belfast Mechanics' Institute.* 8vo.

1830. . . . Resolutions passed at the Meeting at Birmingham,
held on the 25th January 1830, together with the
Declaration, Rules, and Regulations of the *Political Union
for the Protection of Public Rights. Birmingham.* 12mo.

1830–31. **Wm. Carpenter.**   Political Letters and Pamphlets,
published for the avowed purpose of trying with the
Government the Question of Law . . . Stamp Duty of
Fourpence . . . Report of the Editor's Trial . . . 4to.

1831. **William Maclure.**   Opinions on Various Subjects,
dedicated to the Industrious Producers. 2 Vols. *New
Harmony, Indiana.* 8vo.

1831. **Charles Fourier.**   Piéges et Charlatanisme des deux
sectes *Saint-Simon* et *Owen*, qui promettent l'association
et le progrès . . . *Paris.* 8vo.

1830. **Robert Owen.**   Outline of the Rational System of
Society. 4to.
> [Another edn. was published, without date, as No. 7 of Social
> Tracts. 8vo.]

1831. **Charles Rosser.**   Thoughts on the New Era of Society.
A Lecture delivered at *Mr. Owen's* Institution, Burton
Street, Burton Crescent, on Sunday Evening, 13th
November 1831, on the New Era of Society. 1st and
2nd edns. 8vo.

1831. **John Doherty.** A Letter to the Members of the National Association for the Protection of Labour. *Manchester.* 16mo.

1831 (?). **Dr. King.** An Important Address to Trade Unions. [Co-operation, etc.] *Manchester.* 12mo.

1831. The Drones and Bees : a Fable [in Hudibrastic verse— feeble]. *Edinburgh.* 8vo.

1831 (?). Equality. [A Poem written against *Wilmot Horton's* Views.] 16mo.

1831. The Working - Man's Companion. The Results of Machinery, namely, cheap Production and increased Employment, exhibited ; being an Address to the Working-Men of the United Kingdom. [By *Henry Brougham* (?).] 24mo.

1831. —— The Rights of Industry, addressed to the Working-Men of the United Kingdom. By the Author of The Results of Machinery [*Henry Brougham* (?)]. I. Capital and Labour. 24mo.
[Attacks Hodgskin.]

1831. **Lord Brougham** (?). A short Address to Workmen on Combinations to raise Wages. 8vo.

1831. The Ten-Hour Bill. Report of the Proceedings of the Great Leeds Meeting to petition Parliament in favour of *Mr. Sadler's* Bill for the Regulation of the Hours of Children's Labour in Factories, held on Monday, 9th January 1831. 12mo.

1831. The New Charter. Humbly addressed to the King and both Houses of Parliament ; proposed as the Basis of a Constitution for the Government of Great Britain and Ireland, and as a Substitute for the Reform Bill rejected by the Lords. 8vo.

1832. **T. Wayland.** National Advancement and Happiness considered in Reference to the Equalisation of Property, and the Formation of Communities. 8vo.

1832. **William Carpenter.** Proceedings of the Third Co-operative Congress, held in London, and composed of Delegates from the Co-operative Societies of Great Britain and Ireland, on the 23rd of April 1832 . . . 12mo.

1832. On Co-operation. This Article appeared in the *Monthly Repository*, July 1832, as a Review of the Report of the third Co-operative Congress, held in London, April 1832 ; and other Works. 8vo.

1832. The Proceedings of the Fourth Co-operative Congress, held in Liverpool on Monday, 1st October 1832, and by adjournment on each of the five following days. Reported, by Order of Congress, by Mr. W. Pare of Birmingham. *Salford, Manchester.*

1832. **W. Cameron.** An Address to the Disciples of *Robert Owen*, on the Importance and Necessity of speedily establishing a Bond of Union of mutual Interests, for gradually carrying into Operation the New Science of Society.

1832 (?). **Charles Rosser.** Thoughts on the Progress and Prospects of Man, and on the New Era of Society. (Third Edition.) 1st Lecture. 8vo.

1832. Table-Talk on the State of Society, Competition, and Co-operation, Labour and Capital,—Morals and Religion. *Birmingham.* 8vo.

1832. The Rights of Morality : An Essay on the Present State of Society—Moral, Political, and Physical—in England ; with the best means of providing for the poor and those classes of operatives who may be suddenly thrown out of their regular employments by the substitution of new inventions. By *Junius Redivivus.* 24mo.
> 2nd edn., with additions, 1833. 24mo.
> [In the 2nd edn. the title reads, The Producing Man's Companion : an Essay, etc.]

1832. The Reformer's Library. No. IV. The Rights of Nations : A Treatise on Representative Government, Despotism, and Reform. . . . By the Author of " The Reformer's Catechism," and " The People's Charter." 16mo.

1832. The Articles of the Philosophical Co-operative Land Association. 2d.

1832. **Ed. Ducpétiaux.** Économie Politique. De la Situation actuelle des Colonies Agricoles en Belgique. 8vo.

1832. **J. Thimbleby**. Monadelphia : or, The Formation of a New System of Society, without the intervention of a Circulating Medium. *Barnet.* 16mo.

1832. The Circulating Medium, and the Present mode of Exchange, the Cause of Increasing Distress among the Productive Classes—Labour Exchange Banks the only Remedy. By a Co-operator. 8vo.

1832. EQUITABLE LABOR EXCHANGE, *Gray's Inn Road, London :* *Established* 1832. *First Branch, Blackfriars Road.*
To the Storekeeper of the Exchange. No. [——],
1st December 1832.
Deliver to the Bearer Exchange Stores to the Value of Two HOURS, by order of

ROBERT OWEN, *Governor.*
S. AUSTIN, *Director.*
TWO HOURS. [——], *Secretary.*

1833. NATIONAL EQUITABLE LABOUR EXCHANGE. *Birmingham Branch.* Established 1833. No. 3966. 22nd July 1833.
Deliver to the Bearer Exchange Stores to the Value of ONE HOUR by order of

ROBERT OWEN, *Governor.*
BENJAMIN WOOLFIELD, *Director.*
ONE HOUR. CHARLES WEST, *Secretary.*
Charlotte Street, Rathbone Place, London.

1833. **Robert Owen.** Lectures on Charity ; as delivered by *Robert Owen*, at the Institution of New Lanark. Nos. 1-6 (complete).
(The first number was published 7th September 1833.)
1833. —— The Address of *Robert Owen*, delivered at the Great Public Meeting, held at the National Equitable Labour Exchange, Charlotte Street, Fitzroy Square, on 1st May 1833, denouncing the Old System of the World, and announcing the commencement of the New.

1833. **Rev. J. E. Smith.** Lecture on a Christian Community . . . at the Surry Institution. 8vo.

1833. An Address to the Members of Trade Unions, and to the Working Classes generally ; being an Exposition of the relative Situation, Condition, and Future Prospects of Working People in England, Scotland, and Ireland. Together with a . . . Plan. By a Journeyman Bootmaker. [Cf. 1827.] 12mo.

1833. **Seth Luther.** An Address to the Working Men of New England, on the State of Education, and on the Condition of the Producing Classes in Europe and America. With particular Reference to the Effect of Manufacturing (as now conducted) on the Health and Happiness of the Poor. 2nd edn. *New York.* 8vo.

1833. **William Day.** An Inquiry into the Poor Laws and Surplus Labour, and their mutual Reaction; with a Postscript . . . on the Corn Laws. 2nd edn. 8vo.

1833. **Fontana** and **Prati.** St. Simonism in London. On the Pretended Community of Goods, or the Organization of Industry. On the Pretended Community of Women, or Matrimony and Divorce. 8vo.
[2nd edn. 1834. 8vo.]

1833. [**E. G. Wakefield.**] England and America : a Comparison of the Social and Political State of both Nations. 2 Vols. 8vo.
[Another edn. *New York,* 1834. Royal 8vo.]

1833. **Cobbett** and **Fielden.** Rights of Industry [eight-hours' day]. Extracted from *Cobbett's Register,* 14th *December* 1833. 12mo.

1833. Catechism of the *Society for Promoting National Regeneration . . . Bradford.* 8vo.
[Also printed at *Hanley.*]

1833. **Rev. John Bowes.** The Right Use of Money Scripturally stated : or an Answer to the Question, "Ought Christians to Save Money ?" . . . *Dundee.* 12mo.

1833. [**Jane Marcet.**] John Hopkins's Notions on Political Economy. By the Author of *Conversations on Chemistry.* 12mo.
[3rd edn. 1834. 12mo.]

1834. **William Thomson.** The Age of Harmony : or, A New System of Social Economy, eminently calculated to

Improve the Circumstances of the oppressed, enslaved,
and impoverished portion of the People of Great Britain
and Ireland. Addressed to the Industrious Classes. 2nd
edn. *Glasgow.* 12mo.

[William Thomson edited the *Chartist Circular*, the first No.
of which appeared 28th September 1839. *Glasgow.* Folio.]

1834. **Henri de St. Simon.** New Christianity. Translated
from the original French, by the Rev. J. E. Smith, A.M.
12mo.

[Curious coloured plate of a St. Simonian female.]

1834. **[J. Minter Morgan.]** Hampden in the Nineteenth
Century : or, Colloquies on the Errors and Improvement
of Society. 2 Vols. 8vo.

1837. [——] Colloquies on Religion and Religious Education ;
being a Supplement to *Hampden in the Nineteenth
Century.* 8vo.

1834. The Synopsis of the Rational System of Society. 1d.
B. D. Cousins. London.

1834. Public Warnings against *Owen* and Others. No. 1,
4th January 1834. No. 2, 1st February 1834. ½d. each.
D. Murray and Co. London.

1834. **W. Hawkes Smith.** The Errors of the Social System ;
being an Essay on wasted, unproductive, and redundant
Labour. *Birmingham.* 16mo.

1834. **Rev. G. Redford.** A Sermon, by the *Rev. G. Redford,*
A.M., of Angel Street Chapel, Worcester, on the Doctrines
of *Robert Owen,* etc., to which is appended a Reply, by
the *Rev. J. E. Smith,* A.M. of London. *B. D. Cousins.
London.*

1834. An Essay, in Answer to the Question, Whether does
the Principle of Competition, with separate Individual
Interests, or, the Principle of United Exertions, with
combined and equal Interests, form the most secure Basis
for the Formation of Society ? [*Owenite.*] 16mo.

1834. The Charter of the Rights of Humanity of the Productive Classes. Passed at a great Public Meeting of
the Producers of Wealth and Knowledge, held in the
Metropolis on 12th February 1834.

Published for the Social Missionary Union by *B. D. Cousins.*

1834. **William Cobbett.** Legacy to Labourers : or, What is the Right which the Lords, Baronets, and Squires, have to the Lands of England ? In Six Letters, addressed to the Working People of England. With a Dedication to Sir Robert Peel. 12mo.
[3rd edn. 1835. 24mo. New edn. 1872. 8vo.]

1834. *National Regeneration* :—
    1. Letter from Mr. Fitton to Mr. Fielden.
    2. Letter from Mr. Fielden to Mr. Fitton.
    3. Letter from Mr. Holt to Mr. Fielden.
Which Letters contain a development of all the Principles and all the Views connected with this important contemplated change in the Manufacturing Affairs of the Country. 8vo.

1834. **Rev. G. S. Bull.** Mr. Bull and the *Regeneration Society.* To the . . . *Leeds Times.* 16mo.

1834. Rules and Regulations of the Grand National Consolidated Trades' Union of Great Britain and Ireland : Instituted for the purpose of the more effectually enabling the Working Classes to secure, protect, and establish the Rights of Industry. 8vo.

1834. **F. K. S.** Trades' Triumphant, or Unions' Jubilee !! A Plan for the Consolidation of Popular Power, and Restoring to the People their long lost Rights. 8vo.

1834. **Richard Oastler.** A few Words to the Friends and Enemies of Trades Unions. *Huddersfield.* 8vo.

1834. **Kerr.** Kerr's Exposition of Legislative Tyranny and Defence of the Trades Unions. *Belfast.* 8vo.

1834. **John Maxwell,** M.P. Manual Labour *versus* Machinery ; exemplified in a Speech on moving for a Committee of Parliamentary Inquiry into the Condition of Half a Million Hand-loom Weavers in reference to the estabment of Local Guilds of Trade ; with an Appendix. 8vo.

1834. Public Warnings against *Owen* and Others, including the Account of the Illness and Death of *Henry Hurdis Hudson,* Esq. (Containing the monthly numbers complete, 3d. Any of the numbers may be had separate for ½d. each.)

1835. Social Bible. Laws and Regulations of the Association of all Classes of all Nations. Social Hymns for the use of the Friends of the Rational System of Society. *Manchester.* 24mo.

1835. **Graham Hutchison.** An Exposition of the erroneous Nature of *Mr. Owen's* Plan. *Glasgow.* 8vo.

[1835 (?).] The Power of the People : or, the Way to Wealth, Prosperity, and Peace ; a Social Pamphlet, showing how the Working Classes may become possessed of immense landed Estates, in an amazing short time, without doing Injury to any Party . . . *Leeds.* Sm. 8vo.

1836. **Robert Owen.** The Book of the New Moral World. Part I. 8vo.
[Parts II. and III. 1842. IV. VII. 1844.]
1836. —— Manual of the *Association of all Classes of all Nations.* Founded 1st May 1835. No. 2. 12mo.

1836. **Robert Dale Owen.** Address on the Hopes and Destinies of the Human Species. 16mo.
[Another print without title-page, 1836.]
1836 (?). —— Address on Free Inquiry. To which is added Aphorisms on Free Inquiry, by *Thomas Jefferson,* one of the Presidents of the United States. 16mo.

1836. **Phillippo Buonarroti.** History of *Babeuf's* Conspiracy for Equality ; with the Author's Reflections . . . Translated by *Bronterre.* 12mo.

1836. **J. A. Etzler.** The Paradise within the Reach of all Men, without Labour, by Powers of Nature and Machinery. An Address to all intelligent Men. 2 Parts. *London.* 12mo.
[This is a reprint of the original *Pittsburgh* edn. There was a 2nd English edn. 1842. 8vo.]

1836. **John Fielden,** M.P. The Curse of the Factory System : or, A Short Account of the Origin of Factory Cruelties . . . 8vo.

1836. **Henry, Lord Brougham**(?). Lectures on Political Economy read in MS. at the Mechanics' Institution, Glasgow, in the summer of 1835. (Private.) *Glasgow.* Royal 8vo.

1837. **Robert Owen.** The Book of the New Moral World, containing the Rational System of Society, founded on demonstrable Facts, developing the Constitution and Laws of Human Nature and of Society. *Glasgow.* 12mo.

1837. —— Propositions Fondamentales du Système Social, de la Communauté des Biens, fondé sur les Lois de la Nature humaine. Traduit de l'Anglais, par *Jules Gay. Paris.* 8vo.

1837. —— Six Lectures delivered in Manchester previously to the Discussion between *Mr. Robert Owen* and the *Rev. J. H. Roebuck.* And an Address delivered at the Annual Congress of the "Association of all Classes of all Nations." *Manchester.* 16mo.

Another edn. [1839]. *Manchester.* 8vo.

1837. Public Discussion, between *Robert Owen*, late of New Lanark, and the *Rev. J. H. Roebuck*, of Manchester. Revised and authorised by the Speakers. *Manchester.* 12mo.

[1837.] **Samuel Bower.** Competition in Peril: or, The Present Position of the Owenites, or Rationalists, considered ; together with *Miss Martineau's* Account of Communities in America. 12mo.

1837. **John Finch.** The Millennium. The Wisdom of Jesus, and the Foolery of Sectarianism, in Twelve Letters. *Liverpool.* 8vo.

1837 (?). **G. A. Fleming.** A Vindication of the Principles of the Rational System of Society, as proposed by *Robert Owen.* A Lecture delivered in Bywater's Large Room, Peter Street, Manchester. *Manchester.* 16mo.

1837. **Edward Hancock.** *Robert Owen's* Community System, etc., and the horrid Doings of the St. Simonians, in Beaumont Square, Mile End. A new Sect from France. Letter Third. 12mo.

[1837 (?).] **C. J. Haslam.** A Defence of the Social Principles delivered in the Social Institution, Salford. Being an Answer to a Lecture . . . by the *Rev J. R. Beard.* 2nd edn. *Manchester.* 12mo.

1837 (?). —— The Necessity of a Change : or, An Exposure of the Errors and Evils of the present Arrangement of Society ;

with a partial Development of a new Arrangement. 2nd edn. *Manchester* and *London*. 12mo.

1837. **Lloyd Jones.** A Reply to *Mr. R. Carlile's* Objections to the five fundamental Facts as laid down by *Mr. Owen.* An Answer to a Lecture delivered in his Chapel, 27th November 1837. *Manchester.* 16mo.

1837. [**J. Minter Morgan.**] Colloquies on Religion and Religious Education. Being a Supplement to "*Hampden in the Nineteenth Century.*" [See 1834.] 8vo.

1838. [**Francis Place.**] The People's Charter; being the Outline of an Act to provide for the Just Representation of the People of G.B. in the Commons House of Parliament: embracing the principles of Universal Suffrage, No Property Qualification, Annual Parliaments, Equal Representation, Payment of Members, and Vote by Ballot. 36 pp. 12mo.
First issue, 8th May 1838; an amended version, September 1838.

1838. On the Possibility of limiting Populousness. By Marcus. 8vo.

1838. **William Atkinson.** The State of the Science of Political Economy investigated, wherein is shown the defective character of the Arguments advanced for elucidating the Laws of the Formation of Wealth. 8vo.

1838. **Robert Owen.** A Development of the Origin and Effects of Moral Evil, and of the Principles and Practices of Moral Good. *Manchester.* 12mo.

1838. —— A Dialogue, in Three Parts, between the Founder of "The Association of all Classes of all Nations" and a Stranger desirous of being accurately informed respecting its Origin and Objects. *Manchester.* 12mo.

[1838.] —— Synopsis of a Course of Four Lectures [to be delivered at Sunderland] . . . explanatory of the Errors and Evils of . . . Society, etc. [4 pp.] *Birmingham.* 8vo.

1838. —— The Catechism of the New Moral World. 2nd edn. *Leeds.* 16mo.

[1838 (?).] —— Lectures I.-VI. Delivered at the Institution of

New Lanark, upon the 13th Chapter of the 1st Epistle to
the Corinthians. [See 1833.]   12mo.

1838. **Robert Owen.** The Marriage System of the New Moral
World ; with a faint Outline of the present very irrational
System ; as developed in a Course of Ten Lectures. [1834.]
Leeds.   12mo.

[1838.] **Mrs. Frances Morrison.** The Influence of the present
Marriage System upon the Character and Interests of
Females contrasted with that proposed by *Robert Owen,*
Esq.   A Lecture delivered in the Social Institution,
Shudehill, Manchester, on Sunday Evening, 2nd Sep-
tember 1838.   *Manchester.*   8vo.

1838 (?). Exposition of *Mr. Owen's* Views on the Marriage
Question.   *Coventry.*   8vo. leaflet.

1838. Proceedings of the Third Congress of the *Association of
all Classes of all Nations,* and the First of the *National
Community Friendly Society,* . . . held in Manchester, in
May 1838.   6d.   12mo.
    [Fourth Congress, 1839, 1s. ; Fifth Congress, 248 pp., 1840,
    1s. 6d. ; Sixth Congress, 216 pp., 1841, 1s. 6d. ; Seventh Con-
    gress, 208 pp., 1842, 1s. 6d.]

1838. An Analysis of Human Nature : a Lecture delivered
to the Members and Friends of the *Association of all
Classes of all Nations.*   By one of the honorary Mission-
aries to that Institution.   *Leeds.*   16mo.

1838. Socialism examined.   Report of a Public Discussion which
took place at Huddersfield, on . . . 13th, 14th, and 15th
December 1837, between the *Rev. T. Dalton* and *Mr.
Lloyd Jones* upon " The Five Fundamental Facts, and the
Twenty Laws of Human Nature, as found in the Book of
the New Moral World, written by *R. Owen,* Esq." *Manchester.*   8vo.

1838. Authentic Report of the Discussion at the Guildhall,
Bath, on the Evenings of the 13th, 14th, and 15th of
September 1838, between *Mr. Alexander Campbell,* Social
Missionary, and *Mr. W. P. Roberts,* on the Principles of
Mr. Robert Owen.   *Bath.*   8vo.

1838. *Mr. Owen's* Establishment at New Lanark a Failure!! as proved by *Edward Baines*, Esq., M.P., and other Gentlemen, deputed with him by the Parishioners of Leeds, to visit and inspect that Establishment, and Report thereon. *Leeds.* 16mo.

[Report signed by *Edward Baines, Robert Oastler*, and *John Cawood*, and dated *Leeds*, 14th September 1819.]

1838. **Samuel Bower.** The Peopling of Utopia : or, The Sufficiency of Socialism for Human Happiness ; being a Comparison of the Social and Radical Schemes. *Bradford.* 8vo.

1838. —— A Sequel to the Peopling of Utopia ; being an Exposition of the Social Scheme. *Bradford.* 12mo.

1838. **John Garwood.** The Force of Circumstance, a Poem [dedicated to *Robert Owen*]. *Birmingham.* 12mo.

1838. **John Eustace Giles.** Socialism, as a religious Theory, irrational and absurd. The First of Three Lectures on Socialism (as propounded by *Robert Owen* and others), delivered in the Baptist Chapel, South Parade, Leeds, 23rd September 1838. 8vo.

1838. **Joshua Hobson.** Socialism as it is ! Lectures in Reply to the Fallacies and Misrepresentations of the *Rev. John Eustace Giles*, Baptist Minister, Leeds. *Leeds.* 12mo.

1838. **John Hanson.** The Dissection of Owenism dissected : or, A Socialist's Answer to *Mr. Frederick R. Lees's* Pamphlet entitled, "*A Calm Examination of the Fundamental Principles of Robert Owen's misnamed Rational System.*" *Leeds.* 12mo.

1838. **Frederic Richard Lees.** The Owenite Anatomized. An Analysis of the Blunders and Fallacies put forth by one *John Hanson*, in his mis-styled Answer to "*Owenism Dissected.*" *Leeds.* 12mo.

1838. **John Hanson.** The Owenite's Escape from the Charnel-House, and Blow-up of the Ostamachia ; being a Reply to *Mr. F. R. Lees's* Pamphlet entitled, "*The Owenite Anatomized.*" *Manchester.* 16mo.

1838. **H. Howells Horton.** Community the only Salvation for Man. A Lecture delivered in the Social Institution, Salford, . . . 16th September 1838. *Manchester, London,* and *Hulme.* 16mo.

1838. **W. Hawkes Smith.** Letters on the State and Prospects of Society. *Birmingham.* 12mo.

1838. **Robert Cooper.** A Contrast between the New Moral World and the Old Immoral World. A Lecture delivered in the Social Institution, Salford. *Hulme.* 16mo.

1838. **Henry L. Knight.** A Lecture on Irresponsibility, Moral and Natural. . . . *Hulme.* 16mo.

1839. An Address to the Socialists, Radicals, Trades Unions, and the Working Classes generally. . . . Together with a Suggestion and Outlines of a Plan, by which they may gradually and indefinitely improve their Condition. By a Working Man. 12mo.

1839. Combinations Defended : being a Commentary upon . . . the Evidence given before the Parliamentary Committee of Inquiry into Combinations of Employers and Workmen. . . . By the London Trades Combinations Committee. 8vo.

1839. The People's Charter ; and Old England for Ever. 16th thousand. 8vo.

[1839 (?).] **Charles Knowlton,** M.D. Fruits of Philosophy : or, The Private Companion of Young Married People. Price 6d. *Heywood. Manchester.*

[1839 (?).] **H. H. Horton.** Community the Only Salvation for Man. Price 2d. *Heywood. Manchester.*

1839. **R. Buchanan.** The Religion of Past and Present Society founded upon a False Principle. . . . A Lecture . . . Social Institution, Salford . . . 10th March 1839. 12mo.

1839. **T. H. Hudson.** Christian Socialism, explained and enforced, and compared with Infidel Fellowship, especially, as propounded by *Robert Owen,* Esq., and his Disciples. 24mo.

[1839.] **Wm. Martin.** An Exposure of a New System of Irreligion, which is . . . called " *The New Moral World*," promulgated by *R. Owen*, Esq.

1839. **F. R. Lees.** Owenism Dissected. An Examination of the fundamental Principles put forth by *Mr. R. Owen* as the basis of his "*New Moral World.*" . . . 2nd edn. *Leeds.* 12mo.

1839. **Joseph Mather.** Socialism Exposed : or, " The Book of the New Moral World " examined and brought to the Test of Fact and Experience. 2nd edn. 12mo.
[Another edn., abridged.] *Religious Tract Society.* 1840 (?). 12mo.]

1839 (?). An Exposure of *Joseph Mather's* Pamphlet entitled " *Socialism Exposed : or, The Book of the New Moral World examined, and brought to the Test of Fact and Experience.*" By a Lover of practical Christianity. *Bilston.* 16mo.

1839. **George Pearson,** B.D. The Progress and Tendencies of Socialism. A Sermon preached before the University of Cambridge, 17th November 1839. *Cambridge.* 8vo.

1839. **Robert Owen.** Robert Owen on Marriage, Religion, and Private Property, and on the Necessity of immediately carrying into Practice the " Rational System of Society," to prevent the Evils of a Physical Revolution. Large broadside folio.

1839. —— Temple of Free Enquiry. A Report of the Proceedings consequent on laying the Foundation Stone of the Manchester Hall of Science, with an Address by *R. O.* (Reprinted from No. 43, New Series, of the *New Moral World.*) *Leeds.* 16mo.

1839. *Robert Owen* at New Lanark: with a Variety of interesting Anecdotes. . . . By one formerly a Teacher at New Lanark. *Manchester.* 8vo.

1839. **Robert Dale Owen.** Wealth and Misery. Price 2d. *Heywood. Manchester.* 12mo.
[Written 1830.]
[Another edn. Sm. 8vo. 1846 ; date on wrapper given as 1845.]

1839. An Address, with Rules and Regulations of the Social United Interest Colonisation Society.   1d.   *Heywood. Manchester.*   12mo.

1839. Report of the Discussion between *Robert Owen*, Esq., and the *Rev. Wm. Legg*, B.A., which took place in the Town Hall, Reading, 5th and 6th March 1839, on *Mr. Owen's* New Views of Society.   8vo.

1839. Report of the Discussion betwixt *Mr. Troup*, Editor of the *Montrose Review* . . . and *Mr. Lloyd Jones*, of Glasgow . . . in the Watt Institution Hall, Dundee . . . on the Propositions : 1. That Socialism is Atheistical ; and, 2. That Atheism is incredible and absurd.   *Dundee.*   8vo.

1839. [**Charles Bray.**] Socialism.   A Commentary on the Public Discussion on the Subjects of Necessity and Responsibility, between *Mr. A. Campbell*, Social Missionary, and the *Rev. J. T. Bannister*, of Coventry.   By *Jonathan Jonathan* [i.e. *C. Bray*].   *Coventry.*   8vo.

1839. **W. Hawkes Smith.**   Letters on Social Science.   *Birmingham.*   12mo.

1839. The Socialist ; a Tale of Philosophical Religion . . . *Leeds.* 12mo.

1839. The "Fundamental Facts" of Socialism examined.   12mo.

1839. **John Eustace Giles.**   Socialism, in its moral tendencies, compared with Christianity.   The Second of Three Lectures on Socialism (as propounded by *Robert Owen* and others), delivered in the Baptist Chapel, South Parade, Leeds, 30th September 1838.   8vo.

1839. Socialism.   [What is Socialism ?]   12mo.
   [Another edn.   *S.P.C.K.*   1840.]

1839. The Constitution and Laws of the *Universal Community Society.* . . . Established 1st May 1835.   16mo.

1839. Proceedings of the Fourth Congress of the *Association of all Classes of all Nations*, and the Second of the *National Community Friendly Society*, . . . now united and called the *Universal Community Society of Rational Religionists*, held in Birmingham, in May 1839.   *Birmingham.* 12mo.

1839. **J. R. Beard.** The Religion of Jesus Christ defended from the Assaults of Owenism. In Nine Lectures. *London* and *Manchester.* 12mo.

1840. **Wm. Atkinson.** Principles of Political Economy : or, The Laws of the Formation of National Wealth, developed by means of the Christian Law of Government; being the Substance of a Case delivered to the Hand-loom Weavers Commission. 8vo.
[Another edn. With an Introduction by *H. Greeley. New York.* 1843. 8vo.]

1840. **Thomas Carlyle.** Chartism. 1st and 2nd edns. 12mo.
[Another 2nd edn. in 1842. 12mo.]

1840. **William Lovett** and **John Collins.** Chartism ; a New Organisation of the People, embracing a Plan for the Education and Improvement of the People, politically and socially . . . Written in Warwick Gaol. 12mo.

1840. **Thomas Hunt.** Chartism, Trades Unionism, and Socialism ; or, Which is the best calculated to produce permanent relief to the Working Classes ? A Dialogue. 12mo.

1840. A View of a Community as proposed by *Robert Owen.* 8d. plain, and 1s. coloured.

1840. **Albert Brisbane.** Social Destiny of Man : or, Association and Reorganisation of Industry. [*Fourierite.*] *Philadelphia.* 8vo.

1840. **W. King.** Four Letters on the Workings of Money Capital ; showing its present inefficient and limited Agency for Commercial and Social Purposes. [Labour Exchanges.] 12mo.

1840. **John Minter Morgan.** Religion and Crime ; or the Distresses of the People, and the Remedies. 2nd edn. Enlarged royal 8vo. 3rd edn. Royal 8vo.
[Another edn. 1849. 12mo.]

1840 (?). **T. S. Mackintosh.** An Inquiry into the Nature of Responsibility, as deduced from Savage Justice, Civil Justice, and Social Justice ; with some Remarks upon the Doctrine of Irresponsibility, as taught by *Jesus Christ* and *Robert Owen.* . . . *Birmingham.* 12mo.

[1840 (?).] **Robert Dale Owen**. Address on the Hopes and Destinies of the Human Species. 8vo.

1840. **Robert Owen**. Socialism : or, The Rational System of Society. Three Lectures delivered in the Mechanics' Institution, London, in reply to the misrepresentations on the subject of Socialism in Parliament, in the Press, and in the Pulpit. First Lecture. *Effingham Wilson.* 8vo.

1840 (?). —— The Catechism of the New Moral World. *Manchester.* 8vo.

1840. —— Outline of the Rational System of Society, founded on Demonstrable Facts, developing the Constitution and Laws of Human Nature. Authorised edn. 6th edn. revised and amended. *Leeds.* 24mo.
[Another edn. *Manchester.* 12mo. 1840 (?).]

1840. —— Manifesto of *Robert Owen*, the Discoverer, Founder, and Promulgator of the Rational System of Society, and of the Rational Religion. To which is added a Preface and an Appendix. 5th edn. 8vo.

1840 (?). —— Social Bible : or, An Outline of the Rational System of Society. *Manchester* and *London.* 24mo.
[It appeared in 24mo or 48mo in 1835 with Social Hymns.]

1840. Social Hymns for the use of the Friends of the Rational System of Society. 2nd edn. *Leeds.* 24mo.

1840. **Robert Owen**. Lectures on the Marriages of the Priesthood of the Old Immoral World, delivered in the year 1835, before the passing of the New Marriage Act. 4th edn. .With an Appendix, containing the Marriage System of the New Moral World. *Leeds.* 12mo.

1840. Report of the Discussion on Marriage, as advocated by *Robert Owen*, between *L. Jones* and *J. Bowes*, in the Queen's Theatre, Christian Street, Liverpool, on Wednesday, 27th May 1840.
Reprinted from the *Liverpool Journal. Liverpool.* 18mo.

1840. Socialism. Report of a Public Discussion, between *John Bowes* . . . and *Lloyd Jones* . . . in the Queen's Theatre, Christian Street, Liverpool, 5th, 6th, 7th, and 27th May 1840, " On the Five Facts, and Constitution and Laws

of Human Nature, as propounded by *Robert Owen*" . . .
Also on the Marriage System of Socialism. *Liverpool.*
12mo.

1840. **Charles Southwell.** Socialism made Easy : or, A Plain
Exposition of *Mr. Owen's* views. 16mo.

1840. **Sir William Boyd.** A Patriot's Fourth Letter to the
British People ; more particularly addressed to the
Operatives of the United Kingdom, on the Advantages
and Importance of a System of Co-operative Residence.
2nd edn. 8vo.

1840. **John Dunlop.** The Universal Tendency to Association
in Mankind. 16mo.

1840. **C. S. Eyre.** A Few Words on Socialism. *Coventry.*
12mo.

1840. Why am I a Socialist ? or, A Defence of Social Principles
in a Letter to a Christian Friend. By *Ethnicus. Glasgow.* 16mo.

1840. The Elements of Socialism. Compiled by the Author of
" An Essay towards a Science of Consciousness." *Birmingham.* 16mo.

1840 (?). **John Green.** Caspar Hauser : or, The Power of Ex-
ternal Circumstances exhibited in forming the Human
Character, with Remarks. *Manchester* and *London.*
16mo.

1840. **A. Shepheard.** Christianity and Socialism examined,
compared, and contrasted, as means for promoting Human
Improvement and Happiness. 12mo.

1840. **Samuel Bower.** Competition in Peril : or, The Present
Position of the Owenites, or Rationalists, considered ;
together with *Miss Martineau's* Account of Communities
in America. 16mo.

1840. Social Tracts.
No. 1. Observations upon Political and Social Reform . . .
No. 2. A Calculation of the Result of the Industry of
500 Persons of the Working Classes.

No. 3. The Pull all Together.   To the Sober and Industrious of the Working Classes.   16mo.

1840. **James N. Bailey.**   *Social Reformers' Cabinet Library.*
J. Hobson. Leeds.   8vo.
Preliminary Discourse on the Objects, Pleasures, and Ad-
vantages of the Science of Society . . .
Lycurgus and the Spartans historically considered.   Illus-
trating the Power of Circumstances in forming the
Human Character.
The Pleasures and Advantages of Literature and Philo-
sophy briefly illustrated and explained.
A Brief Survey of the Principal Features of Character
exhibited by the Aborigines of North America, illus-
trating the aphorism of the Socialists, " Man is the
Creature of Circumstances."   2 Parts.

1840. Reprint of the Debate in the Lords on Socialism, from
The Times of 5th February, 1840.   For the especial use
of the members of the *Universal Community Society of*
Rational Religionists. Leeds.   4to.
[An extra issue of the *New Moral World* for 15th February
1840.]

1840. **Henry Phillpotts, Bishop of Exeter.**   Progress of
Socialism.   The *Bishop of Exeter's* Speech in the House
of Lords, Friday, 24th January 1840.   8vo.

1840. —— Socialism.   Second Speech of the *Bishop of Exeter*,
in the House of Lords, 4th February 1840.   8vo.

1840. **Rev. J. E. Smith.**   The Little Book : or, Momentous
Crisis of 1840 ; in which the *Bishop of Exeter* and *Robert*
Owen are weighed in the Two Scales of One Balance. . . .
12mo.

1840. **W. N.**   Statement submitted to the Most Noble The
Marquis of Normanby . . . relative to the Principles
and Objects of the *Universal Community Society of*
Rational Religionists.   8vo.

1840. Letter to the Right Honourable *Lord Viscount Mel-*
bourne, on the Presentation of *Mr. Robert Owen* at Court.
By a Member of the Church of England.   8vo.

1840. *Lord Melbourne's* Chain unlinked, with which he intended, through *Robert Owen*, to fetter the People for ever. *Nottingham.* 12mo.

1840 (?). A true Exposure of the noted *Robert Owen!* concerning his late Visit to the Queen . . . With an Account of the Victims of Seduction, and his new Moral Marriage System. 12mo.

1840. Lectures against Socialism . . . under the direction of the . . . *London City Mission.* 8vo.—
1. *Rev. R. Ainslie.* Is there a God ?
2. *Rev. J. Garwood.* Is the Bible of Divine Authority ?
3. *Hon. and Rev. B. W. Noel.* What is Christianity ?
4. *Rev. H. Hughes.* What am I ?
5. *Isaac Taylor.* Am I Responsible, and to Whom ?
6. *Rev. G. Cubitt.* The Power of Circumstances.
7. *Rev. Dr. Hoppus.* The Province of Reason.
8. *R. Matthews.* Is Marriage worth Perpetuating ?
9. *Rev. R. Ainslie.* An Examination of Socialism, with . . . Letter to the *Marquis of Normanby.*

1840. A Budget for the Socialists, containing the Female Socialist : or, The Wise Wench of Whitechapel; a Doggrel, worthy of its Burthen. Also the Lord's Prayer of the Owenites . . . and . . . the Gospel according to *Saint Owen.* 12mo.

1840. **R. Whalley.** A Philosophical Refutation of the Theories of *Robert Owen* and his Followers. . . . Together with an Exposure of the remaining Inconsistencies . . . and Visionary Promises. *Manchester.* 8vo.

1840 (?). **Thomas Powell.** Socialism in its own Colours. A plain Tract on Socialism for Working Men. 12mo.

1840. **Robert Philip.** The Royal Marriage ; an Antidote to Socialism and Oxfordism : A Sermon preached at Maberly Chapel, 12th February 1840. 8vo.

[1840.] **B. Grant.** An Apology for Christianity : or, Modern Infidelity examined in a Series of Letters to *R. Owen* [in Answer to his *Manifesto,* etc.]. 8vo.

1840. **John H. Carter.** The Voice of the Past ; written in Defence of Christianity and the Constitution of England,

with Suggestions on the probable Progress of Society . . .
being a Reply to the Manifesto of *Mr. Robert Owen.*   2nd
edn.   *Portsea.*   8vo.

1840 (?). **John Brindley.**   Tract I. A Refutation of *Robert
Owen's* Fundamental Principles of Socialism ; proving the
free Agency of Man.   *Birmingham.*   12mo.
    [Tract II. Containing a Reply to *Mr. Owen's* Attack upon
    Marriage.
        Tract III. Proving the Existence of a Supreme Intelligent
    Being, whom we call God, as opposed to the Atheistical Principles
    of Socialism.
        Tract IV. In Answer to *Mr. Owen's* Denunciation of all
    Religion.]

[1840.] —— A Reply to *R. Owen's* Fundamental Principles of
Socialism [in his "*Book of the New Moral World*"], etc.
2nd edn.   *Birmingham.*   12mo.

[1840.] —— The Immoralities of Socialism.   Being an Exposure of *Mr. Owen's* Attack upon Marriage [in his "*Book
of the New Moral World*"].   *Birmingham.*   12mo.

1840. **John Bowes.**   The "Social Beasts" : or, An Exposure of
the Principles of *Robert Owen* and the Socialists.   *Liverpool.*   12mo.

1840 (?). An Examination of *Mr. R. Owen's* Doctrines of Human
Responsibility, and the Influence of Circumstances in the
Formation of Character.   8vo.

[1840.] **Rev. J. H. Roebuck.**   Lectures.   No. I. Anti-Owenism.
12mo.

1840. **Joseph Barker.**   The Abominations of Socialism Exposed, in Reply to the *Gateshead Observer.*   *Newcastle.*
12mo.

1840. **H. G. Wright.**   Marriage and its Sanctions.   2nd Thousand.   8vo.

1840. **William Taunton.**   A Record of Facts ; being an Exposure of the wilful Falsehoods and mean Hypocrisy of
the *Rev. John Sibree* of Coventry.   Also an account of
the cowardly conduct of the *Rev. T. Milner* of North-
ampton.   16mo.

1840. A Concise and Convincing Argument against Socialism :
or, The Pernicious Principles of *R. Owen* completely exposed. By a Clerical Gentleman. 12mo.

1840. **Rev. Frederick Sturmer**, M.A.   Socialism, its Immoral
Tendency : or, A Plain Appeal to Common Sense.   8vo.

1841. **Robert Owen.**   A Developement of the Principles and
Plans on which to establish Self - supporting Home
Colonies ; as a most secure and profitable Investment
for Capital. . . . 4to.

1841. —— An Address to the Socialists on the present Position
of the Rational System of Society ; and the measures
required to direct . . . the Operations of the *Universal
Community Society of Rational Religionists ;* being the
substance of Two Lectures delivered . . . in May 1841.
Home Colonisation Society : London.   8vo.

1841. —— Lectures on the Rational System of Society, derived
solely from Nature and Experience, as propounded by
Robert Owen, versus Socialism, derived from Misrepresenta-
tion, as explained by the *Lord Bishop of Exeter* and
others ; and versus the Present System of Society.   8vo.

1841. —— A Lecture delivered in the Mechanics' Institute,
London, on the 30th March 1840, in Reply to the Errors
and Misrepresentations made on the Subject of the
Rational System of Society in both Houses of Parliament.
. . . 2nd edn.   *Home Colonisation Society : London.*   8vo.

1841. —— The Signs of the Times ; or, the Approach of the
Millennium.   An Address . . . 2nd edn.   8vo.

184L(?). **Robert Dale Owen.**   A Lecture on Consistency, as
delivered in New York, Boston, and London.   16mo.

1841. —— Popular Tracts.   8vo.

1841. What is Socialism ?   and what would be its practical
Effects upon Society ?   A Correct Report of the Public
Discussion between *Robert Owen* and *Mr. John Brindley,*
held in Bristol on the 5th, 6th, and 7th of January 1841.
8vo.

1841. **James N. Bailey.**   Sophistry Unmasked.   An Examination of the Arguments contained in a Book written by
John Brindley, and purporting to be a judicious Summary

of the Evidences of Natural Theology and Revealed
Religion. 2 Parts. (Social Reformers' Cabinet Library.
J. Hobson : Leeds.) 8vo.

1841. **Rev. Robert Ainslie.** An Examination of Socialism :
the last of a Series of Lectures against Socialism . . .
27th February 1840, under the Direction of the Committee
of the London City Mission. [A new edn.] 12mo.

1841. **Rev. A. J. Scott.** The Social Systems of the Present
Day, compared with Christianity. In Five Lectures.
Selected from the *Pulpit.* 8vo.

1841. **Charles Bray.** The Philosophy of Necessity . . . [Ap-
pendix on Social Systems by *Mary Hennell*]. 2 Vols.
8vo.

1841. **Hugh Doherty.** *Charles Fourier's* Theory of Attractive
Industry. 8vo.

1841. —— False Association and its Remedy . . . A critical
Introduction to . . . [above]. 8vo.

1841. The Position of Woman in Harmony. No. I. Extracted
. . . from " *The Phalanstery.*" 16mo.

1841. A Prospectus for the Establishment of a Concordium, or
an Industry Harmony College. 8vo.

1841. **J. A. Etzler.** The New World or Mechanical System,
to perform the Labours of Man and Beast by inanimate
Powers, that cost nothing . . . As a Sequel of his
" *Paradise.*" *Philadelphia.* 8vo.

1841. Notes on the Population Question . . . By Anti-Marcus.
16mo.

1841. **G. R. Wythen Baxter.** The Book of the Bastiles : or,
The History of the Working of the New Poor Law. Imp.
8vo.

1841. An Essay on Civilisation. Reprinted from the original
published thirty years ago. 8vo.
[Not *Charles Hall's.*]

1841. Another Plea for the Poor ; a Letter addressed to Christians
of all Denominations, on the Condition of the People, and

the only Effectual Remedy [Home Colonies]. By an
Evangelical Dissenter.   12mo.

1841–42. THE LABOURER'S LIBRARY.   1d. each.   *Leeds.*   12mo.
No. 1.   *William Cobbett.*   The Right of the Poor to the
Suffrage of the People's Charter . . .
Nos. 2 and 3.   *Feargus O'Connor.*   The Remedy for
National Poverty and Impending National Ruin.
No. 4.   *John F. Bray.*   Government and Society con-
sidered in Relation to First Principles.   Reprinted
from *Labour's Wrongs and Labour's Remedy.*

1842. **Robert Owen.**   The Book of the New Moral World
explanatory of the Elements of the Science of Society,
or the Social State of Man.   Part Second.   [1st in 1836.]
8vo.

1842. **Robert Dale Owen.**   Neurology.   An Account of some
Experiments in Cerebral Physiology.   By *Dr. Buchanan.*
Communicated   to   an   American   Newspaper,   at   *Dr.
Buchanan's* Request, by *R. D. Owen.*   16mo.

1842. **William Godwin.**   An Essay on Trades and Professions,
containing   a   forcible   Exposure   of   the   demoralizing
Tendencies of Competition.   *Manchester.*   16mo.
[Extracted from *The Enquirer*, by William Godwin, 1797.]

1842. The Human Eccaleobion : or, The New Moral Warren ;
being a concise but faithful Exposition of Socialism,
instituted by *R. Owen* [in his "*Book of the New Moral
World.*" In verse].   8vo.

1842. **Mme. Gatti de Gamond.**   *Fourier* and his System.
Translated   from   the   4th   French   edn.   by   *C. T. Wood.*
8vo.

1842. **Samuel Wellwood.**   A Letter to *Feargus O'Connor,*
Esq., against his Plan of dividing the Land, and in
favour of the Association of Property, Skill, and Labour.
[*Fourierist.*]   8vo.

1842. **Francis Lieber.**   Essays on Property and Labour, as
connected with Natural Law, and the Constitution of
Society.   *New York.*   12mo.

1842. **O. A. Brownson.** The Labouring Classes, an Article from the *Boston Quarterly Review.* 5th edn. *Boston.* 16mo.

[1842 (?).] **G. J. Holyoake.** The Advantages and Disadvantages of Trades Unions. [*Sheffield.*]

1842. Minutes of the Proceedings at the Conference of Representatives of the Middle and Working Classes . . . Birmingham, 5th April 1842. *Birmingham.* 8vo.

1842. Report of the Proceedings at the Conference of Delegates of the Middle and Working Classes, held at Birmingham, 5th April 1842 . . . *London.* 12mo.

1842. **James N. Bailey.** Essays on Miscellaneous Subjects, Historical, Moral, and Political. *J. Hobson. Leeds.* 12mo.

1842 (?). [**Mullins.**] The Scheme of Universal Brotherhood. Royal 8vo.

1842. The Social Reformers' Almanack for 1842. *J. Hobson. Leeds.* 8vo.

1843. **Thomas Carlyle.** Past and Present. Ernst ist das Leben. Post 8vo.

1843. The Constitution and Laws of the Rational Society, as agreed to at the Annual Congress, held at Harmony Hall, Hants, 10th May 1843. 16mo.

1843. **R. James Reid**, A.M. Exposure of Socialism. A Refutation of the Letter on Harmony Hall, by "One who has whistled at the Plough," which appeared in the *Morning Chronicle* of the 13th December last; with an Appendix of Facts regarding Socialism . . . at Queenwood, Hants. 8vo.

1843. A Brief Account of the First Concordium or Harmonious Industrial College. 8vo.

1843–45. **J. Pierrepont Graves.** Letters and Extracts from the MS. Writings of *J. P. G.* at the *Concordium* and *London.* Cf. 1845. 2 Vols. 8vo.

1843. Rejected Address from the *Concordists' Society* at Ham Common, to the *London Peace Society*, presented at their

Convention, 24th June 1843, at the Freemason's Tavern. And Temper and Diet. (Extracted from the *New Age*, 1st July 1843.) 8vo.

1843. **Goodwyn Barmby.** The Communist Miscellany. A Collection of Tracts, Religious, Political, and Domestic. Edited by *Goodwyn Barmby*, and the Communist Church. [10 numbers.] 8vo.

1843. **[Luke Hansard** (?).] Hints and Reflections for Railway Travellers and others : or, A Journey to the Phalanx. By Minor Hugo. 3 Vols. *London, Ashby de la Zouch* [printed]. 12mo.

1843. **J. A. Etzler.** Dialogue on *Etzler's Paradise :* between Messrs. Clear, Flat, Dunce, and Grudge. By the Author of "*Paradise within the reach of all Men.*" . . . 8vo.

1843. **Thomas Hodgskin.** On Free Trade and Corn Laws. 12mo.

1843. **Thomas Hunt.** Report to a Meeting of intending Emigrants, comprehending a Practical Plan for founding Co-operative Colonies of United Interests in the North-Western Territories of the United States. 8vo.

1843. **John James Metcalfe.** Temporal Prosperity ensured to Mankind, by the Practice of Christianity ; and Proposals for establishing a Society . . . to be entitled the Practical Christian Union. 8vo.

1843. **W. C. C.** Victoriaism : or, A Reorganisation of the People, Moral, Social, Economical, and Political, suggested as a Remedy for the present Distress. Respectfully addressed to the Right Hon. *Sir Robert Peel.* [Collectivism.] 8vo.

1844. **Robert Owen.** Manifesto . . . addressed to all Governments and People who desire to become civilized, and to improve permanently the Condition of all Classes in all Countries, etc. *Washington.* 8vo.

1844. **Alex. Campbell.** The Life and Dying Testimony of *Abram Combe* in Favour of *Robert Owen's* New Views of Man and Society. 12mo.

1844. **G. J. H[olyoake].** A Visit to Harmony Hall! (Reprinted from " *The Movement* ") with Emendations, and a new and curious Vindicatory Chapter. Dedicated to the Socialists of England and Scotland. 12mo.

1844. **Young Germany.** An Account of the Rise, Progress, and present Position of German Communism; with a Memoir of *Wilhelm Weitling*, its Founder: and a Report of the Proceedings at the Banquet given by the English Socialists, in the John Street Institution, London, 22nd September 1844. 12mo.

1844. **Mary Hennell.** An Outline of the various Social Systems and Communities which have been founded on the Principle of Co-operation. With an Introductory Essay by the Author of " *The Philosophy of Necessity* " [C. Bray]. 12mo.
  [First published in 1841, as an Appendix to the " *Philosophy of Necessity*," by C. Bray.]

1844. **Charles Bray.** An Essay upon the Union of Agriculture and Manufactures and upon the Organisation of Industry. [Introduction to Mary Hennell's *Outline*, etc.] 12mo.

1844. **J. A. Etzler.** Two Visions of *J. A. Etzler* . . . a Revelation of Futurity. *Concordium Press.* 8vo.

1844. —— Emigration to the Tropical World for the Melioration of all Classes of People of all Nations. *Concordium Press.* 8vo.

1844. **George Ensor.** Of Property, and of its equal Distribution, as promoting Virtue, Population, Abundance. 8vo.

1844. The Constitutional Rights of Landlords; the Evils springing from the Abuse of them in Ireland; and the Origin and Effects of Banks, of Funds, and of Corn Laws, considered. *Dublin.* 8vo.

1844. **Samuel Laing,** *the younger.* Atlas Prize Essay. National Distress: its Causes and Remedies. 8vo.

1844. **William Thomason.** O'Connorism and Democracy inconsistent with each other; being a Statement of Events in the Life of *Feargus O'Connor. Newcastle.* 8vo.

1844. Tracts for the Times. [A Series of Six Tracts on National Evils and National Remedies.]
I. Foreign Trade *versus* Home Colonisation.
II. Are Great Britain and Ireland incapable of raising food for their Population ?
III. Can our Manufacturing System be extended, beneficially for the Nation ?
IV. Would an Increase of Foreign Trade increase Work and Wages.
V. On the Organisation of Home Colonies.
VI. What good would Home Colonies do ?
Published by the Rational Tract Society.

1845. **Robert Owen.** Letter to the Senate of the 28th Congress . . . requesting permission to deliver a Course of Lectures in its Chamber, etc. *Washington.* 8vo.

1845. —— Address to the Ministers of all Religions . . . as delivered by him in the Chinese Museum, Philadelphia . . . 21st December 1845. *Philadelphia.* S. sh. folio.

1845. **Charles Southwell.** Two-pennyworth of Truth about Owenism and the Owenites.

1845. **J. Minter Morgan.** The Christian Commonwealth. Large 4to.
Another edn. 1845. *London, Paris* [printed]. 12mo.
Another edn. *Phœnix Library,* 1850. 12mo.
Second edn. *Edinburgh,* 1854. 8vo.
(Colonie Chrétienne . . . Traduit de l'Anglais), 1846. 12mo ; and English and French. 1849. 2 Parts. Folio.

1845. **[Wm. King.]** Money Dialogue : or, A Catechism on Currency, Exchanges, etc. By a Member of the Bank of Industry. 12mo.

1845 (?). —— A Note of the *London Bank of Industry, Margaret Street. Wm. King,* Manager. 8vo.

1845 (?). —— To the Thinking Public. No. 3. *Bank of Industry, Margaret Street.* 8vo.
[Originally published in 1821.]

1845 (?). —— [*Bank of Industry Tracts.*] Reasons why Orders are not useful in Promoting the progressive Extension and Concentration of Banks of Interchange. 1 page, 8vo.

1845. **J. Pierrepont Graves.** Letters and Extracts from the MS. Writings of J. P. G. [Cf. 1843.] 2 Vols. 8vo.

1845. An Appeal to the Editors of the *Times* Newspaper in behalf of the Working Classes. By Two Lay Members of the Church. *Hatchard. London.* 8vo.

[A Review of the above appeared in the *North British Review.*]

1845. **Thomas Arnold.** Miscellaneous Works. Collected and republished. 8vo.

1846. **J. Minter Morgan.** Letters to a Clergyman on Institutions for ameliorating the Condition of the People. Chiefly from Paris, in the autumn of 1845. 12mo.

[Another edn. *Phœnix Library.* 1850.]

1846. —— Colonie Chrétienne de 300 Familles . . . Trad. de l'Anglais. 12mo.

1847. **Robert Owen.** Le Livre du Nouveau Monde Moral . . . Abrégé et traduit de l'Anglais, par T. W. Thornton. 12mo.

1847. **W. N.** Equitable Banks of Interchange : a Letter to *T. S. Duncombe*, M.P. . . . [cf. 1845]. 8vo.

1847. **Baron János Dercsenyi.** Researches for a Philanthropical Remedy against Communism. From the German. 8vo.

1848. **Robert Owen.** Dialogue sur le Système Social de *Robert Owen.* Dialogue entre la France, le Monde et Robert Owen, sur la nécessité d'un changement total dans nos Systèmes d'Éducation et de Gouvernement. *Paris.* 12mo.

1848. —— Deuxième Dialogue sur le Système Social, par *Robert Owen.* Dialogue entre les Membres de la Commission Exécutive les Ambassadeurs d'Angleterre, de Russie, d'Autriche, de Prusse, de Hollande, des États-Unis, et Robert Owen. *Paris.* 12mo.

1848. **Michel Chevalier.** The Labour Question. 1. Amelioration of the Condition of the Labouring Classes. 2. Wages. 3. Organisation of Labour. Translated from the French. 32mo.

1848. **Louis Blanc.** Socialism : the Right to Labour. In

Reply to *M. Thiers* . . . With Memoir and Portrait of the Author. 8vo.

1848. **Louis Blanc.** The Organisation of Labour. 32mo.

1848. **Adolphe Thiers.** The Rights of Property; a Refutation of Communism and Socialism. 12mo.

1848. **James Ward.** Threatened Social Disorganisation of France. *Louis Blanc* on the Working Classes; with corrected Notes, and a Refutation of his Destructive Plan. 2nd edn. 12mo.

1848. **Henry Brougham.** Letter to the *Marquess of Lansdowne* . . . on the late Revolution in France. 8vo.
[4th edn., with additions, 1848. 8vo. 5th edn. 1849. 8vo.]

1848. **Robert Dale Owen.** Labour : its History and its Progress. An Address delivered before the *Young Men's Mercantile Library Association* of Cincinnati, etc. *Cincinnati.* 8vo.

1848. **Charles Kingsley,** *jun.* The Saints' Tragedy. Preface by Professor Maurice. 16mo.

[1848.] **Thomas Hodgskin.** A Letter . . . on Free Trade and Slave Labour. 8vo.

1848 (?). **Richard Isham.** Land, Common Property. The People's Right to Land. What "Commonality" is, and its perpetual Existence. By Terrigenous. 12mo.
[3rd edn. 1852. 12mo.]

1848. The People's Charter ; with the Address to the Radical Reformers of Great Britain and Ireland, and a brief Sketch of its Origin. 16mo.

1848. **Alexander Somerville.** The Autobiography of a Working Man, by "One who has whistled at the Plough." 12mo.

1849. **Robert Owen.** The Revolution in the Mind and Practice of the Human Race : or, The Coming Change from Irrationality to Rationality. 8vo.

1849. —— A Supplement to the Revolution in Mind and Practice of the Human Race. . . . To which is added a Discourse delivered to the Socialists of London, 25th October 1849. 8vo.

1849. **James S. Buckingham.** National Evils and Practical Remedies, with the Plan of a model Town . . . Accompanied by an Examination of some important Moral and Political Problems. 8vo.

1849. **J. Minter Morgan.** Tracts: originally published at various Periods, from 1819-38. With an Appendix. *Phœnix Library.* 12mo.
[Another copy, dated 1850.]

1849. **George Mudie.** A Solution of the Portentous Enigma of Modern Civilisation . . . addressed to *Charles Louis Napoleon Bonaparte* . . . Author of a work on the Extinction of Pauperism. 8vo.

1849. **R. W. Russell.** America compared with England. The respective Social Effects of the American and English Systems of Government. 12mo.

1849. **John Gray.** *Edin. Monetary Reform Pamphlet,* No. 1. *Committee of Enquiry* into the validity of the Monetary Principle advocated in *Gray's Lectures . . . Edin.* '16mo.

[1849.] **John Thimbleby.** What is Money? or Man's Birthright, "Time," the only real Wealth; its representative forming the true Medium of Exchange. 8vo.

1849. **Edward Kellogg.** Labor and other Capital. [Currency scheme.] *New York.* 8vo.

1849. **Ebenezer Jones.** The Land Monopoly, the Suffering and Demoralization caused by it; and the Justice and Expediency of its Abolition. 8vo.

1849. **Henry Syme.** Poems and Songs, chiefly for the Encouragement of the Working Classes. *Dunfermline.* Post 8vo.

1849. *North British Review. February* 1849. The Socialist Party in France. 8vo.

1850. **Marx** and **Engels.** The Manifesto of the Communist Party. [This celebrated Paper, written in German, and printed in *London* in February 1848, was published this year by *G. J. Harney,* in an English translation, in his journal the *Red Republican.* See Nos. 21-24, 9th-30th November 1850.]
It was reprinted by *Reeves* in 1888.

1850. **Thomas Carlyle.** Latter-day Pamphlets, edited by T. C. [Nos. i.-viii. original issue.] 8vo.

1850. **Charles Kingsley.** Alton Locke, Tailor and Poet: an Autobiography. 2 Vols. Post 8vo.
[Another edn. 1889.]

1850. [——] Cheap Clothes and Nasty. By Parson Lot. *London* and *Cambridge.* 12mo.
[A Reprint is prefixed to the 1889 edn. of *Alton Locke.*]

1850. **J. Minter Morgan.** The Christian Commonwealth. To which is added, An Inquiry respecting Private Property . . . from a Periodical of 1827. *Phœnix Library.* 12mo.

1850. **John Thimbleby.** A Lecture on the Currency, in which is explained the Represented Time Note Medium of Exchange, in Connexion with a Universal System of Banking; delivered at the Barnet Institute. 8vo.

1850. TEN-DAY NOTE. We of the National Time Bank of England, as by law established, guarantee TEN DAYS' Labour of Head and Hand, in Exchange. On Demand. **2088.** 1st January 1850. **2088.**
Issued by John Thimbleby, JOHNATHAN TRUTH, ⎱ *Directors.*
to the Public. PETER SIMPLE, ⎰ *London.*
Let Man have a Medium by which he can exchange Time for Time, and Hovels shall become Mansions—and Mansions, Temples—and Streets paved with Gold.

1850. **Thomas Clark.** Reflections upon the past Policy and future Prospects of the Chartist Party. Also a Letter condemnatory of Private Assassination as recommended by *Mr. G. J. Harney.* 16mo.

1850. —— A Letter addressed to *G. W. M. Reynolds*, reviewing his Conduct as a professed Chartist, and also explaining who he is and what he is, together with copious Extracts from his most indecent Writings. 16mo.

1850. **Ledru Rollin.** The Decline of England. 2nd edn. 16mo.

1850. **Charles Gourard.** Socialism Unmasked : a Plain Lecture. From the French. 16mo.

1850. **Horace Greeley.** Hints towards Reforms in Lectures, Addresses, and other Writings. *New York.* Cr. 8vo.

1851. **Herbert Spencer.** Social Statics : the Conditions essential to Human Happiness specified. 8vo.

1851. **Charles Kingsley.** Yeast : A Problem. Reprinted from *Fraser's Magazine.* 1st and 2nd edns. 8vo.

1851. **Rev. Charles Kingsley,** *jun.* The Application of Associative Principles and Methods to Agriculture : a Lecture, delivered on behalf of the Society for promoting Working Men's Associations, 28th May 1851. 16mo.

1851. —— The Message of the Church to Labouring Men. A Sermon [on Luke iv. 16-21]. 8vo.

1851. **F. D. Maurice.** On the Reformation of Society, and how all parties may contribute to it ; a Lecture on the opening of the *Southampton Working Tailors' Association,* by the *Rev. F. D. Maurice,* M.A., President of the Society.

1851. —— Reasons for Co-operation : a Lecture, delivered at the Office for Promoting Working Men's Associations, 76 Charlotte Street, Fitzroy Square, 11th December 1850. To which is added, God and Mammon : a Sermon to Young Men . . . 24mo.

1851. **Edward V. Neale.** The Characteristic Features of some of the Leading Systems of Socialism. A Lecture.

1851. **Thomas Ramsay.** Is Christian Socialism a Church Matter ? A Lecture delivered in Blagrove's Rooms, Mortimer Street, Cavendish Square, 8th August 1851, at the Invitation of the Central Co-operative Agency. 16mo.

1851. **J. M. Ludlow.** Christian Socialism and its Opponents : a Lecture. 12mo.

1851. **Tracts on Christian Socialism—**
No. 1. Dialogue between Somebody (a Person of Respectability) and Nobody (the writer).
No. 2. History of the *Working Tailors' Association,* 34 Castle Street, Oxford Street.
No. 3. What Christian Socialism has to do with the Question at present agitating the Church.
No. 4. The Working Associations of Paris.
No. 5. The Society for promoting Working Men's Associations.

No. 6. Prevailing Idolatries: or, Hints for Political Economists.

No. 7. The Doctrine of Circumstances as it affects Priests and People.

No. 8. A Clergyman's Answer to the Question "On what grounds can you associate with men generally?"-

Published by George Bell, 186 Fleet Street. [*Maurice* wrote Nos. 1, 3, 7, 8; *Ludlow*, Nos. 4, 6; *Hughes*, No. 2.]

1851. **Tracts by Christian Socialists—**

No. 1. Series on English History, by a Clergyman [*Maurice*]. No. 1.

No. 2. Cheap Clothes and Nasty, by Parson Lot [*Kingsley*].

No. 3. Labour and the Poor. Part I. By J. T. [*Ludlow*]. Reprinted from *Fraser's Magazine*.

No. 4. Labour and the Poor. Part II.

1851. **James Hole.** Lectures on Social Science and the Organization of Labor. 8vo.

1851. **Stephen Pearl Andrews.** The Science of Society. No. 1. The True Constitution of Government in the Sovereignty of the Individual, as the final Development of Protestantism, Democracy, and Socialism. *New York.* 12mo.

[2nd edn. 1853. 12mo.]

The Science of Society. No. 2. Cost the limit of Price: a Scientific Measure of Honesty in Trade. 12mo.

[Another imprint in 1853.]

1851. **Arthur Bromiley.** A Social Theory: or, A Brief Exposition of the Primary Law in Nature, affecting social Development. Also an Appendix containing an Outline of a Scheme framed in Accordance with the above mentioned Law. 8vo.

1851. Le Banquet des Égaux. Londres, 24 Février 1851. *Paris.* 8vo.

[*G. J. Harney* was present; *Robert Owen* was prevented attending by his bad health. The Banquet took place in Highbury Barn Tavern.]

[1851.] **J. Bronterre O Brien.** To the Oppressed and Mystified People of Great Britain. [A Chartist and Socialist Broadside.] S. sh. 4to.

1852. **Josiah Warren.** Equitable Commerce, a New Development of Principles as Substitutes for Laws and Government, for the harmonious Adjustment and Regulation of the pecuniary, intellectual, and moral Intercourse of Mankind, etc. *New York.* 12mo.

1852. A Brief Inquiry into the Natural Rights of Man, his Duties and Interests; with an Outline of the Principles, Laws, and Institutions by which Liberty, Equality, and Fraternity may be realized throughout the World. 12mo.

1852. **Herbert Spencer.** A Theory of Population deduced from the General Law of Animal Fertility. Republished from the *Westminster Review.* Post 8vo.

1852. **Rev. Charles Kingsley,** *jun.* Who are the Friends of Order? A Reply to certain Observations in a late Number of *Fraser's Magazine* on the so-called " Christian Socialists." 8vo.

1852. First Report of the Society for Promoting Working Men's Associations, with Report of the Co-operative Conference held in London, July 1852. 8vo.

1853. Report of the Co-operative Conference held at Manchester on the 15th and 16th August 1853, at the Cooper Street Institute. With Appendices. 8vo.

1853. **Robert Owen.** The Future of the Human Race; or a great, glorious, and peaceful revolution near at hand, to be effected through the agency of departed spirits of good and superior men and women. 8vo.

1854. **Charles Kingsley.** Who causes Pestilence? Four Sermons, with Preface. *London, Glasgow* [printed]. 8vo.

1854. **George Fitzhugh.** Sociology for the South, or the Failure of Free Society. Sm. 8vo.

1854. **Charles Murray.** A Letter to *Mr. George Jacob Holyoake*; containing a brief Review of that Gentleman's Conduct and Policy as a Reformer, with especial Reference to his Reply to *Mr. Linton* and the " *Boston Liberator* " . . and Defence of the *Cobden Policy.* 8vo.

1854. **Jules Lechevalier St. André.** Five Years in the Land
of Refuge. A Letter on the Prospects of Co-operative
Associations in England, addressed to the Members of
Council of the late Society for Promoting Working Men's
Associations, now reconstituted under the title the "Associa-
tion for Promoting Industrial Provident Societies."   8vo.

1854–55. **Robert Owen.** The New Existence of Man upon
the Earth. To which are added an Outline of *Mr. Owen's*
early Life, and an Appendix containing his Addresses . . .
published in 1815 and 1817.   8 Pts.   8vo.

1855. —— Address delivered at the Meeting in St. Martin's
Hall, Lonc [*sic.*] Acre, London, on the 1st of January
1855.   8vo.

1855. —— Report of the General Preliminary Meeting on the
coming Millennium, on the 1st of January 1855.

1855. —— Tract on the Coming Millennium.   (January 1855.)
[Two series.   1d. each series.]

1855. —— Inauguration of the Millennium.   (May 1855.)

1855. —— Address on Spiritual Manifestations.   (July 1855.)

1855. —— The Millennium in Practice.   (August 1855.)

1855. **[John Frearson.]** The Relative Rights and Interests of
the Employer and Employed discussed ; and a system
proposed by which the Conflicting Interests of all Classes
of Society may be reconciled. By M. Justitia [*i.e.* J. F.].
16mo.

1857. **Robert Owen.** Report of the Meetings of the Congress
of the advanced Minds of the World, convened by *Robert
Owen*, held . . . from the 12th to the 25th of May 1857.
1st and 2nd edns.   8vo.

1857–58. —— The Life of Robert Owen. Written by Himself.
With selections from his writings and correspondence.
Vol. I.   *Effingham Wilson.*   8vo.

A Supplementary Appendix to the First Volume of
the Life of *Robert Owen*, containing a Series of Reports,
Addresses, Memorials, and other Documents referred to in
that volume.   1808-20.   Vol. I. A.   *Effingham Wilson*,
1858.   8vo.   [No more published.   Owen died 17th
November 1858.]

1860. **John Ruskin.** " Unto this Last." (The Four original articles in the *Cornhill Magazine* for August, September, October, and November 1860.)   8vo.
[First collected edn. 1862.   Post 8vo.]

1860. **H. Clinton** and **E. V. Neale.**   Letters on Associated Homes, between Colonel H. C. and E. V. N.   8vo.

1860. *Westminster and Foreign Quarterly Review.   New Series.* Vol. xviii.   No. II.   *October* 1860.   Article III.   Robert Owen.   8vo.

1860. **W. Chambers.**   Co-operation in its different branches. 8vo.

1862. **G. J. Holyoake.**   Moral Errors endangering the Permanence of Co-operative Societies—Paper read at Social Science Congress, Guildhall, London, 1862.   5th edn.

1863. **Josiah Warren.**   True Civilisation an Immediate Necessity, and the last ground of hope for Mankind, etc. *Boston, Mass.*   8vo.

1871. Report . . . Proceedings of the Festival in Commemoration of the Centenary Birthday of *R. Owen* . . . held . . . 16th May 1871 . . . To which is added *Mr. Owen's " Outline of the Rational System of Society."*   8vo.

1874. **Robert Dale Owen.**   Threading my Way.   Twenty-Seven Years of Autobiography.   8vo.

1875. **Henry Travis,** M.D.   Effectual Reform in Man and Society.   8vo.

1877. —— A Manual of Social Science for the Working Classes, explanatory of the . . . True Parts of the Educational, Economical, and Social Views of the late *Robert Owen.*   12mo.

1880. —— English Socialism.   Parts I. and II.   16mo.

1885. **J. Bronterre O'Brien.**   The Rise, Progress, and Phases of Human Slavery : How it came into the World, and How it shall be made to go out.   *Reeves.*   1885.   8vo.
[A posthumous compilation of O'Brien's MS. by the aid of his printed writings.   The first nineteen chapters are a reprint of the twenty-one letters under the same title in *Reynolds's Political Instructor,* 1850.   Letters fifteen and sixteen, and some other references to current politics, are omitted in this reprint.]

N.D. **Thomas Barclay.** The Rights of Labour According to *John Ruskin.* 2nd edn. *Leicester.* 12mo.

N.D. **Rev. Edward Birch.** Remarks on Socialism, designed to show the true Character and licentious Tendency of that System of Infidelity. 12mo.

N.D. **Ernest Jones.** Chartist Songs and Fugitive Pieces. 12mo.

N.D. **Robert Owen's** Reply to the Question "What would you do if you were Prime Minister of England?" 2nd edn. *Stockport.* 12mo.

N.D. **R. D. Owen** and **Frances Wright.** Tracts on Republican Government and National Education. Addressed to the Inhabitants of the United States of America. 16mo.

N.D. **B. Warden.** Rewards of Industry. The Labour Exchange the only true way to Wealth for the Working Classes. 8vo.

N.D. Calculations showing the Facility with which the Paupers and Unemployed, or any other Portion of the Population may be enabled to support themselves within most desirable Circumstances. By Co-operation. Royal 8vo.

N.D. The Power of the People: or, The Way to Wealth, Prosperity and Peace; a social Pamphlet. *Leeds.* Sm. 8vo.

N.D. Sayings and Doings about the New Moral World. *Leeds.* Sm. 8vo.

N.D. Six Letters on the Theory and Practice of Socialism. By *Junius.* Royal 8vo.

N.D. To the Working Classes. Competitive *versus* Co-operative Labour: or, Labour as it is, and Labour as it ought to be. Reprinted from the *New Moral World.* 12mo.

3. PERIODICAL PUBLICATIONS

1794. **Politics for the People**: or, a Salmagundy for Swine.
[Edited by D. J. Eaton.] 2 parts. 8vo.
[The First six Nos. of this work were published under the title
of "Hog's Wash." Part I. contains 15 Nos. Part II. 14.]

1811–43. **The Philanthropist**: or Repository for Hints and
Suggestions calculated to promote the Comfort and Happi-
ness of Man. [Edited by William Allen.] Vols. 1-7.
1811-19. *London.* 8vo.
The Philanthropic Magazine. New Series. Vols. 1
and 2. 1829-30. *Lindfield.* 8vo.
After 17 numbers of this *New Series* had appeared, the work
was discontinued, but it was revived in 1835 under the title of
The Lindfield Reporter: or Philanthropic Magazine,
etc. *Lindfield.* 8vo.
Vol. I. For the years 1835 and 1836. Nos. 1-24, 1836.
Vol. II. For the years 1837 and 1838. Nos. 1-24, 1838.
After 1838, the *Reporter* seems to have been issued less
regularly until Allen's death in 1843.

1817. **The Mirror of Truth.** Published every alternate Friday.
No 1, Friday, Oct. 10. No. 2, Friday, Nov. 7. [Owenite.]
8vo.

1817. **The People.** Nos. 1-15. April 19, 1817—July 26,
1817. 8vo.

1817–18. **The Reformists' Register,** or Weekly Commentary.
Edited by William Hone. Nos. 1-40. 8vo.

1818–19. **The Gorgon,** a Weekly Political Publication. Nos.
1-49. May 23, 1818—April 4, 1819. 8vo.

1821–22. **The Economist**; a Periodical Paper explanatory of
the New System of Society projected by *Robert Owen*, Esq.,
and of a Plan of Association for Improving the Condition

of the Working Classes, during their continuance at their present employments. No. 1, *Jan.* 27, 1821—No. 52, *March* 9, 1822. 2 Vols. Sm. 8vo.

1821. **The Labouring Man's Advocate.** Edited by John Ovington.

1821. **The Labourer's Friend, and Handicrafts' Chronicle,** being a Magazine, published Monthly . . . Price 6d. No. 1, January 1821. 8vo.

1823. **The Unique** : a series of Portraits of Eminent Persons. No. 19. *Robert Owen,* Esq. 24mo.

1823. **The Political Economist and Universal Philanthropist.** Every alternate Saturday, price 6d. ; or once a month, price 1s. No 1, Jan. 11, 1823.
> [In an advertisement of this work, 4 pp. 8vo, there is a vigorous statement of *Hall's* views ; but the object of the paper is to advocate Owenite communities.]

1823–24. **The Mechanics' Weekly Journal** : or, Artisans' Miscellany. 8vo.

1825–28. **The New Harmony Gazette.** [Edited by Frances Wright, afterwards Mme. D'Arusmont, R. D. Owen, and R. L. Jennings.] Vols. I.-III. *New Harmony.* 4to.
Continued after 1828 as
The Free Enquirer. *New York.*

1825–27. **The Register for the First Society of Adherents to Divine Revelation at Orbiston.** Edited by Abram Combe. No. 1, Nov. 10, 1825—No. 34, Sept. 19, 1827. *Edinburgh, Orbiston Press.* 8vo.

1826–27. **The Advocate of the Working Classes.** [George Mudie, Editor.] *Edinburgh.*

1826–30. **The Co-operative Magazine and Monthly Herald.** Vols. I. and II. Jan. 1826—Dec. 1827. 8vo.
The Co-operative Magazine. Vol. III. No. 1, Jan. 1828 —No. 10, Oct. 1829. 8vo.
The London Co-operative Magazine. Vol. IV. 3 Nos. Jan. 1—Mar. 1, 1830. 8vo.
The British Co-operator. Nos. 1-7. April—Oct. 1830.
> [Abram Combe, Wm. Thompson, Wm. Maclure, and Wm. King were among the contributors to this, the leading co-operative periodical.]

1828–30. **The Co-operator.** No 1, *May* 1, 1828—No. 28, *August* 1, 1830. [Edited by W. King, M.D. Usually known as **The Brighton Co-operator.**] *Brighton.* 8vo.

1829–30. **The Associate.** No. 1, Jan. 1, 1829—No. 9, Jan. 1, 1830. 8vo.
The Associate and Co-operative Mirror. Nos. 10-12. 1830. 8vo.

1829 (?). **The Union Exchange Gazette.** By the *Union Exchange Society*, 11 Tottenham Street. 2d. each No.
[The *Union Exchange Society* was founded by W. King, at 36 Red Lion Square. Cf. *Co-operative Mag.* 1827, pp. 421, 499, 547.]

1829–30. **The Birmingham Co-operative Herald.** No. 1, April 1, 1829—No. 9, Dec. 1, 1829. No. 10, Jan. 1, 1830—No. 19, Oct. 1, 1830. *Birmingham.* 8vo.

1830. **The Magazine of Useful Knowledge and Co-operative Miscellany.** No. 1, Oct. 1, 1830—No. 4, Nov. 13, 1830. 8vo.

1830. **The United Trades' Co-operative Journal.** March 6— Oct. 2, 1830. *Manchester.* 8vo.

1830. **The Belfast Co-operative Advocate.**

1830. **The Chester Co-operator.**

1831. **The Lancashire Co-operator.** *Manchester.* 12mo.
No. 1, June 11, 1831—No. 6, Aug. 20, 1831.
[Continued as]
The Lancashire and Yorkshire Co-operator. *Manchester.* 12mo.
No. 1, Sept. 3, 1831—No. 4, Oct. 15, 1831.

1831–35. **The Poor Man's Guardian**; a Weekly Newspaper for the People. Established, contrary to " law " to try the power of " might " against " right." [Edited by H. Hetherington.] Nos. 1-238. *London.* 4to.

1831–32. **Cobbett's Twopenny Trash** : or, Politics for the Poor. 2 Vols. 12mo.
Vol. I. July 1830—June 1831 inclusive.
Vol. II. July 1831 — July 1832 inclusive. [No number for March.]

1831–32. **Carpenter's Monthly Political Magazine.** Vol. I. 8vo.

1831. **The Voice of the People.** *Manchester.* Folio.

The Chief Owenite Organ, 1832–45.

1832–34. **The Crisis** : or, The Change from Error and Misery, to Truth and Happiness. Edited by Robert Owen and Robert Dale Owen. 4 Vols. 4to.

> Vol. I. 44 Nos. Apr. 14, 1832—Jan. 5, 1833 ; Vol. II. 36 Nos. Jan. 12—Aug. 31, 1833 ; Vol. III. 32 Nos. Sept. 7, 1833—Apr. 5, 1834 ; Vol. IV. 20 Nos. Apr. 12—Aug. 23, 1834.
> [The volumes vary in size. In Vol. III. the sub-title becomes *National Co-operative Trades' Union and Equitable Labour Exchange Gazette;* in Vol. IV. the last half of this sub-title disappears. Vol. II. is "under the patronage of Robert Owen" ; Vols. III. and IV. have no indications of editorship.]

1834–45. **The New Moral World,** a London Weekly Publication, developing the Principles of the Rational System of Society. Conducted by Robert Owen and his Disciples. Vol. I. 1835. *London.* 4to.

> Nos. 1-52, Nov. 1, 1834—Oct. 24, 1835.

The New Moral World, or Millennium. A London Weekly Publication, developing the Principles of the Rational System of Society. Conducted by the Disciples of Robert Owen. Vol. II. 1836. *London.* Sm. folio.

> Nos. 53-104, Oct. 31, 1835—Oct. 22, 1836.

The New Moral World, and Manual of Science. Vol. III. 1836-37. *Manchester* and *London.* Sm. folio.

> Nos. 105-136, Oct. 29, 1836—June 3, 1837, published at *London;* Nos. 137-156, June 10, 1837—Oct. 21, 1837, published at *Manchester.*
> [No. 137 is misnumbered 136.]

—— Vol. IV. 1838. *Birmingham.* Sm. folio.

> Nos. 157-208, Oct. 28, 1837—Oct. 20, 1838.
> [Nos. 157-188 published at *Manchester,* Nos. 189-208 at *Birmingham.*]

The New Moral World : or, Gazette of the Universal Community Society of Rational Religionists. Vol. V. 1839. *Leeds.* [*Birmingham.*] Folio.

> *New Series.* Nos. 1-37, Oct. 27, 1838—July 6, 1839.
> [The title and index are the only parts of this volume published at *Leeds.*]

The New Moral World: or, Gazette of the Universal Community Society of Rational Religionists.   Vol. VI. 1839. *Leeds.* Folio.

New Series. Nos. 38-62, July 13, 1839—Dec. 28, 1839.

——Vol. VII.   1839 [1840]. *Leeds.* Folio.

New Series. Nos. 63-88, Jan. 4, 1840—June 27, 1840 ; and Supplements to Nos. 82-88.

—— Vol. I. of Third Series.   Vol. VIII.   1840. *Leeds.* Large folio.

Third Enlarged Series.   Nos. 1-26, July 4, 1840—Dec. 26, 1840.

—— Vol. II. of Third Series.   Vol. IX.   1841. *Leeds.* Large folio.

Third Enlarged Series.   Nos. 1-26, Jan. 2, 1841—June 26, 1841.

The New Moral World: and Gazette of the Rational Society.   Vol. III. of Third Series.   Vol. X.   1842. *London.* Large folio.

Third Enlarged Series.   Nos. 1-52, July 3, 1841—June 25, 1842.

[Nos. 1-16 were published in *Leeds.*]

—— Vol. IV. of Third Series.   Vol. XI.   1843. *London.* Large folio.

Third Series. Nos. 1-52, July 2, 1842—June 24, 1843.

—— Vol. V. of Third Series.   Vol. XII.   1844. *London.* Large folio.

Third Series. Nos. 1-52, July 1, 1843—June 22, 1844.

—— Vol. VI. of Third Series.   Vol. XIII.   1845. *London.* Large folio.

Third Series. Nos. 1-64, June 29, 1844—Sept. 13, 1845.

[The Vol. was at first wrongly numbered XIV.   Nos. 33-61 were printed at *Harmony Hall.*   After the issue of No. 61, Aug. 23, 1845, it passed into the possession of James Hill, and ceased to represent Robert Owen's views.   Accordingly, on Aug. 30, 1845, Owen established a new paper, slightly altering the title, to avoid difficulties of copyright, to *The Moral World.*]

The Moral World, the Advocate of the Rational System of Society, as founded and developed by Robert Owen. *London.* Large folio.

Nos. 1-11, Aug. 30, 1845—Nov. 8, 1845. (All published.)

[The *Herald of Progress* and the *Reasoner* kept alive the Owenite tradition after the collapse of the official journal.]

1832. **The Rational Reformer**: or, Illustrations and Testimonies in favour of the Rational Social System.   8vo.

1832. **The Union Pilot and Co-operative Intelligencer.** *Manchester.*

1832–33. **The British Labourer's Protector, and Factory Child's Friend.** No. 1, Sept. 21, 1832—No. 31, April 19, 1833. [256 pp. complete.] 12mo.

1832–33. **The Poor Man's Advocate** : or, A Full and Fearless Exposure of the Horrors and Abominations of the Factory System in England, in the year 1832 . . . [Edited by J. Doherty.] 1833. *Manchester.* 8vo.
>No. 1, Jan. 21, 1832—No. 50, Jan. 5, 1833.
>[After No. 33, the sub-title is constantly varied, and the issues, except the last, are not numbered.]

1832–33. **The Working Man's Friend and Political Magazine.** Nos. 1-33. 4to.

1833. **The Pioneer** : or, Grand National Consolidated Trades' Union Magazine. Vol. I. 1834. 4to.

1833. **The Birmingham Labour Exchange Gazette.** Nos. 1-5. Jan. 16—Feb. 9, 1833. Sm. 4to.

1833–34. **Gazette of Labour Exchanges.**

1833–34. **The Gauntlet,** a sound Republican Weekly Newspaper. Feb. 9, 1833—Mar. 30, 1834. 4to.

1833–34. **The Destructive and Poor Man's Conservative.** Vol. I. Nos. 1-53. 4to.
>[Continued as]

The People's Conservative and Trades' Union Gazette. Vol. II. Nos. 54-71. 1834. Folio.

1833–38. **The True Sun.** *London.*
>[There was a *Weekly True Sun* and a *Daily True Sun.*]

1834. **The Tradesman,** a Glasgow Weekly Journal.

1834. **The Herald of the Rights of Industry.** *Manchester.* 8vo.
>(No. 1 was published Feb. 8, 1834.)

1834–38. **The Shepherd,** a London Weekly Periodical . . . [Edited by the Rev. J. E. Smith.] Aug. 30, 1834— Mar. 31, 1838. [Owenite, etc.] 4to.

1837. **Bronterre's National Reformer.** Edited by J. Bronterre O'Brien. Vol. I. Nos. 1-11. 4to.

1837-40. **The Star in the East.**

1837-49. **The Northern Star** and Leeds General Advertiser. Edited by Feargus O'Connor. Folio.
[No. 1 was issued Nov. 18, 1837.]

1837. **The Northern Liberator.** Edited by A. H. Beaumont.

1839. *Northern Liberator.* Northern Lights: or, Whims, Oddities, and Digressions of the *"Northern Liberator"* for A.D. 1838. *Newcastle-upon-Tyne.* 8vo.

1839. **The Social Pioneer:** or, Record of the Progress of Socialism. Edited by Epicurus. No. 1, Mar. 9—No. 10, May 11. Complete. 1d. weekly. *A. Heywood. Manchester.* Royal 8vo.

1839. **The National:** a Library for the People. Edited by W. J. Linton. [Contains extracts from *Owen, Fr. Wright, Godwin,* etc.] 26 Nos. Jan. 5—June 29, 1839. 8vo.

1839-40. **The Working Bee.** Printed by John Green, at the Community Press, Manea Fen, Cambridgeshire, for the Trustees of the *Hodsonian Community Society.*
No. 1, July 20, 1839—No. 46, May 30, 1840. 4to.
New Series, Vol. I. Nos. 1-28. Folio.

1839-42. **The Chartist Circular.** Published under the Superintendence of the *Universal Suffrage Central Committee for Scotland.* Edited by William Thomson. No. 1, Sept. 28, 1839—No. 146, July 9, 1842. *Glasgow.* Folio.

1840. **Stephens' Monthly Magazine** of useful Information for the People. Edited by the Rev. J. R. Stephens. *Manchester.* 12mo.

1840. **The London Social Reformer.** No. 1, May 2, 1840.

1840. **The Morning Star, or Phalansterian Gazette.** A Weekly Herald of Universal Principles and Progressive Association, etc. (Edited by H. Doherty.) 4to

1841. **M'Douall's Chartist and Republican Journal.** [Edited
by Dr. P. M. M'Douall.] Royal 8vo.
No. 1, April 3, 1841.
After No. 21, the title is changed to
M'Douall's Chartist Journal and Trades' Advocate.

1841–43. **The London Phalanx,** established for the purpose
of calling public attention to the practical importance of
Universal Principles ; and more particularly to the science
of Attractive Industry, propounded by the late Charles
Fourier, as a component part of the Law of Universal
Unity and Harmony, by him discovered. Published for
the Proprietor, Hugh Doherty.
Vol. I. Nos. 1-57, Apr. 3, 1841—Apr. 30, 1842. Folio.
New Series, Nos. 58-69, June 1842—May 1843. 8vo.

1841–44. **The Fleet Papers** ; being Letters to Thomas Thorn-
hill, Esq., . . . from Richard Oastler, his prisoner in the
Fleet. With occasional Communications from Friends.
Jan. 2, 1841—Sept. 7, 1844. 4 Vols. 8vo.

1841–42. **The Educational Circular and Communist
Apostle.** Edited by Henry Fry. Nos. 1 - 6, Nov.
1841—May 1842. 8vo.

1842–43. **The Union** : A Monthly Record of Moral, Social
and Educational Progress. Edited by G. A. Fleming
8vo.
No. 1, Apr. 1, 1842—No. 10, Jan. 1, 1843.

1842–43. **The Healthian.** A Journal of Human Physiology,
Diet, and Regimen. Vol. I. Nos. 1-14, Jan. 1842—
Feb. 1843. *London* and *Boston, U.S.* 8vo.
[Promoted by Concordists.]

1843–44. **The New Age and Concordium Gazette.** Nos.
1-24, Jan. 1843—Dec. 1844. Vol. I. (published 1845).
8vo.

1843. **The London Chartist Monthly Magazine.** No. 1,
June 1843.

1843. **The Poor Man's Guardian and Repealer's Friend.**
No. 1, June 3, 1843. Edited by H. Hetherington.

1843–45. **The Movement**; and Anti-Persecution Gazette. Edited by G. J. Holyoake. Assisted by M. Q. Ryall. 8vo.

> Nos. 1-68, Dec. 16, 1843—April 2, 1845.
> Followed by
> **The Circular of the Anti - Persecution Union.** Edited by G. J. Holyoake. 4 monthly numbers. May 1 —Aug. 1, 1845. 8vo.

1844. **The Social Pioneer.** [Representing the *New England Social Reform Society.*]

1844–45. **The Communitist.** Published at Skaneateles Community, New York, U.S.A. No. 1, Jan. 1, 1844.

1844–45. **New York Working Men's Advocate.**

1844–47. **The National Reformer.** Edited by J. Bronterre O'Brien. 4to.

> Nos. 1-75, Nov. 1844—April 1846.
> **The National Reformer,** and Manx Weekly Review of Home and Foreign Affairs. Edited by J. Bronterre O'Brien. New Series. *Douglas.* Royal 8vo.
> No. 76 ; No. 1, New Series. Nos. 1-35, Oct. 3, 1846—May 29, 1847.

1845. **The Sunbeam.** "Specially devoted to make known Etzler's System." No. 1, July 1, 1845.

1845–46. **Herald of Progress.** Edited by John Cramp.

> [Ended May 1846, when *The Reasoner* was commenced.]

1846–61. **The Reasoner.** Edited by G. J. Holyoake. Vols. I.-XXVI. 8vo. and folio.

> [According to Mr. Holyoake, *Hist. of Co-operation*, I. p. 311, 30 volumes were published between 1846 and 1872.]

1846–47. **The Ten Hours' Advocate.** Sept. 1846—June 1847. 38 numbers (all published). *Manchester.* 4to.

1847–48. **The Herald of Redemption.** Monthly 1d. [Edited by James Hole.]

> In 1848 the title became
> **The Herald of Co-operation.** It ceased in July 1848.

1847–48. **The Labourer**; a Monthly Magazine of Politics, Literature, etc. Edited by Feargus O'Connor and Ernest Jones. Vols. I.-IV. *London* and *Manchester.* 8vo.

1848. **Politics for the People.**   No. 1, May 6, 1848—No. 17, July 1848.   8vo.

1848. **The Apostle and Chronicle of the Communist Church.** No. 1, Vol I., Aug. 1, 1848.   *Isle of Man.*   8vo.

1849. **The Social Reformer.**   Edited by J. Bronterre O'Brien and Friends.   4to.
Nos. 1-11 (all published), Aug. 11—Oct. 20, 1849.

1849–50. **The Champion** of what is true and right and for the good of all.   [Edited by the Rev. J. R. Stephens.]   8vo.
Vol I. No. 1, Nov. 10, 1849—No. 26, May 4, 1850.
Vol. II.   Nos. 1-26 (no dates given with Vol. II.).

1849. **The Plain Speaker.**   Edited by Thomas Cooper.   4to. Nos. 1-49, Jan. 20—Dec. 22, 1849.

1850. **Cooper's Journal.**   Edited by Thomas Cooper.   No. 1, Jan. 5, 1850—No. 30, Oct. 26, 1850 [all published]. 8vo.

1849–50. **The Democratic Review** of British and Foreign Politics, History, and Literature.   Edited by G. Julian Harney.   Vol. I.   June 1849—May 1850.   Crown 8vo.

1850. **The Red Republican** : Equality, Liberty, Fraternity. Edited by G. Julian Harney.   Nos. 1-24 [all published], June 22 to Nov. 30, 1850.   4to.

1850–51. **The Friend of the People.**   Equality, Liberty, Fraternity.   Edited by G. Julian Harney.   Preliminary No. and Nos. 1-33.   Dec. 7, 1850—July 26, 1851 [all published].   4to.

1852. **The Friend of the People.**   Edited by G. Julian Harney.   [New Series.]   Nos. 1-12.   Feb. 7—April 24, 1852.   Large folio.
[Illustrated with portraits of writers.]
After No. 12, *The Friend of the People* was incorporated together with the *Northern Star* and *The Star*, in a new paper, *The Star of Freedom.*

1850. **Weekly Letters to the Human Race.**   By Robert Owen.   Nos. 1-17.   Royal 8vo.

1850. **The Future**; an Advocate of Social and Democratic Progress. *London: Vickers*, Holywell Street.

1850. **The National Instructor.** [By *Feargus O'Connor, T. Frost*, etc.] No. 1, May 25, 1850—No. 32, Dec. 28, 1850. Price 1d. weekly. 8vo.

1850. **Reynolds's Political Instructor.** Edited by G. W. M. Reynolds. No. 1, Nov. 10, 1849—No. 27, May 11, 1850. [All published.] Folio.

1850. **The Reformers' Almanack and Political Year-Book.** 12mo.

1850. **The Democratic and Social Almanac for 1850.** Presented to the Readers of the "Weekly Tribune" of Dec. 8, 1849. 12mo.

1850–52. **The Christian Socialist**: a Journal of Association conducted by several of the Promoters of the London Working Men's Associations [*i.e.* by *J. Townsend, F. D. Maurice*, and others]. Vols. I. and II. 1851. 4to.
> No. 1 appeared Nov. 2, 1850. In 1852 the first title was dropped, and it became
>
> **The Journal of Association.** January—June 1852.

1851. **Bronterre O'Brien's European Letters** and Tracts for the National Reform League. 8vo.
> No. 1, Sat. Dec. 6, 1851.

1851–52. **Notes to the People.** By Ernest Jones. *J. Pavey, 47 Holywell Street.* 2 Vols. 8vo.

1851–52. **Robert Owen's Journal.** Explanatory of the Means to well-place, well-employ, and well-educate the Population of the *World*. 8vo.
> Vol. I.   Nov. 2—April 26, 1851.
> Vol. II.   May 3—Oct. 25, 1851.
> Vol. III. Nov. 1—April 24, 1851–52.
> Vol. IV.   April 24—Oct. 23, 1852.

1853. **Robert Owen's Rational Quarterly Review and Journal.** Vol. I., containing the First Four Parts, published in 1853. 8vo.

1855. **The English Republic.** A Newspaper and Review. Edited by W. J. Linton. *Brantwood, Coniston.* 8vo.

1856–58. **Millennial Gazette** ; explanatory of the Principles
and Practices by which, in Peace, with Truth, Honesty,
and Simplicity the new Existence of Man upon the Earth
may be easily and speedily commenced.   By Robert
Owen.   No. 1, March 1, 1856—No. 16, July 1, 1858.

1860–63. **The Co-operator.**   A Record of Co-operative Progress : conducted exclusively by Working Men.   No. 1,
June, 1860—No. 39, May, 1863.   Vols. I.-III.   Royal 8vo.

4. BIOGRAPHIES AND HISTORIES

Allen, William, 1770–1843.
1. Life of Willian Allen, with Selections from his Correspondence. 1846. 3 Vols. 8vo.
2. **J. Fayle.** The Spitalfields Genius. The Story of William Allen. 1884. Cr. 8vo.

Frost, Thomas. Forty Years Recollections; Literary and Political. 1880. Cr. 8vo.

Hardy, Thomas. Memoir of Thomas Hardy, Founder of, and Secretary to, the *London Corresponding Society* . . . for Promoting Parliamentary Reform . . . Written by Himself. 1832. 8vo.

Holyoake, G. J. Sixty Years of an Agitator's Life. 3rd edn. 1893. 2 Vols. 8vo.

Lovett, William. 1800–77.
The Life and Struggles of William Lovett . . . with some short account of the different associations he belonged to . . . [an autobiography]. 1876. 8vo.

Owen, Robert. 1771–1858.
1. The Life of Robert Owen. Written by Himself. With Selections from his Writings and Correspondence. 1857-58. 2 Vols. 8vo.
2. **W. L. Sargant.** Robert Owen, and his Social Philosophy. 1860. Post 8vo.
3. **[F. A. Packard.]** Life of Robert Owen. *Philadelphia.* 1866. 12mo.
4. **A. J. Booth.** Robert Owen, the Founder of Socialism in England. 1869. 8vo.

5. **G. J. Holyoake.**   Life and Last Days of Robert Owen, of New Lanark.   Centenary edn.   1871.   12mo.
6. **Lloyd Jones.**   The Life, Times, and Labours of Robert Owen.   [Vol. II. edited by *William C. Jones.*]   1889-90.   2 Vols.   Cr. 8vo.

Place, Francis.   1771-1854.
    Graham, Wallas.   The Life of Francis Place, 1771-1854.   1898.   8vo.

Sadler, Michael Thomas.   1780-1835.
    [**Robert Benton Seeley** (?).]   Memoirs of the Life and Writings of Michael Thomas Sadler, M.P., F.R.S.   1842.   8vo.

Spence, Thomas.   1750-1814.
    Allen Davenport.   The Life, Writings, and Principles of Thomas Spence.   With a Portrait of the Author.   1836.   16mo.

American Communities—
1. **William Alfred Hinds.**   American Communities. Brief Sketches of Economy, Zoar, Bethel . . . the Shakers . . . and the Brotherhood of the New Life. *Office of the American Socialist: Oneida, New York.* 1878.   8vo.
2. **Charles Nordhoff.**   The Communistic Societies of the United States from personal visit and observation; including detailed accounts of the Economists, Zoarites, Shakers . . . and other existing societies.   With Illustrations.   1875.   8vo.
3. **J. H. Noyes.**   History of American Socialisms. *Philadelphia* and *London.*   1870.   Royal 8vo.

Engels, Friedrich.   1. Die Lage der arbeitenden Klasse in England.   *Leipzig.*   1845.   8vo.
    [2te ausgabe.   *Leipzig.*   1848.   8vo.]
2. The Condition of the Working Classes in England in 1844.   With Appendix written 1886, and Preface 1887.   Translated by *Florence K. Wischnewetsky.*   *New York.*   1887.   Sm. 8vo.

Gammage, R. G. The History of the Chartist Movement ; from its commencement down to the present time. With an Appendix. Part I. [all published]. 1854. 16mo.

A new edition, thoroughly revised, and illustrated with numerous portraits of Chartist leaders, was published at *Newcastle-on-Tyne*. 1894. 8vo.

Gibbins, H. de B. English Social Reformers. *Univ. Ext. Series.* 1892. Cr. 8vo.

Held, Adolf. Zwei Bücher zur socialen Geschichte Englands. *Leipzig.* 1881. 8vo.

Holyoake, G. J. 1. History of Co-operation in Rochdale (*The Society of Equitable Pioneers*). Part I., 1844-57 ; Part II., 1857-67. [Part I. dedicated by Permission to Lord Brougham.] 1867. Cr. 8vo.

    2. The History of Co-operation in Halifax ; and of some other Institutions around it. 1867. Cr. 8vo.

    3. The History of Co-operation in England : its Literature and its Advocates. Vol. I., The Pioneer Period, 1812-44. Vol. II., The Constructive Period, 1845-78. 1875-79. 2 Vols. Cr. 8vo.

Jones, Benjamin. Co-operative Production. With Prefatory Note by the Rt. Hon. A. H. Dyke Acland, M.P. *Oxford.* 1894. 2 Vols. Cr. 8vo.

Kaufmann, Rev. M. 1. Christian Socialism. 1888. Cr. 8vo.

    2. Charles Kingsley, Christian Socialist and Social Reformer. 1892. Cr. 8vo.

[Kydd, Samuel.] The History of the Factory Movement, from the year 1802 to the Enactment of the Ten Hours' Bill in 1847. By Alfred [i.e. *Samuel Kydd*]. 1857. 2 Vols. 8vo.

Lurieu, G. de ; et H. Romand. Études sur les Colonies Agricoles de Mendiants, Jeunes Détenus, Orphelins, et Enfants Trouvés. Hollande—Suisse—Belgique—France. *Paris.* 1851. 8vo.

Potter, Beatrice [Mrs. Sidney Webb]. The Co-operative Movement in Great Britain. 1891. 8vo.

Sargant, W. L.   Social Innovators and their Schemes.   1858.
Cr. 8vo.

Seligman, E. R. A.   Owen and the Christian Socialists.   Re-printed from the *Political Science Quarterly*, I. No. 2.
Boston.   1886.   8vo.

Webb, Sidney and **Beatrice.**   The History of Trade Unionism.
1894.   8vo.

INDEX OF AUTHORS